Common European Framework of Reference
for Languages: Learning, teaching, assessment

Other Council of Europe books published by Cambridge University Press

Waystage 1990
Threshold 1990
Vantage

PUBLISHED BY THE PRESS SYNDICATE OF THE UNIVERSITY OF CAMBRIDGE
The Pitt Building, Trumpington Street, Cambridge, United Kingdom

CAMBRIDGE UNIVERSITY PRESS
The Edinburgh Building, Cambridge CB2 2RU, UK
40 West 20th Street, New York, NY 10011–4211, USA
477 Williamstown Road, Port Melbourne, VIC 3207, Australia
Ruiz de Alarcón 13, 28014 Madrid, Spain
Dock House, The Waterfront, Cape Town 8001, South Africa

http://www.cambridge.org

First published 2001
Seventh printing 2004

Printed in the United Kingdom at the University Press, Cambridge

Typeface Swift 9/13pt. *System* QuarkXPress® [SE]

A catalogue record for this book is available from the British Library

Library of Congress Cataloguing in Publication data applied for

ISBN 0 521 80313 6 hardback
ISBN 0 521 00531 0 paperback

Common European Framework of Reference for Languages:
Learning, teaching, assessment

Council for Cultural Co-operation
Education Committee
Modern Languages Division, Strasbourg

Contents

Prefatory note

This restructured edition of the Common European Framework of reference for language learning, teaching and assessment represents the latest stage in a process which has been actively pursued since 1971 and owes much to the collaboration of many members of the teaching profession across Europe and beyond.

The Council of Europe therefore acknowledges with gratitude the contribution made by:

- The Project Group *Language Learning for European Citizenship*, representing all member countries of the Council for Cultural Co-operation with Canada as a participating observer, for their general oversight of its development.
- The Working Party set up by the Project Group, with twenty representatives from member countries representing the different professional interests concerned, as well as representatives of the European Commission and its LINGUA programme, for their invaluable advice and supervision of the project.
- The Authoring Group set up by the Working Party, consisting of Dr J. L. M. Trim (Project Director), Professor D. Coste (Ecole Normale Supérieure de Fontenay/Saint Cloud, CREDIF, France), Dr B. North (Eurocentres Foundation, Switzerland) together with Mr J. Sheils (Secretariat). The Council of Europe expresses its thanks to the institutions mentioned for making it possible for the experts concerned to contribute to this important work.
- The Swiss National Science Foundation for their support of the work by Dr B. North and Professor G. Schneider (University of Fribourg) to develop and scale descriptors of language proficiency for the Common Reference Levels.
- The Eurocentres Foundation for making available their experience in defining and scaling levels of language proficiency
- The U. S. National Foreign Languages Center for providing Mellon Fellowships to Dr Trim and Dr North which facilitated their contribution.
- The many colleagues and institutions across Europe who responded, often with great care and in concrete detail, to the request for feedback on earlier drafts.

The feedback received has been taken into account in revising the Framework and User Guides prior to their adoption on a Europe-wide basis. This revision was carried out by Dr J. L. M. Trim and Dr B. North.

Notes for the user

The aim of these notes is to help you to use the Common European Framework for language learning, teaching and assessment more effectively, either as a language learner or as a member of one of the professions concerned with language teaching and assessment. They will not be concerned with specific ways in which teachers, examiners, textbook writers, teacher trainers, educational administrators, etc. may use the Framework. These are the subject of special guidance addressed to the particular category of user concerned, contained in a fuller User Guide available from the Council of Europe, which can also be consulted on its website. These notes are meant as a first introduction to the Framework for all its users.

You may, of course, use the Framework document in any way you wish, as with any other publication. Indeed, we hope that some readers may be stimulated to use it in ways we have not foreseen. However, it has been written with two main aims in mind:

1. To encourage practitioners of all kinds in the language field, including language learners themselves, to reflect on such questions as:
   - What do we actually do when we speak (or write) to each other?
   - What enables us to act in this way?
   - How much of this do we need to learn when we try to use a new language?
   - How do we set our objectives and mark our progress along the path from total ignorance to effective mastery?
   - How does language learning take place?
   - What can we do to help ourselves and other people to learn a language better?
2. To make it easier for practitioners to tell each other and their clientèle what they wish to help learners to achieve, and how they attempt to do so.

One thing should be made clear right away. We have NOT set out to tell practitioners what to do, or how to do it. We are raising questions, not answering them. It is not the function of the Common European Framework to lay down the objectives that users should pursue or the methods they should employ.

This does not mean that the Council of Europe is indifferent to these issues. Indeed, a great deal of thought and work has been put into the principles and practice of language learning, teaching and assessment over the years by colleagues in our member countries working together in the Council of Europe's Modern Languages Projects. You will find the basic principles and their practical consequences set out in Chapter 1. You will see that the Council is concerned to improve the quality of communication among Europeans of different language and cultural backgrounds. This is because better communication leads to freer mobility and more direct contact, which in turn leads to better understanding and closer co-operation. The Council also supports methods of learning and teaching which help young people and indeed older learners to build up the attitudes, knowledge and skills they need to become more independent in thought and action, and also more responsible and co-operative in relation to other people. In this way the work contributes to the promotion of democratic citizenship.

Given these fundamental aims, the Council encourages all those concerned with the organisation of language learning to base their work on the needs, motivations, characteristics and resources of learners. This means answering questions such as:

- What will learners need to do with the language?
- What do they need to learn in order to be able to use the language to achieve those ends?
- What makes them want to learn?
- What sort of people are they (age, sex, social and educational background, etc.)?
- What knowledge, skills and experiences do their teachers possess?
- What access do they have to course books, works of reference (dictionaries, grammars, etc.), audio-visual aids, computer hardware and software, etc.?
- How much time can they afford (or are willing, or able) to spend?

On the basis of this analysis of the learning/teaching situation, it is seen as fundamentally important to **define, clearly and explicitly, objectives** which are at once **worthwhile** in terms of learner needs and **realistic** in terms of their characteristics and resources. Many parties are concerned with organised language learning, not only the teachers and learners in the classroom, but also educational authorities, examiners, textbook writers and publishers, etc. If they agree on objectives, they can work coherently, even if quite separately, to help learners achieve them. They are also in a position to make their own objectives and methods clear and explicit for the benefit of those who use the products of their work.

As explained in Chapter 1, it is for this purpose that the Common European Framework of reference has been developed. To perform its function it must satisfy certain criteria. It must be comprehensive, transparent and coherent.

These criteria are also set out and explained in Chapter 1. A further word may be useful in respect of 'comprehensive'. This means simply that you should find in it all you need to describe your objectives, methods and products. The scheme of parameters, categories and examples explained in Chapter 2 (most compactly in the boxed text at the beginning) and presented in some detail in Chapters 4 and 5 is intended to give a clear picture of the competences (knowledge, skills, attitudes) which language users build up in the course of their experience of language use and which enable them to meet the challenges of communication across language and cultural boundaries (i.e. to carry out communicative tasks and activities in the various contexts of social life with their conditions and constraints). The common reference levels introduced in Chapter 3 offer a means to map progress as learners build up their proficiency across the parameters of the descriptive scheme.

On the assumption that the aim of language teaching is to make learners competent and proficient in the language concerned, the scheme should enable you to define and describe your objectives clearly and comprehensively. You may well find that this scheme contains more than you yourself need. From Chapter 4 onwards you will find sets of questions at the end of each section, which invite you to consider whether the section is relevant to your objectives and concerns, and if so how. You may decide that it is not relevant, perhaps because it is not appropriate to the learners you have in mind, or that, while it would be useful to them, it is not a priority given limited time and other resources. In that case you can ignore the section. If however it is relevant (and perhaps seeing it in context may draw it to your attention), Chapters 4 and 5 of the Framework will supply names for major parameters and categories for your use, with some examples.

Neither the categories nor the examples claim to be exhaustive. If you want to describe a specialised area, you may well need to sub-categorise further than the present classification goes. The examples are suggestive only. You may well wish to keep some, reject others and add some of your own. You should feel quite free to do so, since it must be for you to decide on your objectives and your product. Remember that what you find unnecessary has its place in the Framework because someone else, with a different background, working in a different situation and responsible for a different set of learners, may find it essential. In the case of 'conditions and constraints' for instance, a school teacher may find it quite unnecessary to take noise levels into account, but a teacher of airline pilots who fails to train them to recognise digits 100% in appallingly noisy ground-to-air communication may condemn them and their passengers to death! On the other hand, the additional categories and exponents you find it necessary to add may well be found useful by other users. For this reason, the taxonomic scheme presented in Chapters 4 and 5 of the Framework is not seen as a closed system, but one which is open to further development in the light of experience.

This principle also applies to the description of levels of proficiency. Chapter 3 explains clearly that the number of levels which a particular user wishes to distinguish is determined by the reason for making the distinction, the use to be made of the resulting information. Levels, like entities, should not be multiplied beyond necessity! The 'hypertext' branching principle, set out in section 3.4, enables practitioners to establish broad- or narrow-band levels in accordance with their need to make finer or coarser distinctions among a population of learners. It is also, of course, possible (even usual) to distinguish between objectives in terms of levels, and the achievement of those objectives in terms of grades.

The six-level frame used throughout is based on the normal practice of a number of public examining bodies. The descriptors proposed are based on those which 'have been found transparent, useful and relevant by groups of non-native and native-speaker teachers from a variety of educational sectors with very different profiles in terms of linguistic training and teaching experience' (p. 30). They are nevertheless presented as recommendations and are not in any way mandatory, 'as a basis for reflection, discussion and further action . . . The aim of the examples is to open new possibilities, not to pre-empt decisions' (ibid.). It is already clear, however, that a set of common reference levels as a calibrating instrument is particularly welcomed by practitioners of all kinds who, as in many other fields, find it advantageous to work with stable, accepted standards of measurement and format.

As a user, you are invited to use the scaling system and associated descriptors critically. The Modern Languages Division of the Council of Europe will be glad to receive a report of your experience in putting them into use. Please note also that scales are provided not only for a global proficiency, but for many of the parameters of language proficiency detailed in Chapters 4 and 5. This makes it possible to specify differentiated profiles for particular learners or groups of learners.

In Chapter 6, attention turns to questions of method. How is a new language acquired or learnt? What can we do to facilitate that learning or acquisition process? Here again, the aim of the Framework is not to prescribe or even recommend a particular method, but to present options, inviting you to reflect on your current practice, to take decisions accordingly and to describe what you actually do. Of course, when considering your aims and objectives we would encourage you to take into consideration the Recommendations of the Committee of Ministers, but the aim of the Framework is to assist you in your own decision-taking. Chapter 7 is devoted to a closer examination of the role of tasks in language learning and teaching, as one of the main areas of advance in recent years.

Chapter 8 discusses the principles of curriculum design involving the differentiation of language learning objectives, especially in the context of building an individual's plurilingual and pluricultural competence in order to deal with the communicative challenges posed by living in a multilingual and multicultural Europe. The chapter deserves close study by those who are devising curricula covering a number of languages and considering the options open to them in seeking the best way to distribute resources for various categories of learners.

Chapter 9 passes finally to questions of assessment, explaining the relevance of the Framework to the assessment of language proficiency and achievement, and then with assessment criteria and different approaches to the assessment process.

The appendices deal with some further aspects of scaling which interested users may find useful. Appendix A deals with some general and theoretical concerns for the benefit of users who wish to develop scales specifically geared to a particular population of learners. Appendix B gives information concerning the Swiss project that developed the scaling descriptors used in this Framework. Appendices C and D present scales developed by other agencies, namely the DIALANG Language Assessment System and the 'Can Do' scales of the Association of Language Testers in Europe (ALTE).

Synopsis

Chapter 1 defines the *aims, objectives and functions* of the proposed Framework in the light of the overall language policy of the Council of Europe and in particular the promotion of *plurilingualism* in response to European linguistic and cultural diversity. It then sets out the *criteria* which the Framework should satisfy.

Chapter 2 explains the *approach* adopted. The descriptive scheme is based on an analysis of language use in terms of the *strategies* used by learners to activate *general* and *communicative competences* in order to carry out the *activities* and *processes* involved in the *production* and *reception* of *texts* and the construction of discourse dealing with particular *themes*, which enable them to fulfil the *tasks* facing them under the given *conditions and constraints* in the *situations* which arise in the various *domains* of social existence. The words in italics designate the parameters for the description of language use and the user/learner's ability to use language.

Chapter 3 introduces the *common reference levels*. Progress in language learning with regard to the parameters of the descriptive scheme can be calibrated in terms of a *flexible series of levels of attainment* defined by appropriate descriptors. This apparatus should be rich enough to accommodate the full range of learner needs and thus the objectives pursued by different providers, or required of candidates for language qualifications.

Chapter 4 establishes in some (but not exhaustive or definitive) detail the categories (scaled where possible) needed for the description of *language use and the language user/learner* according to the parameters identified, covering in turn: the domains and situations providing the context for language use; the themes, tasks and purposes of communication; communicative activities, strategies and processes; and text; especially in relation to activities and media.

Chapter 5 categorises in detail the user/learner's *general and communicative competences,* scaled where possible.

Chapter 6 considers the *processes of language learning and teaching*, dealing with the relation between acquisition and learning and with the nature and development of plurilingual competence, as well as with *methodological options* of a general or more specific kind, in relation to the categories set out in Chapters 3 and 4.

Chapter 7 examines in greater detail the role of *tasks* in language learning and teaching.

Chapter 8   is concerned with the implications of *linguistic diversification* for *curriculum design* and considers such issues as: plurilingualism and pluriculturalism; differentiated learning objectives; principles of curriculum design; curricular scenarios; life-long language learning; modularity and partial competences.

Chapter 9   discusses the various purposes of *assessment* and corresponding assessment types, in the light of the need to reconcile the competing criteria of comprehensiveness, precision and operational feasibility.

The General Bibliography contains a selection of books and articles which users of the Framework may wish to consult in order to go into greater depth with regard to the issues raised. The bibliography contains relevant Council of Europe documents as well as works published elsewhere.

Appendix A discusses development of descriptors of language proficiency. Methods of, and criteria for, scaling, and the requirements for formulating descriptors for the parameters and categories presented elsewhere, are explained.

Appendix B gives an overview of the project in Switzerland which developed and scaled the illustrative descriptors. The illustrative scales in the text are listed with page references.

Appendix C contains the descriptors for self-assessment at series of levels adopted by the DIALANG Project of the European Commission for use on the Internet.

Appendix D contains the 'Can Do' descriptors at the series of levels developed by the Association of Language Testers in Europe (ALTE).

1 The Common European Framework in its political and educational context

1.1 What is the *Common European Framework*?

The Common European Framework provides a common basis for the elaboration of language syllabuses, curriculum guidelines, examinations, textbooks, etc. across Europe. It describes in a comprehensive way what language learners have to learn to do in order to use a language for communication and what knowledge and skills they have to develop so as to be able to act effectively. The description also covers the cultural context in which language is set. The Framework also defines levels of proficiency which allow learners' progress to be measured at each stage of learning and on a life-long basis.

The Common European Framework is intended to overcome the barriers to communication among professionals working in the field of modern languages arising from the different educational systems in Europe. It provides the means for educational administrators, course designers, teachers, teacher trainers, examining bodies, etc., to reflect on their current practice, with a view to situating and co-ordinating their efforts and to ensuring that they meet the real needs of the learners for whom they are responsible.

By providing a common basis for the explicit description of objectives, content and methods, the Framework will enhance the transparency of courses, syllabuses and qualifications, thus promoting international co-operation in the field of modern languages. The provision of objective criteria for describing language proficiency will facilitate the mutual recognition of qualifications gained in different learning contexts, and accordingly will aid European mobility. *(economic + geographic)*

The taxonomic nature of the Framework inevitably means trying to handle the great complexity of human language by breaking language competence down into separate components. This confronts us with psychological and pedagogical problems of some depth. Communication calls upon the whole human being. The competences separated and classified below interact in complex ways in the development of each unique human personality. As a social agent, each individual forms relationships with a widening cluster of overlapping social groups, which together define identity. In an intercultural approach, it is a central objective of language education to promote the favourable development of the learner's whole personality and sense of identity in response to the enriching experience of otherness in language and culture. It must be left to teachers and the learners themselves to reintegrate the many parts into a healthily developing whole.

The Framework includes the description of 'partial' qualifications, appropriate when only a more restricted knowledge of a language is required (e.g. for understanding rather than speaking), or when a limited amount of time is available for the learning of a third or fourth language and more useful results can perhaps be attained by aiming at, say, recognition rather than recall skills. Giving formal recognition to such abilities will help to promote plurilingualism through the learning of a wider variety of European languages.

1.2   The aims and objectives of Council of Europe language policy

CEF serves the overall aim of the Council of Europe as defined in Recommendations R (82) 18 and R (98) 6 of the Committee of Ministers: 'to achieve greater unity among its members' and to pursue this aim 'by the adoption of common action in the cultural field'.
    The work of the Council for Cultural Co-operation of the Council of Europe with regard to modern languages, organised since its foundation in a series of medium-term projects, has derived its coherence and continuity from adherence to three basic principles set down in the preamble to Recommendation R (82) 18 of the Committee of Ministers of the Council of Europe:

- that the rich heritage of diverse languages and cultures in Europe is a valuable common resource to be protected and developed, and that a major educational effort is needed to convert that diversity from a barrier to communication into a source of mutual enrichment and understanding;
- that it is only through a better knowledge of European modern languages that it will be possible to facilitate communication and interaction among Europeans of different mother tongues in order to promote European mobility, mutual understanding and co-operation, and overcome prejudice and discrimination;
- that member states, when adopting or developing national policies in the field of modern language learning and teaching, may achieve greater convergence at the European level by means of appropriate arrangements for ongoing co-operation and co-ordination of policies.

In the pursuit of these principles, the Committee of Ministers called upon member governments

(F14) To promote the national and international collaboration of governmental and non-governmental institutions engaged in the development of methods of teaching and evaluation in the field of modern language learning and in the production and use of materials, including institutions engaged in the production and use of multi-media materials.

(F17) To take such steps as are necessary to complete the establishment of an effective European system of information exchange covering all aspects of language learning, teaching and research, and making full use of information technology.

Consequently, the activities of the CDCC (Council for Cultural Co-operation), its Committee for Education and its Modern Languages Section, have been concerned to encourage, support and co-ordinate the efforts of member governments and non-governmental institutions to improve language learning in accordance with these fundamental principles and in particular the steps which they take to implement the general measures set out in the Appendix to R(82)18:

A. General measures
1. To ensure, as far as possible, that all sections of their populations have access to effective means of acquiring a knowledge of the languages of other member states (or of other communities within their own country) as well as the skills in the use of those languages that will enable them to satisfy their communicative needs and in particular:
    1.1 to deal with the business of everyday life in another country, and to help foreigners staying in their own country to do so;
    1.2 to exchange information and ideas with young people and adults who speak a different language and to communicate their thoughts and feelings to them;
    1.3 to achieve a wider and deeper understanding of the way of life and forms of thought of other peoples and of their cultural heritage.
2. To promote, encourage and support the efforts of teachers and learners at all levels to apply in their own situation the principles of the construction of language-learning systems (as these are progressively developed within the Council of Europe 'Modern languages' programme):
    2.1 by basing language teaching and learning on the needs, motivations, characteristics and resources of learners;
    2.2 by defining worthwhile and realistic objectives as explicitly as possible;
    2.3 by developing appropriate methods and materials;
    2.4 by developing suitable forms and instruments for the evaluating of learning programmes.
3. To promote research and development programmes leading to the introduction, at all educational levels, of methods and materials best suited to enabling different classes and types of student to acquire a communicative proficiency appropriate to their specific needs.

The preamble to R(98)6 reaffirms the political objectives of its actions in the field of modern languages:

- To equip all Europeans for the challenges of intensified international mobility and closer co-operation not only in education, culture and science but also in trade and industry.
- To promote mutual understanding and tolerance, respect for identities and cultural diversity through more effective international communication.
- To maintain and further develop the richness and diversity of European cultural life through greater mutual knowledge of national and regional languages, including those less widely taught.
- To meet the needs of a multilingual and multicultural Europe by appreciably developing the ability of Europeans to communicate with each other across linguistic and cultural boundaries, which requires a sustained, lifelong effort to be encouraged, put on an organised footing and financed at all levels of education by the competent bodies.

3

- To avert the dangers that might result from the marginalisation of those lacking the skills necessary to communicate in an interactive Europe.

Particular urgency was attached to these objectives by the First Summit of Heads of State, which identified xenophobia and ultra-nationalist backlashes as a primary obstacle to European mobility and integration, and as a major threat to European stability and to the healthy functioning of democracy. The second summit made preparation for democratic citizenship a priority educational objective, thus giving added importance to a further objective pursued in recent projects, namely:

> To promote methods of modern language teaching which will strengthen independence of thought, judgement and action, combined with social skills and responsibility.

In the light of these objectives, the Committee of Ministers stressed 'the political importance at the present time and in the future of developing specific fields of action, such as strategies for diversifying and intensifying language learning in order to promote plurilingualism in a pan-European context' and drew attention to the value of further developing educational links and exchanges and of exploiting the full potential of new communication and information technologies.

1.3   What is 'plurilingualism'?

In recent years, the concept of plurilingualism has grown in importance in the Council of Europe's approach to language learning. Plurilingualism differs from multilingualism, which is the knowledge of a number of languages, or the co-existence of different languages in a given society. Multilingualism may be attained by simply diversifying the languages on offer in a particular school or educational system, or by encouraging pupils to learn more than one foreign language, or reducing the dominant position of English in international communication. Beyond this, the plurilingual approach emphasises the fact that as an individual person's experience of language in its cultural contexts expands, from the language of the home to that of society at large and then to the languages of other peoples (whether learnt at school or college, or by direct experience), he or she does not keep these languages and cultures in strictly separated mental compartments, but rather builds up a communicative competence to which all knowledge and experience of language contributes and in which languages interrelate and interact. In different situations, a person can call flexibly upon different parts of this competence to achieve effective communication with a particular interlocutor. For instance, partners may switch from one language or dialect to another, exploiting the ability of each to express themselves in one language and to understand the other; or a person may call upon the knowledge of a number of languages to make sense of a text, written or even spoken, in a previously 'unknown' language, recognising words from a common international store in a new guise. Those with some knowledge, even slight, may use it to help those with none to communicate by mediating between individuals with no common language. In the absence of a mediator, such individuals may nevertheless achieve some degree of communication by bringing the whole of their linguistic equipment into play, experimenting with alternative forms of expression in different languages or dialects, exploiting paralinguistics (mime, gesture, facial expression, etc.) and radically simplifying their use of language.

From this perspective, the aim of language education is profoundly modified. It is no longer seen as simply to achieve 'mastery' of one or two, or even three languages, each taken in isolation, with the 'ideal native speaker' as the ultimate model. Instead, the aim is to develop a linguistic repertory, in which all linguistic abilities have a place. This implies, of course, that the languages offered in educational institutions should be diversified and students given the opportunity to develop a plurilingual competence. Furthermore, once it is recognised that language learning is a lifelong task, the development of a young person's motivation, skill and confidence in facing new language experience out of school comes to be of central importance. The responsibilities of educational authorities, qualifying examining bodies and teachers cannot simply be confined to the attainment of a given level of proficiency in a particular language at a particular moment in time, important though that undoubtedly is.

The full implications of such a paradigm shift have yet to be worked out and translated into action. The recent developments in the Council of Europe's language programme have been designed to produce tools for use by all members of the language teaching profession in the promotion of plurilingualism. In particular, The European Language Portfolio (ELP) provides a format in which language learning and intercultural experiences of the most diverse kinds can be recorded and formally recognised. For this purpose, CEF not only provides a scaling of overall language proficiency in a given language, but also a breakdown of language use and language competences which will make it easier for practitioners to specify objectives and describe achievements of the most diverse kinds in accordance with the varying needs, characteristics and resources of learners.

1.4 Why is CEF needed?

In the words of the Intergovernmental Symposium held in Rüschlikon, Switzerland November 1991, on the initiative of the Swiss Federal Government, on: 'Transparency and Coherence in Language Learning in Europe: Objectives, Evaluation, Certification':

1. A further intensification of language learning and teaching in member countries is necessary in the interests of greater mobility, more effective international communication combined with respect for identity and cultural diversity, better access to information, more intensive personal interaction, improved working relations and a deeper mutual understanding.
2. To achieve these aims language learning is necessarily a life-long task to be promoted and facilitated throughout educational systems, from pre-school through to adult education.
3. It is desirable to develop a Common European Framework of reference for language learning at all levels, in order to:
    *   promote and facilitate co-operation among educational institutions in different countries;
    *   provide a sound basis for the mutual recognition of language qualifications;

- assist learners, teachers, course designers, examining bodies and educational administrators to situate and co-ordinate their efforts.

Plurilingualism has itself to be seen in the context of pluriculturalism. Language is not only a major aspect of culture, but also a means of access to cultural manifestations. Much of what is said above applies equally in the more general field: in a person's cultural competence, the various cultures (national, regional, social) to which that person has gained access do not simply co-exist side by side; they are compared, contrasted and actively interact to produce an enriched, integrated pluricultural competence, of which plurilingual competence is one component, again interacting with other components.

1.5   For what uses is CEF intended?

The uses of the Framework include:

The planning of language learning programmes in terms of:

- their assumptions regarding prior knowledge, and their articulation with earlier learning, particularly at interfaces between primary, lower secondary, upper secondary and higher/further education;
- their objectives;
- their content.

The planning of language certification in terms of:

- the content syllabus of examinations;
- assessment criteria, in terms of positive achievement rather than negative deficiencies.

The planning of self-directed learning, including:

- raising the learner's awareness of his or her present state of knowledge;
- self-setting of feasible and worthwhile objectives;
- selection of materials;
- self-assessment.

Learning programmes and certification can be:

- *global*, bringing a learner forward in all dimensions of language proficiency and communicative competence;
- *modular*, improving the learner's proficiency in a restricted area for a particular purpose;
- *weighted*, emphasising learning in certain directions and producing a 'profile' in which a higher level is attained in some areas of knowledge and skill than others;
- *partial*, taking responsibility only for certain activities and skills (e.g. reception) and leaving others aside.

The Common European Framework is constructed so as to accommodate these various forms.

In considering the role of a common framework at more advanced stages of language learning it is necessary to take into account changes in the nature of needs of learners and the context in which they live, study and work. There is a need for general qualifications at a level beyond threshold, which may be situated with reference to the CEF. They have, of course, to be well defined, properly adapted to national situations and embrace new areas, particularly in the cultural field and more specialised domains. In addition, a considerable role may be played by modules or clusters of modules geared to the specific needs, characteristics and resources of learners.

1.6 What criteria must CEF meet?

In order to fulfil its functions, such a Common European Framework must be comprehensive, transparent and coherent.

By 'comprehensive' is meant that the Common European Framework should attempt to specify as full a range of language knowledge, skills and use as possible (without of course attempting to forecast *a priori* all possible uses of language in all situations – an impossible task), and that all users should be able to describe their objectives, etc., by reference to it. CEF should differentiate the various dimensions in which language proficiency is described, and provide a series of reference points (levels or steps) by which progress in learning can be calibrated. It should be borne in mind that the development of communicative proficiency involves other dimensions than the strictly linguistic (e.g. sociocultural awareness, imaginative experience, affective relations, learning to learn, etc.).

By 'transparent' is meant that information must be clearly formulated and explicit, available and readily comprehensible to users.

By 'coherent' is meant that the description is free from internal contradictions. With regard to educational systems, coherence requires that there is a harmonious relation among their components:

- the identification of needs;
- the determination of objectives;
- the definition of content;
- the selection or creation of material;
- the establishment of teaching/learning programmes;
- the teaching and learning methods employed;
- evaluation, testing and assessment.

The construction of a comprehensive, transparent and coherent framework for language learning and teaching does not imply the imposition of one single uniform system. On the contrary, the framework should be open and flexible, so that it can be applied, with such adaptations as prove necessary, to particular situations. CEF should be:

- *multi-purpose*: usable for the full variety of purposes involved in the planning and provision of facilities for language learning
- *flexible*: adaptable for use in different circumstances

- *open*: capable of further extension and refinement
- *dynamic*: in continuous evolution in response to experience in its use
- *user-friendly*: presented in a form readily understandable and usable by those to whom it is addressed
- *non-dogmatic*: not irrevocably and exclusively attached to any one of a number of competing linguistic or educational theories or practices.

2 Approach adopted

2.1 An action-oriented approach

A comprehensive, transparent and coherent frame of reference for language learning, teaching and assessment must relate to a very general view of language use and learning. The approach adopted here, generally speaking, is an action-oriented one in so far as it views users and learners of a language primarily as 'social agents', i.e. members of society who have tasks (not exclusively language-related) to accomplish in a given set of circumstances, in a specific environment and within a particular field of action. While acts of speech occur within language activities, these activities form part of a wider social context, which alone is able to give them their full meaning. We speak of 'tasks' in so far as the actions are performed by one or more individuals strategically using their own specific competences to achieve a given result. The action-based approach therefore also takes into account the cognitive, emotional and volitional resources and the full range of abilities specific to and applied by the individual as a social agent.

Accordingly, any form of language use and learning could be described as follows:

Language use, embracing language learning, comprises the actions performed by persons who as individuals and as social agents develop a range of **competences**, both **general** and in particular **communicative language competences**. They draw on the competences at their disposal in various contexts under various **conditions** and under various **constraints** to engage in **language activities** involving **language processes** to produce and/or receive **texts** in relation to **themes** in specific **domains**, activating those **strategies** which seem most appropriate for carrying out the **tasks** to be accomplished. The monitoring of these actions by the participants leads to the reinforcement or modification of their competences.

- *Competences* are the sum of knowledge, skills and characteristics that allow a person to perform actions.
- *General competences* are those not specific to language, but which are called upon for actions of all kinds, including language activities.
- *Communicative language competences* are those which empower a person to act using specifically linguistic means.
- *Context* refers to the constellation of events and situational factors (physical and others), both internal and external to a person, in which acts of communication are embedded.

- *Language activities* involve the exercise of one's communicative language competence in a specific domain in processing (receptively and/or productively) one or more texts in order to carry out a task.
- *Language processes* refer to the chain of events, neurological and physiological, involved in the production and reception of speech and writing.
- *Text* is any sequence or discourse (spoken and/or written) related to a specific domain and which in the course of carrying out a task becomes the occasion of a language activity, whether as a support or as a goal, as product or process.
- *Domain* refers to the broad sectors of social life in which social agents operate. A higher order categorisation has been adopted here limiting these to major categories relevant to language learning/teaching and use: the educational, occupational, public and personal domains.
- A *strategy* is any organised, purposeful and regulated line of action chosen by an individual to carry out a task which he or she sets for himself or herself or with which he or she is confronted.
- A *task* is defined as any purposeful action considered by an individual as necessary in order to achieve a given result in the context of a problem to be solved, an obligation to fulfil or an objective to be achieved. This definition would cover a wide range of actions such as moving a wardrobe, writing a book, obtaining certain conditions in the negotiation of a contract, playing a game of cards, ordering a meal in a restaurant, translating a foreign language text or preparing a class newspaper through group work.

If it is accepted that the different dimensions highlighted above are interrelated in all forms of language use and learning, then any act of language learning or teaching is in some way concerned with each of these dimensions: strategies, tasks, texts, an individual's general competences, communicative language competence, language activities, language processes, contexts and domains.

At the same time, it is also possible in learning and teaching that the objective, and therefore assessment, may be focused on a particular component or sub-component (the other components then being considered as means to an end, or as aspects to be given more emphasis at other times, or as not being relevant to the circumstances). Learners, teachers, course designers, authors of teaching material and test designers are inevitably involved in this process of focusing on a particular dimension and deciding on the extent to which other dimensions should be considered and ways of taking account of these: this is illustrated with examples below. It is immediately clear, however, that although the often stated aim of a teaching/learning programme is to develop communication skills (possibly because this is most representative of a methodological approach?), certain programmes in reality strive to achieve a qualitative or quantitative development of language activities in a foreign language, others stress performance in a particular domain, yet others the development of certain general competences, while others are primarily concerned with refining strategies. The claim that 'everything is connected' does not mean that the objectives cannot be differentiated.

Each of the main categories outlined above can be divided into sub-categories, still very generic, which will be looked at in the following chapters. Here, we are looking only at the various components of general competences, communicative competence, language activities and domains.

2.1.1 The general competences of an individual

The **general competences** of language learners or users (see section 5.1.) consist in particular of their *knowledge, skills* and *existential competence* and also their *ability to learn*:
Knowledge, i.e. declarative knowledge (*savoir*, see 5.1.1.), is understood as knowledge resulting from experience (empirical knowledge) and from more formal learning (academic knowledge). All human communication depends on a shared knowledge of the world. As far as language use and learning are concerned, the knowledge which comes into play is not directly related exclusively to language and culture. Academic knowledge in a scientific or technical educational field, and academic or empirical knowledge in a professional field clearly have an important part to play in the reception and understanding of texts in a foreign language relating to those fields. Empirical knowledge relating to day-to-day living (organisation of the day, mealtimes, means of transport, communication and information), in the public or private domains is, however, just as essential for the management of language activities in a foreign language. Knowledge of the shared values and beliefs held by social groups in other countries and regions, such as religious beliefs, taboos, assumed common history, etc., are essential to intercultural communication. These multiple areas of knowledge vary from individual to individual. They may be culture-specific, but nevertheless also relate to more universal parameters and constants.

Any new knowledge is not simply added onto the knowledge one had before but is conditioned by the nature, richness and structure of one's previous knowledge and, furthermore, serves to modify and restructure the latter, however partially. Clearly, the knowledge which an individual has already acquired is directly relevant to language learning. In many cases, methods of teaching and learning pre-suppose this awareness of the world. However, in certain contexts (e.g. immersion, attending school or university where the language of tuition is not one's mother tongue), there is simultaneous and correlated enrichment of linguistic and other knowledge. Careful consideration must then be given to the relationship between knowledge and communicative competence.

Skills and **know-how** (*savoir-faire*, see section 5.1.2.), whether it be a matter of driving a car, playing the violin or chairing a meeting, depend more on the ability to carry out procedures than on declarative knowledge, but this skill may be facilitated by the acquisition of 'forgettable' knowledge and be accompanied by forms of existential competence (for example relaxed attitude or tension in carrying out a task). Thus, in the example quoted above, driving a car, which through repetition and experience becomes a series of almost automatic processes (declutching, changing gear, etc.), initially requires an explicit break-down of conscious and verbalisable operations ('Slowly release the clutch pedal, slip into third gear, etc.') and the acquisition of certain facts (there are three pedals in a manual car set out as follows, etc.) which one does not have to consciously think about once one 'knows how to drive'. When one is learning to drive, one generally needs a high level of concentration and heightened self-awareness since one's own self-image is particularly vulnerable (risk of failure, of appearing incompetent). Once the skills have been mastered, the driver can be expected to be much more at ease and self-confident; otherwise this would be disconcerting for passengers and other motorists. Clearly, it would not be difficult to draw parallels with certain aspects of language learning (e.g. pronunciation and some parts of grammar, such as inflexional morphology).

Existential competence (*savoir-être,* see 5.1.3.) may be considered as the sum of the individual characteristics, personality traits and attitudes which concern, for example, self-image and one's view of others and willingness to engage with other people in social interaction. This type of competence is not seen simply as resulting from immutable personality characteristics. It includes factors which are the product of various kinds of acculturation and may be modified.

These personality traits, attitudes and temperaments are parameters which have to be taken into account in language learning and teaching. Accordingly, even though they may be difficult to define, they should be included in a framework of reference. They are considered to be part of an individual's general competences and therefore an aspect of his or her abilities. In so far as they are capable of being acquired or modified in use and through learning (for example, of one or more languages), attitude formation may be an objective. As has frequently been noted, existential competences are culture-related and therefore sensitive areas for inter-cultural perceptions and relations: the way one member of a specific culture expresses friendliness and interest may be perceived by someone from another culture as aggressive or offensive.

Ability to learn (*savoir apprendre*, see 5.1.4.) mobilises existential competence, declarative knowledge and skills, and draws on various types of competence. Ability to learn may also be conceived as 'knowing how, or being disposed, to discover "otherness"' – whether the other is another language, another culture, other people or new areas of knowledge.

Whilst the notion of ability to learn is of general application, it is particularly relevant to language learning. Depending on the learners in question, the ability to learn may involve varying degrees and combinations of such aspects of existential competence, declarative knowledge and skills and know-how as:

*   Existential competence: e.g. a willingness to take initiatives or even risks in face-to-face communication, so as to afford oneself the opportunity to speak, to prompt assistance from the people with whom one is speaking, such as asking them to rephrase what they have said in simpler terms, etc; also listening skills, attention to what is said, heightened awareness of the risks of cultural misunderstanding in relations with others.
*   Declarative knowledge: e.g. knowledge of what morpho-syntactical relations correspond to given declension patterns for a particular language; or, awareness that there may be a taboo or particular rituals associated with dietary or sexual practices in certain cultures or that they may have religious connotations.
*   Skills and know-how: e.g. facility in using a dictionary or being able to find one's way easily around a documentation centre; knowing how to manipulate audiovisual or computer media (e.g. the Internet) as learning resources.

For the same individual there can be many variations in the use of skills and know-how and the ability to deal with the unknown:

*   Variations according to the event, depending on whether the individual is dealing with new people, a totally unknown area of knowledge, an unfamiliar culture, a foreign language.
*   Variations according to context: faced with the same event (e.g. parent/child relationships in a given community), the processes of discovery and seeking meaning will doubtless be different for an ethnologist, tourist, missionary, journalist, educator or doctor, each acting according to his or her own discipline or outlook.

- Variations according to the prevailing circumstances and past experience: it is quite probable that the skills applied in learning a fifth foreign language will be different from those applied in learning the first.

Such variations should be considered alongside concepts such as 'learning styles' or 'learner profiles' as long as the latter are not regarded as being immutably fixed once and for all.

For learning purposes, the strategies selected by the individual in order to accomplish a given task will depend on the diversity of the various abilities to learn at his/her disposal. But it is also through the diversity of learning experiences, provided they are not compartmentalised nor strictly repetitive, that the individual extends his/her ability to learn.

2.1.2 Communicative language competence

Communicative language competence can be considered as comprising several components: *linguistic, sociolinguistic* and *pragmatic.* Each of these components is postulated as comprising, in particular, knowledge and skills and know-how. *Linguistic competences* include lexical, phonological, syntactical knowledge and skills and other dimensions of language as system, independently of the sociolinguistic value of its variations and the pragmatic functions of its realisations. This component, considered here from the point of view of a given individual's communicative language competence, relates not only to the range and quality of knowledge (e.g. in terms of phonetic distinctions made or the extent and precision of vocabulary) but also to cognitive organisation and the way this knowledge is stored (e.g. the various associative networks in which the speaker places a lexical item) and to its accessibility (activation, recall and availability). Knowledge may be conscious and readily expressible or may not (e.g. once again in relation to mastery of a phonetic system). Its organisation and accessibility will vary from one individual to another and vary also within the same individual (e.g. for a plurilingual person depending on the varieties inherent in his or her plurilingual competence). It can also be held that the cognitive organisation of vocabulary and the storing of expressions, etc. depend, amongst other things, on the cultural features of the community or communities in which the individual has been socialised and where his or her learning has occurred.

Sociolinguistic competences refer to the sociocultural conditions of language use. Through its sensitivity to social conventions (rules of politeness, norms governing relations between generations, sexes, classes and social groups, linguistic codification of certain fundamental rituals in the functioning of a community), the sociolinguistic component strictly affects all language communication between representatives of different cultures, even though participants may often be unaware of its influence.

Pragmatic competences are concerned with the functional use of linguistic resources (production of language functions, speech acts), drawing on scenarios or scripts of interactional exchanges. It also concerns the mastery of discourse, cohesion and coherence, the identification of text types and forms, irony, and parody. For this component even more than the linguistic component, it is hardly necessary to stress the major impact of interactions and cultural environments in which such abilities are constructed.

All the categories used here are intended to characterise areas and types of competences internalised by a social agent, i.e. internal representations, mechanisms and capacities, the cognitive existence of which can be considered to account for observable behaviour and performance. At the same time, any learning process will help to develop or transform these same internal representations, mechanisms and capacities.

Each of these components will be examined in more detail in Chapter 5.

2.1.3 Language activities

The language learner/user's communicative language competence is activated in the performance of the various *language activities*, involving **reception**, **production**, **interaction** or **mediation** (in particular interpreting or translating). Each of these types of activity is possible in relation to texts in oral or written form, or both.

As processes, *reception* and *production* (oral and/or written) are obviously primary, since both are required for interaction. In this Framework, however, the use of these terms for language activities is confined to the role they play in isolation. Receptive activities include silent reading and following the media. They are also of importance in many forms of learning (understanding course content, consulting textbooks, works of reference and documents). Productive activities have an important function in many academic and professional fields (oral presentations, written studies and reports) and particular social value is attached to them (judgements made of what has been submitted in writing or of fluency in speaking and delivering oral presentations).

In *interaction* at least two individuals participate in an oral and/or written exchange in which production and reception alternate and may in fact overlap in oral communication. Not only may two interlocutors be speaking and yet listening to each other simultaneously. Even where turn-taking is strictly respected, the listener is generally already forecasting the remainder of the speaker's message and preparing a response. Learning to interact thus involves more than learning to receive and to produce utterances. High importance is generally attributed to interaction in language use and learning in view of its central role in communication.

In both the receptive and productive modes, the written and/or oral activities of *mediation* make communication possible between persons who are unable, for whatever reason, to communicate with each other directly. Translation or interpretation, a paraphrase, summary or record, provides for a third party a (re)formulation of a source text to which this third party does not have direct access. Mediating language activities – (re)processing an existing text – occupy an important place in the normal linguistic functioning of our societies.

2.1.4 Domains

Language activities are contextualised within *domains*. These may themselves be very diverse, but for most practical purposes in relation to language learning they may be broadly classified as fourfold: the *public domain*, the *personal domain*, the *educational domain* and the *occupational domain*.

The *public* domain refers to everything connected with ordinary social interaction (business and administrative bodies, public services, cultural and leisure activities of a public nature, relations with the media, etc.). Complementarily, the *personal* domain comprises family relations and individual social practices.

The *occupational* domain embraces everything concerned with a person's activities and relations in the exercise of his or her occupation. The *educational* domain is concerned with the learning/training context (generally of an institutional nature) where the aim is to acquire specific knowledge or skills.

2.1.5 Tasks, strategies and texts

Communication and learning involve the performance of *tasks* which are not solely language tasks even though they involve language activities and make demands upon the individual's communicative competence. To the extent that these tasks are neither routine nor automatic, they require the use of *strategies* in communicating and learning. In so far as carrying out these tasks involves language activities, they necessitate the processing (through reception, production, interaction or mediation) of oral or written *texts.*

The overall approach outlined above is distinctly action-oriented. It is centred on the relationship between, on the one hand, the agents' use of strategies linked to their competences and how they perceive or imagine the situation to be and on the other, the task or tasks to be accomplished in a specific context under particular conditions.

Thus someone who has to **move a wardrobe** (task) may try to push it, take it to pieces so as to carry it more easily and then reassemble it, call on outside labour or give up and convince himself or herself that it can wait until tomorrow, etc. (all strategies). Depending on the strategy adopted, the performance (or avoidance, postponement or redefinition) of the task may or may not involve a language activity and text processing (reading instructions for dismantling, making a telephone call, etc.). Similarly, a learner at school who has to translate a text from a foreign language (task) may look to see if a translation already exists, ask another learner to show what he or she has done, use a dictionary, try to work out some kind of meaning on the basis of the few words or structures he or she knows, think of a good excuse for not handing in this exercise, etc. (all possible strategies). For all the cases envisaged here there will necessarily be language activity and text processing (translation/mediation, verbal negotiation with a classmate, letter or verbal excuses to the teacher, etc.).

The relationship between strategies, task and text depends on the nature of the task. This may be primarily language-related, i.e. it may require largely language activities and the strategies applied relate primarily to these language activities (e.g. reading and commenting on a text, completing a 'fill in the gaps'-type exercise, giving a lecture, taking notes during a presentation). It may include a language component, i.e. where language activities form only part of what is required and where the strategies applied relate also or primarily to other activities (e.g. cooking by following a recipe). It is possible to carry out many tasks without recourse to a language activity. In these cases, the activities involved are not necessarily language-related at all and the strategies applied relate to other types of activity. For instance, erecting a tent can be carried out in silence by several people who know what they are doing. They may perhaps engage in a few oral exchanges relating to technique, or they may at the same time hold a conversation having nothing at all to do with the task, or they may carry out the task while one of them is humming a tune. The use of language becomes necessary when one of the group does not know what to do next, or when for some reason the established routine does not work.

In this type of analysis communication strategies and learning strategies are but strategies among others, just as communicative tasks and learning tasks are but tasks among others. Similarly, 'authentic' texts or texts specially designed for teaching purposes, texts in textbooks or texts produced by learners are but texts among others.

In the following chapters a detailed account is offered for each dimension and subcategory in turn, with examples and scaling where appropriate. Chapter 4 deals with the dimension of language use – what a language user or learner is required to *do*, whilst Chapter 5 deals with the competences that enable a language user to act.

2.2 Common reference levels of language proficiency

In addition to the descriptive scheme glossed above, Chapter 3 provides a 'vertical dimension' and outlines an ascending series of common reference levels for describing learner proficiency. The set of descriptive categories introduced in Chapters 4 and 5 map out a 'horizontal dimension' made up of parameters of communicative activity and communicative language competence. It is quite common to present a series of levels in a series of parameters as a profiling grid with a horizontal and a vertical dimension. This is, of course, a considerable simplification since just the addition of domain, for example, would give a third dimension turning such a grid into a notional cube. A full diagrammatic representation of the degree of multidimensionality involved would in fact be very challenging, if not impossible.

The addition of a vertical dimension to the Framework nevertheless enables learning space to be mapped or profiled, even if simply, and this is useful for a number of reasons:

- The development of definitions of learner proficiency related to categories used in the Framework may assist in making more concrete what it may be appropriate to expect at different levels of achievement in terms of those categories. This in turn may aid the development of transparent and realistic statements of overall learning objectives.
- Learning which takes place over a period of time needs to be organised into units which take account of progression and can provide continuity. Syllabuses and materials need to be situated in relation to one another. A framework of levels may help in this process.
- Learning efforts in relation to those objectives and those units need also to be situated on this vertical dimension of progress, i.e. assessed in relation to gains in proficiency. The provision of proficiency statements may help in this process.
- Such assessment should take account of incidental learning, of out-of-school experience, of the kind of lateral enrichment outlined above. The provision of a set of proficiency statements going beyond the scope of a particular syllabus may be helpful in this respect.
- The provision of a common set of proficiency statements will facilitate comparisons of objectives, levels, materials, tests and achievement in different systems and situations.

- A framework including both horizontal and vertical dimensions facilitates the definition of partial objectives and the recognition of uneven profiles, partial competencies.
- A framework of levels and categories facilitating profiling of objectives for particular purposes may aid inspectors. Such a framework may help to assess whether learners are working at an appropriate level in different areas. It may inform decisions on whether performance in those areas represents a standard appropriate to the stage of learning, immediate future goals and wider longer-term goals of effective language proficiency and personal development.
- Finally, in their learning career students of the language will pass through a number of educational sectors and institutions offering language services, and the provision of a common set of levels may facilitate collaboration between those sectors. With increased personal mobility, it is more and more common for learners to switch between educational systems at the end of or even in the middle of their period in a particular educational sector, making the provision of a common scale on which to describe their achievement an issue of ever wider concern.

In considering the vertical dimension of the Framework, one should not forget that the process of language learning is continuous and individual. No two users of a language, whether native speakers or foreign learners, have exactly the same competences or develop them in the same way. Any attempt to establish 'levels' of proficiency is to some extent arbitrary, as it is in any area of knowledge or skill. However, for practical purposes it is useful to set up a scale of defined levels to segment the learning process for the purposes of curriculum design, qualifying examinations, etc. Their number and height will depend largely on how a particular educational system is organised and for which purposes scales are established. It is possible to set down procedures and criteria for scaling and for the formulation of the descriptors used to characterise successive levels of proficiency. The issues and options concerned are discussed in depth in Appendix A. Users of this framework are strongly advised to consult that section and the supporting bibliography before taking independent policy decisions on scaling.

One also needs to remember that levels only reflect a vertical dimension. They can take only limited account of the fact that learning a language is a matter of horizontal as well as vertical progress as learners acquire the proficiency to perform in a wider range of communicative activities. Progress is not merely a question of moving up a vertical scale. There is no particular logical requirement for a learner to pass through all the lower levels on a sub-scale. They may make lateral progress (from a neighbouring category) by broadening their performance capabilities rather than increasing their proficiency in terms of the same category. Conversely, the expression 'deepening one's knowledge' recognises that one may well feel the need at some point to underpin such pragmatic gains by having a look at 'the basics' (that is: lower level skills) in an area into which one has moved laterally.

Finally, one should be careful about interpreting sets of levels and scales of language proficiency as if they were a linear measurement scale like a ruler. No existing scale or set of levels can claim to be linear in this way. Talking in terms of the series of Council of Europe content specifications, even if *Waystage* is situated halfway to *Threshold Level* on a scale of levels, and *Threshold* half way to *Vantage Level,* experience with existing scales suggests that many learners will take more than twice as long to reach *Threshold Level* from *Waystage* than they needed to reach *Waystage*. They will then probably need more than twice as long to reach *Vantage Level* from *Threshold Level* than they needed to reach *Threshold Level* from *Waystage*, even if the levels appear to be equidistant on the scale. This is because of the necessary broadening of the range of activities, skills and language involved. This fact of life is reflected in the frequent presentation of a scale of levels with a diagram like an ice cream cornet – a three-dimensional cone which broadens towards the top. Extreme caution should be exercised in using any scale of levels to calculate the 'mean seat time' necessary to meet particular objectives.

2.3 Language learning and teaching

2.3.1   Such statements of learning objectives say nothing about the processes by which learners come to be able to act in the required ways, or the processes by which they develop/build up the competences that make the actions possible. They say nothing about the ways in which teachers facilitate the processes of language acquisition and learning. Yet, since it is one of the principal functions of the Framework to encourage and enable all the different partners to the language teaching and learning processes to inform others as transparently as possible not only of their aims and objectives but also of the methods they use and the results actually achieved, it seems clear that the Framework cannot confine itself to the knowledge, skills and attitudes learners will need to develop in order to act as competent language users, but must also deal with the processes of language acquisition and learning, as well as with the teaching methodology. These matters are dealt with in Chapter 6.

2.3.2   The role of the Framework in respect of language acquisition, learning and teaching must however be made clear once more. In accordance with the basic principles of pluralist democracy, the Framework aims to be not only comprehensive, transparent and coherent, but also open, dynamic and non-dogmatic. For that reason it cannot take up a position on one side or another of current theoretical disputes on the nature of language acquisition and its relation to language learning, nor should it embody any one particular approach to language teaching to the exclusion of all others. Its proper role is to encourage all those involved as partners to the language learning/teaching process to state as explicitly and transparently as possible their own theoretical basis and their practical procedures. In order to fulfil this role it sets out parameters, categories, criteria and scales which users may draw upon and which may possibly stimulate them to consider a wider range of options than previously or to question the previously unexamined assumptions of the tradition in which they are working. This is not to say that such assumptions are wrong, but only that all those responsible for planning should benefit from a re-examination of theory and practice in which they can take into account decisions other practitioners have taken in their own and, particularly, in other European countries.

An open, 'neutral' framework of reference does not of course imply an absence of policy. In providing such a framework the Council of Europe is not in any way retreating from the principles set out in Chapter 1 above as well as in Recommendations R (82) 18 and R (98) 6 of the Committee of Ministers addressed to member governments.

2.3.3 Chapters 4 and 5 are mainly concerned with the actions and competences required of a language user/learner in respect of any one language in order to communicate with other users of that language. Much of Chapter 6 relates to ways in which the necessary abilities can be developed and how that development can be facilitated. Chapter 7 takes a closer look at the role of tasks in language use and language learning. However, the full implications of adopting a plurilingual and pluricultural approach have yet to be explored. Chapter 6 therefore also examines the nature and development of plurilingual competence. Its implications for the diversification of language teaching and educational policies are then explored in some detail in Chapter 8.

2.4   Language assessment

The CEF is 'A common European framework for language learning, teaching and assessment'. Up to this point, the focus has been upon the nature of language use and the language user and the implications for learning and teaching.

In Chapter 9, the final chapter, attention is concentrated on the functions of the Framework in relation to the assessment of language proficiency. The chapter outlines three main ways in which the Framework can be used:

1.   for the specification of the content of tests and examinations.
2.   for stating the criteria for the attainment of a learning objective, both in relation to the assessment of a particular spoken or written performance, and in relation to continuous teacher-, peer- or self-assessment.
3.   for describing the levels of proficiency in existing tests and examinations thus enabling comparisons to be made across different systems of qualifications.

The chapter then lays out in some detail the choices that have to be made by those conducting assessment procedures. The choices are presented in the form of contrasting pairs. In each case the terms used are clearly defined and the relative advantages and disadvantages are discussed in relation to the purpose of the assessment in its educational context. The implications of exercising one or another of the alternative options are also stated.

The chapter proceeds to consider questions of feasibility in assessment. The approach is based on the observation that a practical scheme of assessment cannot be over elaborate. Judgement must be used as to the amount of detail to be included, for instance, in a published examination syllabus, in relation to the very detailed decisions that have to be made in setting an actual examination paper or establishing a test bank. Assessors, particularly of oral performance, have to work under considerable time pressure and can only handle a strictly limited number of criteria. Learners who wish to assess their own proficiency, say as a guide to what they should tackle next, have more time, but will need to be selective concerning the components of overall communicative competence relevant to them. This illustrates the more general principle that the Framework must be comprehensive, but all its users must be selective. Selectivity may well involve the use of a simpler classificatory scheme which, as we have seen in relation to 'communicative activities' may well collapse categories separated in the general scheme. On the other hand, the user's purposes may well mean expanding some categories and their exponents in areas of special relevance. The chapter discusses the issues raised and illustrates the discussion by presenting the schemes adopted by a number of examining bodies for proficiency assessment criteria.

For many users, Chapter 9 will enable them to approach public examination syllabuses in a more insightful and critical manner, raising their expectations of what information examining bodies should provide concerning the objectives, content, criteria and procedures for qualifying examinations at national and international level (e.g. ALTE, ICC). Teacher trainers will find it useful for raising awareness of assessment issues among teachers in initial and in-service training. However, teachers are becoming increasingly responsible for the assessment of their pupils and students at all levels, both formative and summative. Learners, too, are increasingly called upon to carry out self-assessment, whether to chart and plan their learning or to report their ability to communicate in languages which they have not been formally taught, but which contribute to their plurilingual development.

The introduction of a **European Language Portfolio** with international currency is now under consideration. The Portfolio would make it possible for learners to document their progress towards plurilingual competence by recording learning experiences of all kinds over a wide range of languages, much of which would otherwise be unattested and unrecognised. It is intended that the Portfolio will encourage learners to include a regularly updated statement of their self-assessed proficiency in each language. It will be of great importance for the credibility of the document for entries to be made responsibly and transparently. Here reference to CEF will be particularly valuable.

Those professionally involved in test development as well as in the administration and conduct of public examinations may wish to consult Chapter 9 in conjunction with the more specialised *Guide for Examiners* (document CC-Lang(96)10 rev). This guide, which deals in detail with test development and evaluation is complementary to Chapter 9. It also contains suggestions for further reading, an appendix on item analysis and a glossary of terms.

3 Common Reference Levels

3.1 Criteria for descriptors for Common Reference Levels

One of the aims of the Framework is to help partners to describe the levels of proficiency required by existing standards, tests and examinations in order to facilitate comparisons between different systems of qualifications. For this purpose the Descriptive Scheme and the Common Reference Levels have been developed. Between them they provide a conceptual grid which users can exploit to describe their system. Ideally a scale of reference levels in a common framework should meet the following four criteria. Two relate to description issues, and two relate to measurement issues:

Description Issues
- A common framework scale should be *context-free* in order to accommodate generalisable results from different specific contexts. That is to say that a common scale should not be produced specifically for, let us say, the school context and then applied to adults, or vice-versa. Yet at the same time the descriptors in a common Framework scale need to be *context-relevant*, relatable to or translatable into each and every relevant context – and appropriate for the function they are used for in that context. This means that the categories used to describe what learners can do in different contexts of use must be relatable to the target contexts of use of the different groups of learners within the overall target population.
- The description also needs to be *based on theories* of language competence. This is difficult to achieve because the available theory and research is inadequate to provide a basis for such a description. Nevertheless, the categorisation and description needs to be theoretically grounded. In addition, whilst relating to theory, the description must also remain *user-friendly* – accessible to practitioners. It should encourage them to think further about what competence means in their context.

Measurement Issues
- The points on the scale at which particular activities and competences are situated in a common framework scale should be *objectively determined* in that they are based on a theory of measurement. This is in order to avoid systematising error through adopting unfounded conventions and 'rules of thumb' from the authors, particular groups of practitioners or existing scales that are consulted.
- The *number of levels* adopted should be adequate to show progression in different sectors, but, in any particular context, should not exceed the number of levels between which people are capable of making reasonably consistent distinctions. This may mean adopting different sizes of scale step for different dimensions, or a

two-tier approach between broader (common, conventional) and narrower (local, pedagogic) levels.

These criteria are very difficult to meet, but are useful as a point of orientation. They can in fact be met by a combination of intuitive, qualitative and quantitative methods. This is in contrast to the purely intuitive ways in which scales of language proficiency are normally developed. Intuitive, committee authorship may work well for the development of systems for particular contexts, but have certain limitations in relation to the development of a common framework scale. The main weakness of reliance on intuition is that the placement of a particular wording at a particular level is subjective. Secondly there is also the possibility that users from different sectors may have valid differences of perspective due to the needs of their learners. A scale, like a test, has validity in relation to contexts in which it has been shown to work. Validation – which involves some quantitative analysis – is an ongoing and, theoretically never-ending, process. The methodology used in developing the Common Reference Levels, and their illustrative descriptors, has therefore been fairly rigorous. A systematic combination of intuitive, qualitative and quantitative methods was employed. First, the content of existing scales was analysed in relation to categories of description used in the Framework. Then, in an intuitive phase, this material was edited, new descriptors were formulated, and the set discussed by experts. Next a variety of qualitative methods were used to check that teachers could relate to the descriptive categories selected, and that descriptors actually described the categories they were intended to describe. Finally, the best descriptors in the set were scaled using quantitative methods. The accuracy of this scaling has since been checked in replication studies.

Technical issues connected with the development and scaling of descriptions of language proficiency are considered in the appendices. Appendix A gives an introduction to scales and scaling plus methodologies which can be adopted in development. Appendix B gives a brief overview of the Swiss National Science Research Council project which developed the Common Reference Levels, and their illustrative descriptors, in a project covering different educational sectors. Appendices C and D then introduce two related European projects which have since used a similar methodology to develop and validate such descriptors in relation to young adults. In Appendix C the DIALANG project is described. As part of a wider assessment instrument, DIALANG has extended and adapted for self-assessment descriptors from the CEF. In Appendix D the ALTE (Association of Language Testers in Europe) 'Can Do' project is described. This project has developed and validated a large set of descriptors, which can also be related to the Common Reference Levels. These descriptors complement those in the Framework itself in that they are organised in relation to domains of use which are relevant to adults.

The projects described in the appendices demonstrate a very considerable degree of communality with regard both to the Common Reference Levels themselves and to the concepts scaled to different levels in the illustrative descriptors. That is to say that there is already a growing body of evidence to suggest that the criteria outlined above are at least partially fulfilled.

3.2 The Common Reference Levels

There does appear in practice to be a wide, though by no means universal, consensus on the number and nature of levels appropriate to the organisation of language learning and the public recognition of achievement. It seems that an outline framework of six broad levels gives an adequate coverage of the learning space relevant to European language learners for these purposes.

- **Breakthrough**, corresponding to what Wilkins in his 1978 proposal labelled '*Formulaic Proficiency*', and Trim in the same publication[1] '*Introductory*'.
- **Waystage**, reflecting the Council of Europe content specification.
- **Threshold**, reflecting the Council of Europe content specification.
- **Vantage**, reflecting the third Council of Europe content specification, a level described as '*Limited Operational Proficiency*' by Wilkins, and '*adequate response to situations normally encountered*' by Trim.
- **Effective Operational Proficiency** which was called '*Effective Proficiency*' by Trim, '*Adequate Operational Proficiency*' by Wilkins, and represents an advanced level of competence suitable for more complex work and study tasks.
- **Mastery** (Trim: '*comprehensive mastery*'; Wilkins: '*Comprehensive Operational Proficiency*'), corresponds to the top examination objective in the scheme adopted by ALTE (Association of Language Testers in Europe). It could be extended to include the more developed intercultural competence above that level which is achieved by many language professionals.

When one looks at these six levels, however, one sees that they are respectively higher and lower interpretations of the classic division into basic, intermediate and advanced. Also, some of the names given to Council of Europe specifications for levels have proved resistant to translation (e.g. *Waystage*, *Vantage*). The scheme therefore proposed adopts a 'hypertext' branching principle, starting from an initial division into three broad levels – A, B and C:

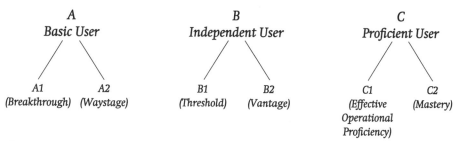

Figure 1

3.3 Presentation of Common Reference Levels

The establishment of a set of common reference points in no way limits how different sectors in different pedagogic cultures may choose to organise or describe their system of levels and modules. It is also to be expected that the precise formulation of the set of common reference points, the wording of the descriptors, will develop over time as the

[1] Trim, J. L. M. 1978 *Some Possible Lines of Development of an Overall Structure for a European Unit Credit Scheme for Foreign Language Learning by Adults*, Council of Europe.

experience of member states and of institutions with related expertise is incorporated into the description.

It is also desirable that the common reference points are presented in different ways for different purposes. For some purposes it will be appropriate to summarise the set of proposed Common Reference Levels in single holistic paragraphs, as shown in Table 1. Such a simple 'global' representation will make it easier to communicate the system to non-specialist users and will also provide teachers and curriculum planners with orientation points:

Table 1. *Common Reference Levels: global scale*

Proficient User	C2	Can understand with ease virtually everything heard or read. Can summarise information from different spoken and written sources, reconstructing arguments and accounts in a coherent presentation. Can express him/herself spontaneously, very fluently and precisely, differentiating finer shades of meaning even in more complex situations.
	C1	Can understand a wide range of demanding, longer texts, and recognise implicit meaning. Can express him/herself fluently and spontaneously without much obvious searching for expressions. Can use language flexibly and effectively for social, academic and professional purposes. Can produce clear, well-structured, detailed text on complex subjects, showing controlled use of organisational patterns, connectors and cohesive devices.
Independent User	B2	Can understand the main ideas of complex text on both concrete and abstract topics, including technical discussions in his/her field of specialisation. Can interact with a degree of fluency and spontaneity that makes regular interaction with native speakers quite possible without strain for either party. Can produce clear, detailed text on a wide range of subjects and explain a viewpoint on a topical issue giving the advantages and disadvantages of various options.
	B1	Can understand the main points of clear standard input on familiar matters regularly encountered in work, school, leisure, etc. Can deal with most situations likely to arise whilst travelling in an area where the language is spoken. Can produce simple connected text on topics which are familiar or of personal interest. Can describe experiences and events, dreams, hopes and ambitions and briefly give reasons and explanations for opinions and plans.
Basic User	A2	Can understand sentences and frequently used expressions related to areas of most immediate relevance (e.g. very basic personal and family information, shopping, local geography, employment). Can communicate in simple and routine tasks requiring a simple and direct exchange of information on familiar and routine matters. Can describe in simple terms aspects of his/her background, immediate environment and matters in areas of immediate need.
	A1	Can understand and use familiar everyday expressions and very basic phrases aimed at the satisfaction of needs of a concrete type. Can introduce him/herself and others and can ask and answer questions about personal details such as where he/she lives, people he/she knows and things he/she has. Can interact in a simple way provided the other person talks slowly and clearly and is prepared to help.

In order to orient learners, teachers and other users within the educational system for some practical purpose, however, a more detailed overview is likely to be necessary. Such an overview can be presented in the form of a grid showing major categories of language use at each of the six levels. The example in Table 2 (on the next two pages) is a draft for a self-assessment orientation tool based on the six levels. It is intended to help learners to profile their main language skills, and decide at which level they might look at a checklist of more detailed descriptors in order to self-assess their level of proficiency.

For other purposes, it may be desirable to focus on a particular spectrum of levels, and a particular set of categories. By restricting the range of levels and categories covered to those relevant to a particular purpose, it will be possible to add more detail: finer levels and categories. Such detail would enable a set of modules to be 'mapped' relative to one another – and also to be situated in relation to the Common Framework.

Alternatively, rather than profiling categories of communicative activities, one may *Analytic* wish to assess a performance on the basis of the aspects of communicative language competence one can deduce from it. The chart in Table 3 was designed to assess spoken performances. It focuses on different qualitative aspects of language use.

3.4   Illustrative descriptors

The three tables used to introduce the Common Reference Levels (Tables 1, 2 and 3) are summarised from a bank of 'illustrative descriptors' developed and validated for the CEF in the research project described in Appendix B. These formulations have been mathematically scaled to these levels by analysing the way in which they have been interpreted in the assessment of large numbers of learners.

For ease of consultation, scales of descriptors are juxtaposed to the relevant categories of the descriptive scheme in Chapters 4 and 5. The descriptors refer to the following three metacategories in the descriptive scheme:

Communicative activities

'Can Do' descriptors are provided for reception, interaction and production. There may not be descriptors for all sub-categories for every level, since some activities cannot be undertaken until a certain level of competence has been reached, whilst others may cease to be an objective at higher levels.

Strategies

'Can Do' descriptors are provided for some of the strategies employed in performing communicative activities. Strategies are seen as a hinge between the learner's resources (competences) and what he/she can do with them (communicative activities). The principles of a) planning action, b) balancing resources and compensating for deficiencies during execution and c) monitoring results and undertaking repair as necessary are described in the sections dealing with interaction and production strategies in Chapter 4.

Table 2. *Common Reference Levels: self-assessment grid*

		A1	A2	B1
U N D E R S T A N D I N G	**Listening**	I can recognise familiar words and very basic phrases concerning myself, my family and immediate concrete surroundings when people speak slowly and clearly.	I can understand phrases and the highest frequency vocabulary related to areas of most immediate personal relevance (e.g. very basic personal and family information, shopping, local area, employment). I can catch the main point in short, clear, simple messages and announcements.	I can understand the main points of clear standard speech on familiar matters regularly encountered in work, school, leisure, etc. I can understand the main point of many radio or TV programmes on current affairs or topics of personal or professional interest when the delivery is relatively slow and clear.
	Reading	I can understand familiar names, words and very simple sentences, for example on notices and posters or in catalogues.	I can read very short, simple texts. I can find specific, predictable information in simple everyday material such as advertisements, prospectuses, menus and timetables and I can understand short simple personal letters.	I can understand texts that consist mainly of high frequency everyday or job-related language. I can understand the description of events, feelings and wishes in personal letters.
S P E A K I N G	**Spoken Interaction**	I can interact in a simple way provided the other person is prepared to repeat or rephrase things at a slower rate of speech and help me formulate what I'm trying to say. I can ask and answer simple questions in areas of immediate need or on very familiar topics.	I can communicate in simple and routine tasks requiring a simple and direct exchange of information on familiar topics and activities. I can handle very short social exchanges, even though I can't usually understand enough to keep the conversation going myself.	I can deal with most situations likely to arise whilst travelling in an area where the language is spoken. I can enter unprepared into conversation on topics that are familiar, of personal interest or pertinent to everyday life (e.g. family, hobbies, work, travel and current events).
	Spoken Production	I can use simple phrases and sentences to describe where I live and people I know.	I can use a series of phrases and sentences to describe in simple terms my family and other people, living conditions, my educational background and my present or most recent job.	I can connect phrases in a simple way in order to describe experiences and events, my dreams, hopes and ambitions. I can briefly give reasons and explanations for opinions and plans. I can narrate a story or relate the plot of a book or film and describe my reactions.
W R I T I N G	**Writing**	I can write a short, simple postcard, for example sending holiday greetings. I can fill in forms with personal details, for example entering my name, nationality and address on a hotel registration form.	I can write short, simple notes and messages relating to matters in areas of immediate need. I can write a very simple personal letter, for example thanking someone for something.	I can write simple connected text on topics which are familiar or of personal interest. I can write personal letters describing experiences and impressions.

B2	C1	C2
I can understand extended speech and lectures and follow even complex lines of argument provided the topic is reasonably familiar. I can understand most TV news and current affairs programmes. I can understand the majority of films in standard dialect.	I can understand extended speech even when it is not clearly structured and when relationships are only implied and not signalled explicitly. I can understand television programmes and films without too much effort.	I have no difficulty in understanding any kind of spoken language, whether live or broadcast, even when delivered at fast native speed, provided I have some time to get familiar with the accent.
I can read articles and reports concerned with contemporary problems in which the writers adopt particular attitudes or viewpoints. I can understand contemporary literary prose.	I can understand long and complex factual and literary texts, appreciating distinctions of style. I can understand specialised articles and longer technical instructions, even when they do not relate to my field.	I can read with ease virtually all forms of the written language, including abstract, structurally or linguistically complex texts such as manuals, specialised articles and literary works.
I can interact with a degree of fluency and spontaneity that makes regular interaction with native speakers quite possible. I can take an active part in discussion in familiar contexts, accounting for and sustaining my views.	I can express myself fluently and spontaneously without much obvious searching for expressions. I can use language flexibly and effectively for social and professional purposes. I can formulate ideas and opinions with precision and relate my contribution skilfully to those of other speakers.	I can take part effortlessly in any conversation or discussion and have a good familiarity with idiomatic expressions and colloquialisms. I can express myself fluently and convey finer shades of meaning precisely. If I do have a problem I can backtrack and restructure around the difficulty so smoothly that other people are hardly aware of it.
I can present clear, detailed descriptions on a wide range of subjects related to my field of interest. I can explain a viewpoint on a topical issue giving the advantages and disadvantages of various options.	I can present clear, detailed descriptions of complex subjects integrating sub-themes, developing particular points and rounding off with an appropriate conclusion.	I can present a clear, smoothly flowing description or argument in a style appropriate to the context and with an effective logical structure which helps the recipient to notice and remember significant points.
I can write clear, detailed text on a wide range of subjects related to my interests. I can write an essay or report, passing on information or giving reasons in support of or against a particular point of view. I can write letters highlighting the personal significance of events and experiences.	I can express myself in clear, well-structured text, expressing points of view at some length. I can write about complex subjects in a letter, an essay or a report, underlining what I consider to be the salient issues. I can select style appropriate to the reader in mind.	I can write clear, smoothly flowing text in an appropriate style. I can write complex letters, reports or articles which present a case with an effective logical structure which helps the recipient to notice and remember significant points. I can write summaries and reviews of professional or literary works.

Table 3. *Common Reference Levels: qualitative aspects of spoken language use*

	RANGE	ACCURACY	FLUENCY	INTERACTION	COHERENCE
C2	Shows great flexibility reformulating ideas in differing linguistic forms to convey finer shades of meaning precisely, to give emphasis, to differentiate and to eliminate ambiguity. Also has a good command of idiomatic expressions and colloquialisms.	Maintains consistent grammatical control of complex language, even while attention is otherwise engaged (e.g. in forward planning, in monitoring others' reactions).	Can express him/herself spontaneously at length with a natural colloquial flow, avoiding or backtracking around any difficulty so smoothly that the interlocutor is hardly aware of it.	Can interact with ease and skill, picking up and using non-verbal and intonational cues apparently effortlessly. Can interweave his/her contribution into the joint discourse with fully natural turntaking, referencing, allusion making, etc.	Can create coherent and cohesive discourse making full and appropriate use of a variety of organisational patterns and a wide range of connectors and other cohesive devices.
C1	Has a good command of a broad range of language allowing him/her to select a formulation to express him/ herself clearly in an appropriate style on a wide range of general, academic, professional or leisure topics without having to restrict what he/she wants to say.	Consistently maintains a high degree of grammatical accuracy; errors are rare, difficult to spot and generally corrected when they do occur.	Can express him/herself fluently and spontaneously, almost effortlessly. Only a conceptually difficult subject can hinder a natural, smooth flow of language.	Can select a suitable phrase from a readily available range of discourse functions to preface his remarks in order to get or to keep the floor and to relate his/her own contributions skilfully to those of other speakers.	Can produce clear, smoothly flowing, well-structured speech, showing controlled use of organisational patterns, connectors and cohesive devices.
B2+					
B2	Has a sufficient range of language to be able to give clear descriptions, express viewpoints on most general topics, without much conspicuous searching for words, using some complex sentence forms to do so.	Shows a relatively high degree of grammatical control. Does not make errors which cause misunderstanding, and can correct most of his/her mistakes.	Can produce stretches of language with a fairly even tempo; although he/she can be hesitant as he/she searches for patterns and expressions. There are few noticeably long pauses.	Can initiate discourse, take his/her turn when appropriate and end conversation when he/she needs to, though he/she may not always do this elegantly. Can help the discussion along on familiar ground confirming comprehension, inviting others in, etc.	Can use a limited number of cohesive devices to link his/her utterances into clear, coherent discourse, though there may be some 'jumpiness' in a long contribution.

B1+					
B1	Has enough language to get by, with sufficient vocabulary to express him/herself with some hesitation and circumlocutions on topics such as family, hobbies and interests, work, travel, and current events.	Uses reasonably accurately a repertoire of frequently used 'routines' and patterns associated with more predictable situations.	Can keep going comprehensibly, even though pausing for grammatical and lexical planning and repair is very evident, especially in longer stretches of free production.	Can initiate, maintain and close simple face-to-face conversation on topics that are familiar or of personal interest. Can repeat back part of what someone has said to confirm mutual understanding.	Can link a series of shorter, discrete simple elements into a connected, linear sequence of points.
A2+					
A2	Uses basic sentence patterns with memorised phrases, groups of a few words and formulae in order to communicate limited information in simple everyday situations.	Uses some simple structures correctly, but still systematically makes basic mistakes.	Can make him/herself understood in very short utterances, even though pauses, false starts and reformulation are very evident.	Can answer questions and respond to simple statements. Can indicate when he/she is following but is rarely able to understand enough to keep conversation going of his/her own accord.	Can link groups of words with simple connectors like 'and', 'but' and 'because'.
A1	Has a very basic repertoire of words and simple phrases related to personal details and particular concrete situations.	Shows only limited control of a few simple grammatical structures and sentence patterns in a memorised repertoire.	Can manage very short, isolated, mainly pre-packaged utterances, with much pausing to search for expressions, to articulate less familiar words, and to repair communication.	Can ask and answer questions about personal details. Can interact in a simple way but communication is totally dependent on repetition, rephrasing and repair.	Can link words or groups of words with very basic linear connectors like 'and' or 'then'.

Communicative language competences

Scaled descriptors are provided for aspects of linguistic competence and pragmatic competence, and for sociolinguistic competence. Certain aspects of competence do not seem to be amenable to definition at all levels; distinctions have been made where they have been shown to be meaningful.

Descriptors need to remain holistic in order to give an overview; detailed lists of microfunctions, grammatical forms and vocabulary are presented in language specifications for particular languages (e.g. *Threshold Level 1990*). An analysis of the functions, notions, grammar and vocabulary necessary to perform the communicative tasks described on the scales could be part of the process of developing new sets of language specifications. General competences implied by such a module (e.g. Knowledge of the World, Cognitive skills) could be listed in similar fashion.

The descriptors juxtaposed with the text in Chapters 4 and 5:

• Draw, in their formulation, upon the experience of many bodies active in the field of defining levels of proficiency.

• Have been developed in tandem with the development of the model presented in Chapters 4 and 5 through an interaction between (a) the theoretical work of the authoring group, (b) the analysis of existing scales of proficiency and (c) the practical workshops with teachers. Whilst not providing fully comprehensive coverage of the categories presented in Chapters 4 and 5, the set gives an indication of the possible appearance of a set of descriptors which would do so.

• Have been matched to the set of Common Reference Levels: A1 *(Breakthrough)*, A2 *(Waystage)*, B1 *(Threshold)*, B2 *(Vantage)*, C1 *(Effective Operational Proficiency)* and C2 *(Mastery)*.

• Meet the criteria outlined in Appendix A for effective descriptors in that each is brief, is clear and transparent, is positively formulated, describes something definite and has independent, stand-alone integrity – not relying on the formulation of other descriptors for its interpretation.

• Have been found transparent, useful and relevant by groups of non-native and native-speaker teachers from a variety of educational sectors with very different profiles in terms of linguistic training and teaching experience. Teachers appear to understand the descriptors in the set, which has been refined in workshops with them from an initial pool of some thousands of examples.

• Are relevant to the description of actual learner achievement in lower and upper secondary, vocational and adult education, and could thus represent realistic objectives.

• Have been (with noted exceptions) 'objectively calibrated' to a common scale. This means that the position of the vast majority of the descriptors on the scale is the product of the way in which they have been interpreted to assess the achievement of learners, and *not* just on the basis of the opinion of the authors.

• Provide a bank of criterion statements about the continuum of foreign language proficiency which can be exploited flexibly for the development of criterion-referenced assessment. They can be matched to existing local systems, elaborated by local experience and/or used to develop new sets of objectives.

The set as a whole, whilst not being fully comprehensive and having been scaled in one (admittedly multi-lingual, multi-sector) context of foreign language learning in instructional settings:

- **is flexible**. The same set of descriptors can be organised – as here – into the set of broad 'conventional levels' identified at the Rüschlikon Symposium, used by the European Commission's DIALANG Project (see Appendix C), as well as by ALTE (The Association of Language Testers in Europe) (see Appendix D). They can also be presented as narrower 'pedagogic levels'.
- **is coherent** from the point of view of content. Similar or identical elements which were included in different descriptors proved to have very similar scale values. These scale values also, to a very large extent, confirm the intentions of authors of the scales of language proficiency used as sources. They also appear to relate coherently to the content of Council of Europe specifications, as well as the levels being proposed by DIALANG and ALTE.

3.5   Flexibility in a branching approach

Level A1 (*Breakthrough*) is probably the lowest 'level' of generative language proficiency which can be identified. Before this stage is reached, however, there may be a range of specific tasks which learners can perform effectively using a very restricted range of language and which are relevant to the needs of the learners concerned. The 1994–5 Swiss National Science Research Council Survey, which developed and scaled the illustrative descriptors, identified a band of language use, limited to the performance of isolated tasks, which can be presupposed in the definition of Level A1. In certain contexts, for example with young learners, it may be appropriate to elaborate such a 'milestone'. The following descriptors relate to simple, general tasks, which were scaled below Level A1, but can constitute useful objectives for beginners:

- can make simple purchases where pointing or other gesture can support the verbal reference;
- can ask and tell day, time of day and date;
- can use some basic greetings;
- can say yes, no, excuse me, please, thank you, sorry;
- can fill in uncomplicated forms with personal details, name, address, nationality, marital status;
- can write a short, simple postcard.

The descriptors above concern 'real life' tasks of a tourist nature. In a school learning context, one could imagine a separate list of 'pedagogic tasks', including ludic aspects of language – especially in primary schools.   *playful*

Secondly, the Swiss empirical results suggest a scale of 9 more or less equally sized, coherent levels as shown in Figure 2. This scale has steps between A2 (*Waystage*) and B1 (*Threshold*), between B1 (*Threshold*) and B2 (*Vantage*), and between B2 (*Vantage*) and C1 (*Effective Operational Proficiency*). The possible existence of such narrower levels may be of interest in *learning* contexts, but can still be related to the broader levels conventional in *examining* contexts.

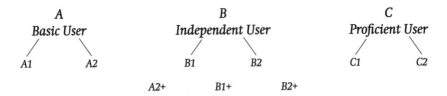

Figure 2

In the illustrative descriptors a distinction is made between the 'criterion levels' (e.g. A2 or A2.1) and the 'plus levels' (e.g. A2+ or A2.2). The latter are distinguished from the former by a horizontal line, as in this example for overall listening comprehension.

Table 4. *Levels A2.1 and A2.2 (A2+): listening comprehension*

	Can understand enough to be able to meet needs of a concrete type provided speech is clearly and slowly articulated.
A2	Can understand phrases and expressions related to areas of most immediate priority (e.g. very basic personal and family information, shopping, local geography, employment) provided speech is clearly and slowly articulated.

Establishing cut-off points between levels is always a subjective procedure; some institutions prefer broad levels, others prefer narrow ones. The advantage of a branching approach is that a common set of levels and/or descriptors can be 'cut' into practical local levels at different points by different users to suit local needs and yet still relate back to a common system. The numbering allows further subdivisions to be made without losing the reference to the main objective being referred to. With a flexible branching scheme such as that proposed, institutions can develop the branches relevant to them to the appropriate degree of delicacy in order to situate the levels used in their system in terms of the common framework.

Example 1:
A primary to lower secondary school system, for example, or system for adult evening classes in which the provision of visible progress at low levels is felt necessary, could develop the *Basic User* stem to produce a set of perhaps six milestones with finer differentiation at *A2* (*Waystage*) where large numbers of learners would be found.

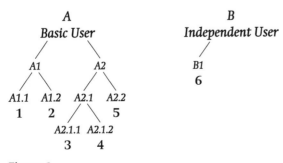

Figure 3

Example 2:

In an environment for learning the language in the area where it is spoken one might tend to develop the *Independence* branch, adding a further layer of delicacy by subdividing the levels in the middle of the scale:

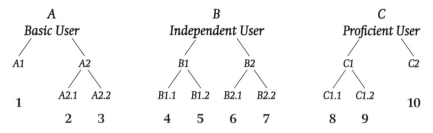

Figure 4

Example 3:

Frameworks for encouraging higher level language skills for professional needs would probably develop the *Proficient User* branch:

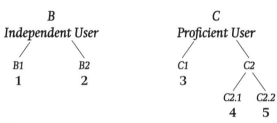

Figure 5

3.6   Content coherence in Common Reference Levels

An analysis of the functions, notions, grammar and vocabulary necessary to perform the communicative tasks described on the scales could be part of the process of developing new sets of language specifications.

- **Level A1 (Breakthrough)** – is considered the lowest level of generative language use – the point at which the learner can *interact in a simple way, ask and answer simple questions about themselves, where they live, people they know, and things they have, initiate and respond to simple statements in areas of immediate need or on very familiar topics,* rather than relying purely on a very finite rehearsed, lexically organised repertoire of situation-specific phrases.
- **Level A2** does appear to reflect the level referred to by the **Waystage** specification. It is at this level that the majority of descriptors stating social functions are to be found, like *use simple everyday polite forms of greeting and address; greet people, ask how they are and react to news; handle very short social exchanges; ask and answer questions about what they do at work and in free time; make and respond to invitations; discuss what to do, where to go and make arrangements to meet; make and accept offers.* Here too are to be found

descriptors on **getting out and about**: the simplified cut-down version of the full set of transactional specifications in 'The Threshold Level' for adults living abroad, like: *make simple transactions in shops, post offices or banks; get simple information about travel; use public transport: buses, trains, and taxis, ask for basic information, ask and give directions, and buy tickets; ask for and provide everyday goods and services.*

- The next band represents a **strong Waystage (A2+)** performance. What is noticeable here is **more active participation in conversation** given some assistance and certain limitations, for example: *initiate, maintain and close simple, restricted face-to-face conversation; understand enough to manage simple, routine exchanges without undue effort; make him/herself understood and exchange ideas and information on familiar topics in predictable everyday situations, provided the other person helps if necessary; communicate successfully on basic themes if he/she can ask for help to express what he wants to; deal with everyday situations with predictable content, though he/she will generally have to compromise the message and search for words; interact with reasonable ease in structured situations, given some help, but participation in open discussion is fairly restricted;* plus **significantly more ability to sustain monologues,** for example: *express how he/she feels in simple terms; give an extended description of everyday aspects of his/her environment e.g. people, places, a job or study experience; describe past activities and personal experiences; describe habits and routines; describe plans and arrangements; explain what he/she likes or dislikes about something; give short, basic descriptions of events and activities; describe pets and possessions; use simple descriptive language to make brief statements about and compare objects and possessions.*

- **Level B1** reflects the **Threshold Level** specification for a visitor to a foreign country and is perhaps most categorised by two features. The first feature is the **ability to maintain interaction and get across what you want to, in a range of contexts,** for example: *generally follow the main points of extended discussion around him/her, provided speech is clearly articulated in standard dialect; give or seek personal views and opinions in an informal discussion with friends; express the main point he/she wants to make comprehensibly; exploit a wide range of simple language flexibly to express much of what he or she wants to; maintain a conversation or discussion but may sometimes be difficult to follow when trying to say exactly what he/she would like to; keep going comprehensibly, even though pausing for grammatical and lexical planning and repair is very evident, especially in longer stretches of free production.* The second feature is the **ability to cope flexibly with problems in everyday life,** for example *cope with less routine situations on public transport; deal with most situations likely to arise when making travel arrangements through an agent or when actually travelling; enter unprepared into conversations on familiar topics; make a complaint; take some initiatives in an interview/consultation (e.g. to bring up a new subject) but is very dependent on interviewer in the interaction; ask someone to clarify or elaborate what they have just said.*

- The subsequent band seems to be a **Strong Threshold (B1+)**. The same two main features continue to be present, with the addition of a number of descriptors which focus on **the exchange of quantities of information,** for example: *take messages communicating enquiries, explaining problems; provide concrete information required in an interview/consultation (e.g. describe symptoms to a doctor) but does so with limited precision; explain why something is a problem; summarise and give his or her opinion about a short story, article, talk, discussion, interview, or documentary and answer further questions of detail; carry out a prepared interview, checking and confirming information, though he/she may occasionally have to ask for repetition if the other person's response is rapid or extended; describe how to do some-*

thing, giving detailed instructions; exchange accumulated factual information on familiar routine and non-routine matters within his/her field with some confidence.

- **Level B2** represents a new level as far above B1 (Threshold) as A2 (Waystage) is below it. It is intended to reflect the Vantage Level specification. The metaphor is that, having been progressing slowly but steadily across the intermediate plateau, the learner finds he has arrived somewhere, things look different, he/she acquires a new perspective, can look around him/her in a new way. This concept does seem to be borne out to a considerable extent by the descriptors calibrated at this level. They represent quite a break with the content so far. For example at the lower end of the band there is a focus on effective argument: *account for and sustain his opinions in discussion by providing relevant explanations, arguments and comments; explain a viewpoint on a topical issue giving the advantages and disadvantages of various options; construct a chain of reasoned argument; develop an argument giving reasons in support of or against a particular point of view; explain a problem and make it clear that his/her counterpart in a negotiation must make a concession; speculate about causes, consequences, hypothetical situations; take an active part in informal discussion in familiar contexts, commenting, putting point of view clearly, evaluating alternative proposals and making and responding to hypotheses.* Secondly, running right through the level there are two new focuses. The first is being able to more than hold your own in social discourse: e.g. *converse naturally, fluently and effectively; understand in detail what is said to him/her in the standard spoken language even in a noisy environment; initiate discourse, take his/her turn when appropriate and end conversation when he/she needs to, though he/she may not always do this elegantly; use stock phrases (e.g. 'That's a difficult question to answer') to gain time and keep the turn whilst formulating what to say; interact with a degree of fluency and spontaneity that makes regular interaction with native speakers quite possible without imposing strain on either party; adjust to the changes of direction, style and emphasis normally found in conversation; sustain relationships with native speakers without unintentionally amusing or irritating them or requiring them to behave other than they would with a native speaker.* The second new focus is a new degree of language awareness: *correct mistakes if they have led to misunderstandings; make a note of 'favourite mistakes' and consciously monitor speech for it/them; generally correct slips and errors if he/she becomes conscious of them; plan what is to be said and the means to say it, considering the effect on the recipient/s.* In all, this does seem to be a new threshold for a language learner to cross.

- At the next band – representing a **Strong Vantage** (B2+) performance – the focus on argument, effective social discourse and on language awareness which appears at B2 (Vantage) continues. However, the focus on argument and social discourse can also be interpreted as a new focus on discourse skills. This new degree of discourse competence shows itself in conversational management (co-operating strategies): *give feedback on and follow up statements and inferences by other speakers and so help the development of the discussion; relate own contribution skilfully to those of other speakers.* It is also apparent in relation to coherence/cohesion: *use a limited number of cohesive devices to link sentences together smoothly into clear, connected discourse; use a variety of linking words efficiently to mark clearly the relationships between ideas; develop an argument systematically with appropriate highlighting of significant points, and relevant supporting detail.* Finally, it is at this band that there is a concentration of items on negotiating: *outline a case for compensation, using persuasive language and simple arguments to demand satisfaction; state clearly the limits to a concession.*

- **Level C1**, the next band, was labelled *Effective Operational Proficiency*. What seems to characterise this level is good access to a broad range of language, which allows fluent, spontaneous communication, as illustrated by the following examples: *Can express him/herself fluently and spontaneously, almost effortlessly. Has a good command of a broad lexical repertoire allowing gaps to be readily overcome with circumlocutions. There is little obvious searching for expressions or avoidance strategies; only a conceptually difficult subject can hinder a natural, smooth flow of language.* The discourse skills characterising the previous band continue to be evident at Level C1, with an emphasis on more fluency, for example: *select a suitable phrase from a fluent repertoire of discourse functions to preface his remarks in order to get the floor, or to gain time and keep it whilst thinking; produce clear, smoothly flowing, well-structured speech, showing controlled use of organisational patterns, connectors and cohesive devices.*

- **Level C2**, whilst it has been termed 'Mastery', is not intended to imply native-speaker or near native-speaker competence. What is intended is to characterise the degree of precision, appropriateness and ease with the language which typifies the speech of those who have been highly successful learners. Descriptors calibrated here include: *convey finer shades of meaning precisely by using, with reasonable accuracy, a wide range of modification devices; has a good command of idiomatic expressions and colloquialisms with awareness of connotative level of meaning; backtrack and restructure around a difficulty so smoothly the interlocutor is hardly aware of it.*

The Common Reference Levels can be presented and exploited in a number of different formats, in varying degrees of detail. Yet the existence of fixed points of common reference offers transparency and coherence, a tool for future planning and a basis for further development. The intention of providing a concrete illustrative set of descriptors, together with criteria and methodologies for the further development of descriptors, is to help decision-makers design applications to suit their contexts.

3.7   How to read the scales of illustrative descriptors

The levels used are the six main levels introduced in Chapter 3: A1 *(Breakthrough)*, A2 *(Waystage)*, B1 *(Threshold)*, B2 *(Vantage)*, C1 *(Effective Operational Proficiency)* and C2 *(Mastery)*. The levels in the middle part of the scale – *Waystage, Threshold* and *Vantage* – often have a subdivision represented by a thin line, as mentioned above. Where this is the case, descriptors below the thin line represent the criterion level concerned. Descriptors placed above the line define a level of proficiency which is significantly higher than that represented by the criterion level, but which does not achieve the standard for the following level. The basis for this distinction is the empirical calibration. Where there is no subdivision of A2 *(Waystage)*, B1 *(Threshold)* or B2 *(Vantage)*, the descriptor represents the criterion level. In those cases no formulation was found to fall between the two criterion levels concerned.

   Some people prefer to read a scale of descriptors from the lowest to the highest levels; some prefer the reverse. For consistency all scales are presented with C2 *(Mastery)* at the top, and A1 *(Breakthrough)* at the bottom.

   Each level should be taken to subsume the levels below it on the scale. That is to say, someone at B1 *(Threshold)* is considered also to be able to do whatever is stated at A2

(*Waystage*), to be better than what is stated at A2 (*Waystage*). That means that provisos attached to a performance placed at A2 (*Waystage*) for example '*provided speech is clearly and slowly articulated*' will have less force, or be non-applicable to a performance at B1 (*Threshold*).

Not every element or aspect in a descriptor is repeated at the following level. That is to say that entries at each level describe selectively what is seen as salient or new at that level. They do not systematically repeat all the elements mentioned at the level below with a minor change of formulation to indicate increased difficulty.

Not every level is described on all scales. It is difficult to draw conclusions from the absence of a particular area at a particular level, since this could be due to one of several different reasons, or to a combination of them:

- The area exists at this level: some descriptors were included in the research project, but were dropped in quality control;
- The area probably exists at this level: descriptors could presumably be written, but haven't been;
- The area may exist at this level: but formulation seems to be very difficult if not impossible;
- The area doesn't exist or isn't relevant at this level; a distinction cannot be made here.

If users of the Framework wish to exploit the descriptor bank they will need to take a view on the question of what to do about gaps in the descriptors provided. It may well be the case that gaps can be plugged by further elaboration in the context concerned, and/or by merging material from the user's own system. On the other hand some gaps may still – rightly – remain. It might be the case that a particular category is not relevant towards the top or bottom of the set of levels. A gap in the middle of a scale may, on the other hand, indicate that a meaningful distinction cannot easily be formulated.

3.8 How to use scales of descriptors of language proficiency

The Common Reference Levels exemplified in Tables 1, 2 and 3 constitute a verbal scale of proficiency. Technical issues concerned with the development of such a scale are discussed in Appendix A. Chapter 9 on assessment describes ways in which the scale of Common Reference Levels can be used as a resource in relation to the assessment of language proficiency.

However, a very important issue in discussing scales of language proficiency is the accurate identification of the purpose the scale is to serve, and an appropriate matching of the formulation of scale descriptors to that purpose.

A functional distinction has been made between three types of scales of proficiency: (a) user-oriented, (b) assessor-oriented and (c) constructor-oriented scales (Alderson 1991). Problems can arise when a scale designed for one function is used for another – unless the formulation can be shown to be adequate.

(a) **user-oriented scales** report typical or likely behaviours of learners at any given level. Statements tend to talk about **what the learner can do** and to be positively worded, even at low levels:

> Can understand simple English spoken slowly and carefully to him/her and catch the main points in short, clear, simple messages and announcements.
> *Eurocentres Certificate Scale of Language Proficiency 1993: Listening: Level 2*[2]

though limitations may also be expressed:

> Manages to communicate in simple and routine tasks and situations. With the help of a dictionary can understand simple written messages and without one can get the gist. Limited language proficiency causes frequent breakdowns and misunderstandings in non-routine situations.
> *Finnish Nine Level Scale of Language Proficiency 1993: Level 2*

User-oriented scales are often *holistic*, offering one descriptor per level. The Finnish scale referred to is of this type. Table 1, shown earlier in this chapter in order to introduce the Common Reference Levels, also offers users a holistic summary of typical proficiency at each level. User scales may also report the four skills, as in the Eurocentres scale referred to above, but simplicity is a major characteristic of scales with this purpose.

(b)   **assessor-oriented scales** guide the rating process. Statements are typically expressed in terms of aspects of the quality of the performance expected. Here assessment in the sense of summative, proficiency assessment of a particular performance is meant. Such scales concentrate on **how well the learner performs** and are often negatively worded even at high levels, particularly when the formulation is norm-referenced around a pass grade for an examination:

> Disconnected speech and/or frequent hesitations impeded communication and constantly strain the listener.
> *Certificate in Advanced English 1991 (University of Cambridge Local Examinations Syndicate), Paper 5 (Oral) Criteria for Assessment: Fluency: Band 1–2 (bottom of 4 bands)*

Negative formulation can, however, be to a great extent avoided if a qualitative development approach is used in which informants analyse and describe features of key performance samples.

Some assessor-oriented scales are *holistic scales,* offering one descriptor per level. Others on the other hand are *analytic* scales, focusing on different aspects of the performance such as Range, Accuracy, Fluency, Pronunciation. Table 3, presented earlier in this chapter, is an example of a positively worded *analytic* assessor-oriented scale drawn from the CEF illustrative descriptors.

Some analytic scales have a large number of categories in order to profile achievement. Such approaches have been argued to be less appropriate for assessment because assessors tend to find it difficult to cope with more than 3–5 categories. Analytic scales like Table 3 have been therefore described as **diagnosis-oriented** since one of their purposes is to profile current position, profile target needs in relevant categories and provide a diagnosis of what needs to be covered to get there.

---

[2] All the scales mentioned in this chapter are reviewed in detail with full references in North, B. (1994) *Scales of language proficiency: a survey of some existing systems*, Strasbourg, Council of Europe CC-LANG (94) 24.

(c) **constructor-oriented scales** guide the construction of tests at appropriate levels. *Test specs?* Statements are typically expressed in terms of specific communication tasks the learner might be asked to perform in tests. These types of scales, or lists of specifications, also concentrate on *what the learner can do*.

> Can give detailed information about own family, living conditions, educational background; can describe and converse on everyday things in his environment (e.g., his suburb, the weather); can describe present or most recent job or activity; can communicate on the spot with fellow workers or immediate superior (e.g., ask questions about job, make complaints about work conditions, time off, etc.); can give simple messages over the telephone; can give directions and instructions for simple tasks in his everyday life (e.g., to tradesmen). Has tentative use of polite request forms (e.g., involving could, would). May sometimes offend by unintended blandness or aggressiveness or irritate by over-deference where native speakers expect informality.
>
> *Australian Second Language Proficiency Ratings 1982; Speaking; Level 2: Examples of Specific ESL tasks (one of three columns)*

This holistic descriptor could be deconstructed into short, constituent descriptors for the categories *Information Exchange (Personal Domain; Work Domain), Description, Conversation, Telephoning, Directing/Instructing, Sociocultural*.

Finally, checklists or scales of descriptors used for continuous teacher-assessment – or self-assessment – work best when the descriptors say not only *what* the learners can do but also *how well* they can do it. The failure to include adequate information on how well learners should perform tasks caused problems with earlier versions of both the English National Curriculum attainment targets and the Australian curriculum profiles. Teachers appear to prefer some detail, related to curriculum tasks (a link to constructor-orientation) on the one hand, and related to qualitative criteria (a link to diagnosis-oriented) on the other hand. Descriptors for self-assessment will also typically be more effective if they indicate how well one should be able to perform tasks at different levels.

To summarise, scales of language proficiency can thus be seen as having one or more of the following orientations:

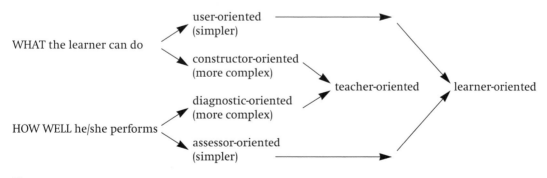

Figure 6

All these orientations can be considered relevant to a common framework.

Another way of looking at the orientations discussed above is to say that a user-oriented scale is a less detailed version of a constructor-oriented scale which is intended to give an overview. Similarly, an assessor-oriented scale is a less detailed version of a diagnostic-oriented scale which helps an assessor to arrive at an overview. Some user-oriented scales take this process of reducing detail into an overview to its logical conclusion and present a 'global' scale describing typical achievement at each level. In some cases this is instead of reporting detail (e.g. the Finnish scale cited above). In some cases it is to give meaning to a profile of numbers reported for particular skills (e.g. IELTS: International English Language Testing System). In other cases it is to give an entry point or overview to a more detailed specification (e.g. Eurocentres). In all these cases, the view taken is similar to that in hypertext computer presentations. The user is presented with an information pyramid and can get an overview by considering the top layer of the hierarchy (here the 'global' scale). More detail can be presented by going down layers of the system, but at any one point, what is being looked at is confined to one or two screens – or pieces of paper. In this way complexity can be presented without blinding people with irrelevant detail, or simplifying to the point of banality. Detail is there – if it is required.

Hypertext is a very useful analogy in thinking of a descriptive system. It is the approach taken in the ESU (English-speaking Union) Framework scale for examinations in English as a Foreign Language. In the scales presented in Chapters 4 and 5 the approach is developed further. For example, in relation to communicative activities, a scale for *Interaction* is a summary of sub-scales in this category.

Users of the Framework may wish to consider and where appropriate state:

- *to what extent their interest in levels relates to learning objectives, syllabus content, teacher guidelines and continuous assessment tasks (constructor-oriented);*
- *to what extent their interest in levels relates to increasing consistency of assessment by providing defined criteria for degree of skill (assessor-oriented);*
- *to what extent their interest in levels relates to reporting results to employers, other educational sectors, parents and learners themselves (user-oriented), providing defined criteria for degrees of skill (assessor-oriented);*
- *to what extent their interest in levels relates to reporting results to employers, other educational sectors, parents and learners themselves (user-oriented).*

3.9 Proficiency levels and achievement grades

An important distinction in relation to scaling can be made between the definition of levels of proficiency, as in a scale of Common Reference Levels, and the assessment of degrees of achievement in relation to an objective at one particular level. A proficiency scale, like the Common Reference Levels, defines a series of ascending bands of proficiency. It may cover the whole conceptual range of learner proficiency, or it may just cover the range of proficiency relevant to the sector or institution concerned. Being assessed as Level B2 may represent a tremendous achievement for one learner (assessed as Level B1 only two months previously), but a mediocre performance for another (already assessed as Level B2 two years previously).

Proficiency
Scale

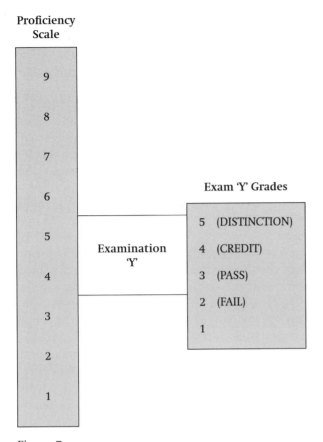

Figure 7

A particular objective may be situated at a certain level. In Figure 7, examination 'Y' aims to cover the band of proficiency represented by Levels 4 and 5 on the proficiency scale. There may be other examinations aimed at different levels, and the proficiency scale may be used to help make transparent the relationship between them. This is the idea behind the English-speaking Union (ESU) Framework project for examinations in English as a Foreign Language, and of the ALTE scheme to relate examinations for different European languages to each other.

Achievement in examination 'Y' may be assessed in terms of a grading scale, let us say 1–5, in which a '3' is the norm representing a Pass. Such a grading scale may be used for direct assessment of performance in subjectively marked papers – typically for Speaking and for Writing – and/or may be used to report the examination result. Examination 'Y' may be part of a suite of examinations 'X', 'Y' and 'Z'. Each examination may well have a grading scale in a similar style. But it is obvious that a Grade 4 in Examination X does not mean the same thing as a Grade 4 in Examination Y in terms of proficiency in the language.

If Examinations 'X', 'Y', and 'Z' have all been situated onto a common proficiency scale, then it should be possible, over a period of time, to establish the relationship between the grades on one examination in the series with the grades on the others. This can be achieved through a process of pooling expertise, analysing specifications, comparing official samples and scaling candidates' results.

It is possible to establish the relationship between examination grades and proficiency levels in this way because examinations have, by definition, a standard and a group of trained assessors capable of interpreting that standard. It is necessary to make the common standards explicit and transparent, provide examples which operationalise the standards, and then scale them.

Assessment of achievement in schools in many countries is through achievement grades (*notes, Noten*), sometimes 1–6, with 4 as the Pass, norm or 'satisfactory' grade. What is meant by the various grades is internalised by the teachers in the context concerned, but rarely defined. The nature of the relationship between teacher assessment grades and proficiency levels is in principle the same as that between examination grades and proficiency levels. But the issue is further complicated by the fact that there will be a myriad of standards involved. This is because, apart from the question of the form of assessment used and degree of common interpretation of grades by teachers in any one context, each school year in each type of school in each educationally distinct region will naturally constitute a different standard. A '4' at the end of the fourth year obviously does not mean the same as a '4' at the end of the third year in the same secondary school. Nor will a '4' for the end of the fourth year mean the same thing in two different kinds of school.

Nevertheless, it is possible to establish an approximate relationship between the range of standards in use in a particular sector and proficiency levels. This can be achieved through a cumulative process employing such techniques as the following. Standard definitions can be provided for different grades of achievement of the same objective. Teachers can be asked to profile average achievement onto an existing proficiency scale or grid such as Table 1 and Table 2. Representative samples of performance can be collected and calibrated to a scale in joint rating sessions. Teachers can be asked to rate previously standardised videos with the grades they normally give their students.

Users of the Framework may wish to consider and where appropriate state:

- *to what extent their concern relates to the establishment of a set of profiling levels to record progress in proficiency within their system as a whole*
- *to what extent their concern relates to the provision of transparent criteria for the award of grades of achievement in the objectives set for a particular proficiency level, perhaps operationalised by an examination, perhaps assessed by teachers*
- *to what extent their concern relates to the development of a common framework to establish coherent relationships between a range of educational sectors, proficiency levels, and assessment types within their system.*

---

4 Language use and the language user/learner

Following the first three introductory and explanatory chapters, Chapters 4 and 5 now present a fairly detailed scheme of categories for the description of language use and the language user. In accordance with the action-oriented approach taken, it is assumed that the language learner is in the process of becoming a language user, so that the same set of categories will apply. There is, however, an important modification which must be made. The learner of a second or foreign language and culture does not cease to be competent in his or her mother tongue and the associated culture. Nor is the new competence kept entirely separate from the old. The learner does not simply acquire two distinct, unrelated ways of acting and communicating. The language learner becomes *plurilingual* and develops *interculturality*. The linguistic and cultural competences in respect of each language are modified by knowledge of the other and contribute to intercultural awareness, skills and know-how. They enable the individual to develop an enriched, more complex personality and an enhanced capacity for further language learning and greater openness to new cultural experiences. Learners are also enabled to mediate, through interpretation and translation, between speakers of the two languages concerned who cannot communicate directly. A place is of course given to these activities (section 4.4.4) and competences (sections 5.1.1.3, 5.1.2.2 and 5.1.4), which differentiate the language learner from the monolingual native speaker.

Question boxes. Readers will see that from this point on, each section is followed by a box in which the Framework user is invited: 'to consider and where appropriate state' the answers to one or more questions that follow. The alternatives in the phrase 'need/be equipped/be required' relate to learning, teaching and assessment respectively. The content of the box is phrased as an invitation rather than as an instruction in order to emphasise the non-directive character of the Framework enterprise. If a user decides that a whole area is not of concern, there is no need to consider each section within that area in detail. In most cases, however, we expect that the Framework user will reflect on the question posed in each box and take a decision one way or another. If the decision taken is of significance, it can be formulated using the categories and examples supplied, supplemented as may be found necessary for the purpose in hand.

The analysis of language use and the language user contained in Chapter 4 is fundamental to the use of the Framework, since it offers a structure of parameters and categories which should enable all those involved in language learning, teaching and assessment to consider and state in concrete terms and in whatever degree of detail they wish, what they expect the learners towards whom they undertake responsibilities to be able to do with a language, and what they should know in order to be able to act. Its aim is to be comprehensive in its coverage, but not of course exhaustive. Course designers, textbook writers, teachers and examiners will have to make very detailed concrete decisions on the content of texts, exercises, activities, tests, etc. This process can never be reduced simply to choosing from a pre-determined menu. That level of decision must, and should, be in the hands of the practitioners concerned, calling on their judgement and creativity. They should, however, find represented here all the major aspects of language use and competence they need to take into consideration. The overall structure of Chapter 4 is thus a kind of checklist and for this reason is presented at the beginning of the chapter. Users are recommended to familiarise themselves with this overall structure and to refer to it when asking themselves such questions as:

- Can I predict the domains in which my learners will operate and the situations which they will have to deal with? If so, what roles will they have to play?
- What sort of people will they have to deal with?
- What will be their personal or professional relations in what institutional frameworks?
- What objects will they need to refer to?
- What tasks will they have to accomplish?
- What themes will they need to handle?
- Will they have to speak, or simply listen and read with understanding?
- What sort of things will they be listening to or reading?
- Under what conditions will they have to act?
- What knowledge of the world or of another culture will they need to call on?
- What skills will they need to have developed? How can they still be themselves without being misinterpreted?
- For how much of this can I take responsibility?
- If I cannot predict the situations in which the learners will use the language, how can I best prepare them to use the language for communication without over-training them for situations that may never arise?
- What can I give them that will be of lasting value, in whatever different ways their careers may later diverge?
- How can language learning best contribute to their personal and cultural development as responsible citizens in a pluralist democratic society?

Clearly, the Framework cannot give the answers to these questions. Indeed, it is precisely because the answers depend entirely upon a full appreciation of the learning/teaching situation and above all upon the needs, motivations, characteristics and resources of the learners and other parties concerned that the diversification of provision is necessary. The role of the following chapters is to articulate the problem in such a way that the issues can be considered and if need be debated in a transparent and rational way and the decisions communicated to all those affected in a clear and concrete manner.

Where possible, reference is made at the end of each section to relevant items in the General Bibliography for further reading.

4.1 The context of language use

It has long been recognised that language in use varies greatly according to the requirements of the context in which it is used. In this respect, language is not a neutral instrument of thought like, say, mathematics. The need and the desire to communicate arise in a particular situation and the form as well as the content of the communication is a response to that situation. The first section of Chapter 4 is therefore devoted to different aspects of context.

4.1.1 Domains

Each act of language use is set in the context of a particular situation within one of the *domains* (spheres of action or areas of concern) in which social life is organised. The choice of the domains in which learners are being prepared to operate has far-reaching implications for the selection of situations, purposes, tasks, themes and texts for teaching and testing materials and activities. Users may have to bear in mind the motivational effects of choosing domains of present relevance in relation to their future utility. For instance, children may be better motivated by a concentration on their present centres of interest, which may then leave them ill-prepared to communicate later in an adult environment. In adult education, conflicts of interest can arise between employers, who may be funding courses and who look for concentration on the occupational domain, and students who may be mostly interested in developing personal relations.

The number of possible domains is indeterminate, since any definable sphere of activity or area of concern may constitute the domain of concern to a particular user or course of instruction. For general purposes of language learning and teaching it may be useful to distinguish at least the following:

* the *personal* domain, in which the person concerned lives as a private individual, centred on home life with family and friends, and engages in individual practices such as reading for pleasure, keeping a personal diary, pursuing a special interest or hobby, etc.;
* the *public* domain, in which the person concerned acts as a member of the general public, or of some organisation, and is engaged in transactions of various kinds for a variety of purposes;
* the *occupational* domain, in which the person concerned is engaged in his or her job or profession;
* the *educational* domain, in which the person concerned is engaged in organised learning, especially (but not necessarily) within an educational institution.

It should be noted that in many situations more than one domain may be involved. For a teacher, the occupational and educational domains largely coincide. The public domain, with that which is involved in terms of social and administrative interactions and transactions, and contact with the media, opens up to the other domains. In both the educational and professional domains, many interactions and language activities fall under the ordinary social functioning of a group rather than reflect a connection with occupational or learning tasks; similarly, the personal domain should by no means be considered as a sphere apart (media penetration into family and personal life, distribution of various 'public' documents in 'private' letter-boxes, advertising, public texts on the packaging of products used in private daily life, etc.).

On the other hand, the personal domain individualises or personalises actions in the other domains. Without ceasing to be social agents, the persons involved situate themselves as individuals; a technical report, a class presentation, a purchase made can – fortunately – enable a 'personality' to be expressed other than solely in relation to the professional, educational or public domain of which, in a specific time and place, its language activity forms part.

> *Users of the Framework may wish to consider and where appropriate state:*
>
> * *in which domains the learner will need/be equipped/be required to operate.*

4.1.2 Situations

In each domain, the external situations which arise may be described in terms of:

* the *locations* in which, and the *times* at which, they occur;
* the *institutions* or *organisations* – the structure and procedures of which control much of what can normally occur;
* the *persons* involved, especially in their relevant social roles in relation to the user/ learner;
* the *objects* (animate and inanimate) in the environment;
* the *events* that take place;
* the *operations* performed by the persons involved;
* the *texts* encountered within the situation.

Table 5 (on pages 48–49) gives some examples of the above situational categories, classified according to domains, likely to be met in most European countries. The table is purely illustrative and suggestive. It makes no claim to be exhaustive. In particular it cannot deal with the dynamic aspects of interactive situations, in which the participants identify the relevant features of the situation as it develops and are concerned to change rather than to describe it. More is said regarding the relations between partners in acts of communication in sections 4.1.4 and 4.1.5. On the internal structure of communicative interaction, see 5.2.3.2. On sociocultural aspects, see 5.1.1.2, for user strategies, 4.4.

> *Users of the Framework may wish to consider and where appropriate state:*
>
> * *the situations which the learner will need/be equipped/be required to handle;*
> * *the locations, institutions/organisations, persons, objects, events and actions with which the learner will be concerned.*

4.1.3 Conditions and constraints

The external conditions under which communication occurs impose various constraints on the user/learner and his/her interlocutors, e.g.:

- Physical conditions:
  a) for speech:
    - clarity of pronunciation;
    - ambient noise (trains, aircraft, 'static', etc.);
    - interference (crowded street, markets, pubs, parties, discos, etc.);
    - distortions (poor telephone lines, radio reception, public address systems);
    - weather conditions (wind, extreme cold, etc.).
  b) for writing:
    - poor reproduction of print;
    - difficult handwriting;
    - poor lighting, etc.
- Social conditions:
  - number and familiarity of interlocutors;
  - relative status of participants (power and solidarity, etc.);
  - presence/absence of audience or eavesdroppers;
  - social relationships between participants (e.g. friendliness/hostility, co-operativeness).
- Time pressures:
  - different pressures for speaker/listener (real time) and writer/reader (more flexible);
  - preparation time (e.g. improvised vs routinised vs prepared in advance) for speeches, reports, etc.;
  - limitations on time allowed (e.g. by rules, expense, competing events and commitments, etc.) for turns and interactions;
  - other pressures: financial; anxiety-producing situations (e.g. examinations), etc.

The ability of all speakers, especially learners, to put their language competence into action depends greatly on the physical conditions under which communication takes place. Speech recognition is made much more difficult by noise, interference and distortion, examples of which are given. The ability to function efficiently and reliably under difficult conditions may be of crucial importance, say for airline pilots receiving landing instructions, where there is no margin of error. Those learning to make public announcements in foreign languages need to use a particularly clear pronunciation, to repeat key words, etc., to ensure understanding. Language laboratories have often employed tapes copied from copies in which noise and distortion are at levels which would be rejected as unacceptable in a visual channel and seriously impede language learning.

Care has to be taken to ensure that all candidates in listening comprehension tests enjoy equal conditions. Similar considerations may apply, *mutatis mutandis*, to reading comprehension and written production. Teachers and testers need also to be aware of the effect of social conditions and time pressures upon the processes of learning, classroom interaction and their effect upon a learner's competence and his or her ability to perform on a particular occasion.

Common European Framework of Reference for Languages: learning, teaching, assessment

Table 5. *External context of use: descriptive categories*

Domain	Locations	Institutions	Persons

Personal	Home: house, rooms, garden
	    own
	    of family
	    of friends
	    of strangers
	Own space in hostel, hotel
	The countryside, seaside
		The family
		Social networks
			(Grand)Parents, offspring, siblings, aunts, uncles, cousins, in-laws, spouses, intimates, friends, acquaintances

Public	Public spaces: street, square, park Public transport Shops (super)markets Hospitals, surgeries, clinics Sports stadia, fields, halls Theatre, cinema, entertainment Restaurant, pub, hotel Places of worship	Public authorities Political bodies The law Public health Services clubs Societies Political parties Denominations	Members of the public Officials Shop personnel Police, army, security Drivers, conductors Passengers Players, fans, spectators Actors, audiences Waiters, barpersons Receptionists Priests, congregation
Occupational	Offices Factories Workshops Ports, railways Farms Airports Stores, shops Service industries Hotels Civil Service	Firms Multinational corporations Nationalised industries Trade unions	Employers/ees Managers Colleagues Subordinates Workmates Clients Customers Receptionists, secretaries Cleaners
Educational	Schools: hall classrooms, playground, Sports fields, corridors Colleges Universities Lecture theatres Seminar rooms Student Union Halls of residence Laboratories Canteen	School College University Learned societies Professional Institutions Adult education bodies	Class teachers Teaching staff Caretakers Assistant staff Parents Classmates Professors, lecturers (Fellow) students Library and laboratory staff Refectory staff, cleaners Porters, secretaries

Objects	Events	Operations	Texts
Furnishing and furniture Clothing Household equipment Toys, tools, personal hygiene Objets d'art, books, Wild/domestic animals, pets Trees, plants, lawn, ponds Household goods Handbags Leisure/sports equipment	Family occasions Encounters Incidents, accidents Natural phenomena Parties, visits Walking, cycling motoring Holidays, excursions Sports events	Living routines: dressing, undressing cooking, eating, washing DIY, gardening Reading, radio and TV Entertaining Hobbies Games and sports	Teletext Guarantees Recipes Instructional material Novels, magazines Newspapers Junk mail Brochures Personal letters Broadcast and recorded spoken texts
Money, purse, wallet Forms Goods Weapons Rucksacks Cases, grips Balls Programmes Meals, drinks, snacks Passports, licences	Incidents Accidents, illnesses Public meetings Law-suits, court trials Rag-days, fines, arrests Matches, contests Performances Weddings, funerals	Buying and obtaining public services Using medical services Journeys by road/ rails/ship/air Public entertainment and leisure activities Religious services	Public announcements and notices Labels and packaging Leaflets, graffiti Tickets, timetables Notices, regulations Programmes Contracts Menus Sacred texts, sermons, hymns
Business machinery Industrial machinery Industrial and craft tools	Meetings Interviews Receptions Conferences Trade fairs Consultations Seasonal sales Industrial accidents Industrial disputes	Business admin. Industrial management Production operations Office procedures Trucking Sales operations Selling, marketing Computer operation Office maintenance	Business letter Report memorandum Life and safety notices Instructional manuals Regulations Advertising material Labelling and packaging Job description Sign posting Visiting cards
Writing material School uniforms Games equipment and clothing Food Audio-visual equipment Blackboard & chalk Computers Briefcases and school bags	Return to school / entry Breaking up Visits and exchanges Parents' days / evenings Sports days, matches Disciplinary problems	Assembly Lessons Games Playtime Clubs and societies Lectures, essay writing Laboratory work Library work Seminars and tutorials Homework Debates and discussions	Authentic texts (as above) Textbooks, readers Reference books Blackboard text OP text Computer screen text Videotext Exercise materials Journal articles Abstracts Dictionaries

> *Users of the Framework may wish to consider and where appropriate state:*
>
> - *how the physical conditions under which the learner will have to communicate will affect what he/she is required to do;*
> - *how the number and nature of the interlocutors will affect what the learner is required to do;*
> - *under what time pressure the learner will have to operate.*

4.1.4 The user/learner's mental context

The external context is highly organised independently of the individual. This organisation is extremely rich. It provides a very fine articulation of the world, closely reflected in the language of the community concerned and acquired by its speakers in the course of their maturation, education and experience, at least in so far as it is seen to be relevant to them. As a factor in the participation of a communicative event, however, we must distinguish between this external context, which is far too rich to be acted upon or even perceived in its full complexity by any individual, and the user/learner's mental context.

The external context is filtered and interpreted through the user's:

perceptual apparatus;
attention mechanisms;
long-term experience, affecting memory, associations and connotations;
practical classification of objects, events, etc.;
linguistic categorisation.

These factors influence the user's *observation* of the context. The extent to which the observed context provides the mental context for the communicative event is further determined by considerations of relevance in the light of the user's

intentions in entering into communication;
line of thought: the stream of thoughts, ideas, feelings, sense, impressions, etc., attended to in consciousness;
expectations in the light of previous experience;
reflection: the operation of thought processes upon experience (e.g. deduction, induction);
needs, drives, motivations, interests, which lead to a decision to act;
conditions and constraints, limiting and controlling the choices of action;
state of mind (fatigue, excitement, etc.), health and personal qualities (see section 5.1.3).

The mental context is thus not limited to reducing the information content of the immediately observable external context. Line of thought may be more powerfully influenced by memory, stored knowledge, imagination and other internal cognitive (and emotive) processes. In that case the language produced is only marginally related to the observable external context. Consider, for example, an examinee in a featureless hall, or a mathematician or poet in his or her study.

External conditions and constraints are also relevant mainly in so far as the user/learner recognises, accepts and adjusts to them (or fails to do so). This is very much a matter of the individual's interpretation of the situation in the light of his or her general competences (see section 5.1) such as prior knowledge, values and beliefs.

Users of the Framework may wish to consider and where appropriate state:

- *what assumptions are made about the learner's ability to observe and identify relevant features of the external contexts of communication;*
- *how communicative and learning activities relate to the learner's drives, motivations and interests;*
- *how far the learner is required to reflect on experience;*
- *in what ways the mental characteristics of the learner condition and constrain communication.*

4.1.5   The mental context of the interlocutor(s)

In a communicative event we have also to consider the user's interlocutor. The need for communication presupposes a 'communication gap', which can however be bridged because of the overlap, or partial congruence, between the mental context of the user in focus and the mental context of the interlocutor(s).

In face-to-face interaction, user and interlocutor(s) share the same external context (except, crucially, for the presence of the other), but for the reasons given above their observation and interpretation of the context differ. The effect – and often all or part of the function – of a communicative act is to increase the area of congruence in the understanding of the situation in the interest of effective communication so as to serve the purposes of the participants. This may be a matter of an exchange of factual information. More difficult to bridge are differences in values and beliefs, politeness conventions, social expectations, etc., in terms of which the parties interpret the interaction, unless they have acquired the relevant intercultural awareness.

The interlocutor(s) may be subject to partially or wholly different conditions and constraints from the user/learner, and react to them in different ways. For instance, an employee using a public address system may be unaware how poor its output is. One partner to a telephone conversation may have time to kill whilst the other has a client waiting, etc. These differences greatly affect the pressures upon the user.

Users of the Framework may wish to consider and where appropriate state:

- *to what extent the learners will need to adjust to the interlocutor's mental context;*
- *how learners can best be prepared to make the necessary adjustments.*

4.2   Communication themes

Within the various domains we may distinguish *themes*, the topics which are the subjects of discourse, conversation, reflection or composition, as the focus of attention in particular communicative acts. Thematic categories can be classified in many different ways. One influential classification, into themes, sub-themes and 'specific notions' is that presented in *Threshold Level 1990*, Chapter 7:

1. personal identification
2. house and home, environment
3. daily life
4. free time, entertainment
5. travel
6. relations with other people
7. health and body care
8. education
9. shopping
10. food and drink
11. services
12. places
13. language
14. weather

In each of these thematic areas, subcategories are established. For example, area 4, 'free time and entertainment', is subcategorised in the following way:

4.1 leisure
4.2 hobbies and interests
4.3 radio and TV
4.4 cinema, theatre, concert, etc.
4.5 exhibitions, museums, etc.
4.6 intellectual and artistic pursuits
4.7 sports
4.8 press

For each sub-theme, 'specific notions' are identified. In this respect, the categories represented in Table 5, covering the locations, institutions etc. to be treated, are particularly relevant. For instance, under 4.7. 'sports', *Threshold Level 1990* specifies:

1. locations: field, ground, stadium
2. institutions and organisations: sport, team, club
3. persons: player
4. objects: cards, ball
5. events: race, game
6. actions: to watch, to play (+name of sport), to race, to win, to lose, to draw

Clearly, this particular selection and organisation of themes, sub-themes and specific notions is not definitive. It results from the authors' decisions in the light of their assessment of the communicative needs of the learners concerned. It will be seen that the above themes relate mostly to the personal and public domains, as is appropriate to temporary visitors who are unlikely to enter into the vocational and educational life of the country. Some (e.g. area 4) are partly in the personal and partly in the public domain. Users of the Framework, including where possible the actual learners concerned, will of course make their own decisions based on their assessment of learner needs, motivations, characteristics and resources in the relevant domain or domains with which they are concerned For example, vocationally-oriented language learning (VOLL) may develop themes in the occupational area relevant to the students concerned. Students in upper secondary education may explore scientific, technological, economic, etc. themes in some depth. The use of a foreign language as medium of instruction will necessarily entail a close concern with the thematic content of the subject area taught.

Users of the Framework may wish to consider and where appropriate state:

- *which themes learners will need/be equipped/be required to handle in the selected domains;*
- *which sub-themes they will handle with respect to each theme;*
- *which specific notions relating to locations, institutions/organisations, persons, objects, events and operations they will need/be equipped/be required to handle in order to deal with each (sub)theme.*

4.3 Communicative tasks and purposes

4.3.1 Acts of communication with one or more interlocutors are generally undertaken by a language user in pursuance of his or her needs in a given situation. In the personal domain, the intention may be to entertain a visitor by exchanging information on families, friends, likes and dislikes, to compare experiences and attitudes, etc. In the public domain, it will usually be to transact business, say to buy clothes of good quality at a reasonable price. In the occupational domain, it may be to understand new regulations and their implications for a client. In the educational domain it may be to contribute to a roleplay or a seminar, or write a paper on a specialised topic for a conference or for publication, etc.

4.3.2 Over the years, needs analyses and language audits have produced an extensive literature on the language-using tasks a learner may be equipped or required to tackle in order to deal with the exigencies of the situations which arise in the various domains. As examples among many others, the following tasks in the *vocational* domain from *Threshold Level 1990* (Chapter 2, section 1.12) may be helpful.

> **Communicating at work:**
> As temporary residents learners should be able to:
>
> - seek work permits etc. as required;
> - enquire (e.g. from employment agencies) about the nature, availability and conditions of employment (e.g. job description, pay, laws of work, free time and holidays, length of notice);

- read employment advertisements;
- write letters of application and attend interviews giving written or spoken information about own personal data, qualifications and experience and answer questions about them;
- understand and follow joining procedures;
- understand and ask questions concerning the tasks to be performed on starting work;
- understand safety and security regulations and instructions;
- report an accident and make an insurance claim;
- make use of welfare facilities;
- communicate appropriately with superiors, colleagues and subordinates;
- participate in the social life of the enterprise or institution (e.g. canteen, sports and social clubs, etc.).

As a member of the host community, a learner should be able to assist an English-speaking (native or non-native) person with the tasks listed above.

Threshold Level 1990, Chapter 7, Section 1 gives examples of tasks in the *personal* domain.

Personal identification
The learners can say who they are, spell their name, state their address, give their telephone number, say when and where they were born, state their age, sex, state whether they are married or not, state their nationality, say where they are from, what they do for a living, describe their family, state their religion, if any, state their likes and dislikes, say what other people are like; elicit/understand similar information from others.

Practitioners (teachers, course-writers, examiners, curriculum designers, etc.) and users (parents, school governors, employers, etc.) as well as learners themselves have found these highly concrete task specifications very meaningful and motivating as learning objectives. Tasks are, however, indefinitely large in number. It is not possible for a general framework to specify *in extenso* all the communicative tasks that may be required in real-life situations. It is for practitioners to reflect upon the communicative needs of the learners with whom they are concerned and then, using as appropriate the full resources of the Framework model (e.g. as detailed in Chapter 7), to specify the communicative tasks they should be equipped to face. Learners should also be brought to reflect on their own communicative needs as one aspect of awareness-raising and self-direction.

Users of the Framework may wish to consider and where appropriate state:

- *the communicative tasks in the personal, public, occupational and/or educational domains that the learner will need/be equipped/be required to tackle;*
- *the assessment of learner needs on which the choice of tasks is based.*

4.3.3 In the educational domain it may be helpful to distinguish between the tasks which learners are equipped/required to tackle as language *users* and those in which they engage as part of the language *learning process* itself.

With regard to tasks as vehicles for planning, carrying out and reporting on language learning and teaching, information can be given as appropriate concerning:

- *Types of task*, e.g. simulations, roleplay, classroom interaction etc.;
- *Goals*, e.g. the group-based learning goals in relation to the differing, less predictable goals of participants;
- *Input*, e.g. instructions, materials, etc. selected or produced by teachers and/or learners;
- *Outcomes*, e.g. output artefacts such as texts, summaries, tables, presentations, etc. and learning outcomes such as improved competences, awareness, insights, strategies, experience in decision-making and negotiation, etc.;
- *Activities*, e.g. cognitive/affective, physical/reflective, group/pair/individual, processes: receptive and productive, etc. (see section 4.5);
- *Roles*, the roles of participants both in the tasks themselves and in task planning and management;
- *Monitoring and evaluation* of the relative success of the task conceived and as carried out using such criteria as relevance, difficulty expectations and constraints, and appropriateness.

A fuller account of the role of tasks in language learning and teaching is given in Chapter 7.

> *Users of the Framework may wish to consider and where appropriate state:*
>
> - *the tasks that learners will need/be equipped/be required to undertake in the educational domain, a) as participants in guided, goal-oriented interactions, projects, simulations, roleplays, etc., b) in other ways when the L2 (second language) is used as the medium of instruction in teaching of i) the language itself ii) other curricular subjects, etc.*

4.3.4 Ludic uses of language

The use of language for playful purposes often plays an important part in language learning and development, but is not confined to the educational domain. Examples of ludic activities include:

Social language games:
- oral (story with mistakes; how, when, where, etc.);
- written (consequences, hangman, etc.);
- audio-visual (picture lotto, snap, etc.);

- board and card games (Scrabble, Lexicon, Diplomacy, etc.);
- charades, miming, etc.

Individual activities:
- puzzles (crossword, rebus, anagram, etc.);
- media games (TV and radio: chiffres et lettres, Catchword, etc.).

Verbal joking (punning, etc.) e.g. in:
- advertisements e.g. (for a car) '*Make your money go a long way*';
- newspaper headlines e.g. '*Feminism or bust!*';
- graffiti e.g. '*Grammar rules – O.K.?*'.

4.3.5   Aesthetic uses of language

Imaginative and artistic uses of language are important both educationally and in their own right. Aesthetic activities may be productive, receptive, interactive or mediating (see 4.4.4 below), and may be oral or written. They include such activities as:

- singing (nursery rhymes, folk songs, pop songs, etc.)
- retelling and rewriting stories, etc.
- listening to, reading, writing and speaking imaginative texts (stories, rhymes, etc.) including audio-visual texts, cartoons, picture stories, etc.
- performing scripted or unscripted plays, etc.
- the production, reception and performance of literary texts, e.g.: reading and writing texts (short stories, novels, poetry, etc.) and performing and watching/listening to recitals, drama, opera, etc.

This summary treatment of what has traditionally been a major, often dominant, aspect of modern language studies in upper secondary and higher education may appear dismissive. It is not intended to be so. National and regional literatures make a major contribution to the European cultural heritage, which the Council of Europe sees as 'a valuable common resource to be protected and developed'. Literary studies serve many more educational purposes – intellectual, moral and emotional, linguistic and cultural – than the purely aesthetic. It is much to be hoped that teachers of literature at all levels may find many sections of the Framework relevant to their concerns and useful in making their aims and methods more transparent.

Users of the Framework may wish to consider and where appropriate state:

- *which ludic and aesthetic uses of language the learner will need/be equipped/be required to make.*

4.4 Communicative language activities and strategies

To carry out communicative tasks, users have to engage in communicative language activities and operate communication strategies.

Many communicative activities, such as conversation and correspondence, are *interactive,* that is to say, the participants alternate as producers and receivers, often with several turns.

In other cases, as when speech is recorded or broadcast or written texts are sent out or published, producers are separated from receivers, whom they may not even know and who are unable to respond. In these cases the communicative event can be regarded as *the speaking, writing, listening* to or *reading* of a text.

In most cases, the user as speaker or writer is producing his own text to express his own meanings. In others, he/she is acting as a channel of communication (often, but not necessarily, in different languages) between two or more persons who for one reason or another cannot communicate directly. This process, *mediation,* may be interactive or not.

Many if not most situations involve a mixture of activity types. In a school language class, for instance, a learner may be required to listen to a teacher's exposition, to read a textbook, silently or aloud, to interact with fellow pupils in group or project work, to write exercises or an essay, and even to mediate, whether as an educational activity or in order to assist another pupil.

Strategies are a means the language user exploits to mobilise and balance his or her resources, to activate skills and procedures, in order to fulfil the demands of communication in context and successfully complete the task in question in the most comprehensive or most economical way feasible depending on his or her precise purpose. Communication strategies should therefore *not* be viewed simply with a disability model – as a way of making up for a language deficit or a miscommunication. Native speakers regularly employ communication strategies of all kinds (which will be discussed below) when the strategy is appropriate to the communicative demands placed upon them.

The use of communication strategies can be seen as the application of the metacognitive principles: *Pre-planning, Execution, Monitoring,* and *Repair Action* to the different kinds of communicative activity: Reception, Interaction, Production and Mediation. The word 'strategies' has been used in different ways. Here what is meant is the adoption of a particular line of action in order to maximise effectiveness. Skills that are an inevitable part of the process of understanding or articulating the spoken and written word (e.g. chunking a stream of sound in order to decode it into a string of words carrying propositional meaning) are treated as lower-level skills, in relation to the appropriate communicative process (see section 4.5).

Progress in language learning is most clearly evidenced in the learner's ability to engage in observable language activities and to operate communication strategies. They are therefore a convenient basis for the scaling of language ability. A suggested scaling is given in this chapter for various aspects of the activities and strategies discussed.

4.4.1 *Productive activities and strategies*

Productive activities and strategies include both speaking and writing activities.

4.4.1.1 In ***oral production (speaking)*** activities the language user produces an oral text which is received by an audience of one or more listeners. Examples of speaking activities include:

- public address (information, instructions, etc.)
- addressing audiences (speeches at public meetings, university lectures, sermons, entertainment, sports commentaries, sales presentations, etc.).

They may involve, for example:

- reading a written text aloud;
- speaking from notes, or from a written text or visual aids (diagrams, pictures, charts, etc.);
- acting out a rehearsed role;
- speaking spontaneously;
- singing.

Illustrative scales are provided for:

- Overall spoken production;
- Sustained monologue: describing experience;
- Sustained monologue: putting a case (e.g. in debate);
- Public announcements;
- Addressing audiences.

[handwritten left margin note: Don't seem especially distinct]

		OVERALL ORAL PRODUCTION
C2		*Can produce clear, smoothly flowing well-structured speech with an effective logical structure which helps the recipient to notice and remember significant points.*
C1		*Can give clear, detailed descriptions and presentations on complex subjects, integrating sub-themes, developing particular points and rounding off with an appropriate conclusion.*
B2		*Can give clear, systematically developed descriptions and presentations, with appropriate highlighting of significant points, and relevant supporting detail.*
		Can give clear, detailed descriptions and presentations on a wide range of subjects related to his/her field of interest, expanding and supporting ideas with subsidiary points and relevant examples.
B1		*Can reasonably fluently sustain a straightforward description of one of a variety of subjects within his/her field of interest, presenting it as a linear sequence of points.*
A2		*Can give a simple description or presentation of people, living or working conditions, daily routines, likes/dislikes, etc. as a short series of simple phrases and sentences linked into a list.*
A1		*Can produce simple mainly isolated phrases about people and places.*

	SUSTAINED MONOLOGUE: Describing experience
C2	*Can give clear, smoothly flowing, elaborate and often memorable descriptions.*
C1	*Can give clear, detailed descriptions of complex subjects.* *Can give elaborate descriptions and narratives, integrating sub-themes, developing particular points and rounding off with an appropriate conclusion.*
B2	*Can give clear, detailed descriptions on a wide range of subjects related to his/her field of interest.*
B1	*Can give straightforward descriptions on a variety of familiar subjects within his/her field of interest.* *Can reasonably fluently relate a straightforward narrative or description as a linear sequence of points.* *Can give detailed accounts of experiences, describing feelings and reactions.* *Can relate details of unpredictable occurrences, e.g. an accident.* *Can relate the plot of a book or film and describe his/her reactions.* *Can describe dreams, hopes and ambitions.* *Can describe events, real or imagined.* *Can narrate a story.*
A2	*Can tell a story or describe something in a simple list of points. Can describe everyday aspects of his/her environment e.g. people, places, a job or study experience.* *Can give short, basic descriptions of events and activities.* *Can describe plans and arrangements, habits and routines, past activities and personal experiences.* *Can use simple descriptive language to make brief statements about and compare objects and possessions.* *Can explain what he/she likes or dislikes about something.*
	Can describe his/her family, living conditions, educational background, present or most recent job. *Can describe people, places and possessions in simple terms.*
A1	*Can describe him/herself, what he/she does and where he/she lives.*

	SUSTAINED MONOLOGUE: Putting a case (e.g. in a debate)
C2	*No descriptor available*
C1	*No descriptor available*
B2	*Can develop an argument systematically with appropriate highlighting of significant points, and relevant supporting detail.* *Can develop a clear argument, expanding and supporting his/her points of view at some length with subsidiary points and relevant examples.* *Can construct a chain of reasoned argument:* *Can explain a viewpoint on a topical issue giving the advantages and disadvantages of various options.*
B1	*Can develop an argument well enough to be followed without difficulty most of the time.* *Can briefly give reasons and explanations for opinions, plans and actions.*
A2	*No descriptor available*
A1	*No descriptor available*

	PUBLIC ANNOUNCEMENTS
C2	*No descriptor available*
C1	*Can deliver announcements fluently, almost effortlessly, using stress and intonation to convey finer shades of meaning precisely.*
B2	*Can deliver announcements on most general topics with a degree of clarity, fluency and spontaneity which causes no strain or inconvenience to the listener.*
B1	*Can deliver short, rehearsed announcements on a topic pertinent to everyday occurrences in his/her field which, despite possibly very foreign stress and intonation, are nevertheless clearly intelligible.*
A2	*Can deliver very short, rehearsed announcements of predictable, learnt content which are intelligible to listeners who are prepared to concentrate.*
A1	*No descriptor available*

Note: The descriptors on this sub-scale have not been empirically calibrated.

	ADDRESSING AUDIENCES
C2	*Can present a complex topic confidently and articulately to an audience unfamiliar with it, structuring and adapting the talk flexibly to meet the audience's needs.* *Can handle difficult and even hostile questioning.*
C1	*Can give a clear, well-structured presentation of a complex subject, expanding and supporting points of view at some length with subsidiary points, reasons and relevant examples.* *Can handle interjections well, responding spontaneously and almost effortlessly.*
B2	*Can give a clear, systematically developed presentation, with highlighting of significant points, and relevant supporting detail.* *Can depart spontaneously from a prepared text and follow up interesting points raised by members of the audience, often showing remarkable fluency and ease of expression.* *Can give a clear, prepared presentation, giving reasons in support of or against a particular point of view and giving the advantages and disadvantages of various options.* *Can take a series of follow up questions with a degree of fluency and spontaneity which poses no strain for either him/herself or the audience.*
B1	*Can give a prepared straightforward presentation on a familiar topic within his/her field which is clear enough to be followed without difficulty most of the time, and in which the main points are explained with reasonable precision.* *Can take follow up questions, but may have to ask for repetition if the speech was rapid.*
A2	*Can give a short, rehearsed presentation on a topic pertinent to his/her everyday life, briefly give reasons and explanations for opinions, plans and actions.* *Can cope with a limited number of straightforward follow up questions.* *Can give a short, rehearsed, basic presentation on a familiar subject.* *Can answer straightforward follow up questions if he/she can ask for repetition and if some help with the formulation of his/her reply is possible.*
A1	*Can read a very short, rehearsed statement – e.g. to introduce a speaker, propose a toast.*

Note: The descriptors on this sub-scale have been created by recombining elements of descriptors from other scales.

> *Users of the Framework may wish to consider and where appropriate state:*
>
> • *in what range of oral production (speaking) activities the learner will need/be equipped/be required to engage.*

4.4.1.2 In ***written production (writing)*** activities the language user as writer produces a written text which is received by a readership of one or more readers.

Examples of writing activities include:

• completing forms and questionnaires;
• writing articles for magazines, newspapers, newsletters, etc.;
• producing posters for display;
• writing reports, memoranda, etc.;
• making notes for future reference;
• taking down messages from dictation, etc.;
• creative and imaginative writing;
• writing personal or business letters, etc.

Illustrative scales are provided for:

• Overall written production;
• Creative writing;
• Reports and essays.

	OVERALL WRITTEN PRODUCTION
C2	*Can write clear, smoothly flowing, complex texts in an appropriate and effective style and a logical structure which helps the reader to find significant points.*
C1	*Can write clear, well-structured texts of complex subjects, underlining the relevant salient issues, expanding and supporting points of view at some length with subsidiary points, reasons and relevant examples, and rounding off with an appropriate conclusion.*
B2	*Can write clear, detailed texts on a variety of subjects related to his/her field of interest, synthesising and evaluating information and arguments from a number of sources.*
B1	*Can write straightforward connected texts on a range of familiar subjects within his field of interest, by linking a series of shorter discrete elements into a linear sequence.*
A2	*Can write a series of simple phrases and sentences linked with simple connectors like 'and', 'but' and 'because'.*
A1	*Can write simple isolated phrases and sentences.*

Note: The descriptors on this scale and on the two sub-scales which follow (Creative Writing; Reports and Essays) have not been empirically calibrated with the measurement model. The descriptors for these three scales have therefore been created by recombining elements of descriptors from other scales.

	CREATIVE WRITING
C2	*Can write clear, smoothly flowing, and fully engrossing stories and descriptions of experience in a style appropriate to the genre adopted.*
C1	*Can write clear, detailed, well-structured and developed descriptions and imaginative texts in an assured, personal, natural style appropriate to the reader in mind.*
B2	*Can write clear, detailed descriptions of real or imaginary events and experiences, marking the relationship between ideas in clear connected text, and following established conventions of the genre concerned.*
	Can write clear, detailed descriptions on a variety of subjects related to his/her field of interest. *Can write a review of a film, book or play.*
B1	*Can write straightforward, detailed descriptions on a range of familiar subjects within his/her field of interest.* *Can write accounts of experiences, describing feelings and reactions in simple connected text.* *Can write a description of an event, a recent trip – real or imagined.* *Can narrate a story.*
A2	*Can write about everyday aspects of his/her environment, e.g. people, places, a job or study experience in linked sentences.* *Can write very short, basic descriptions of events, past activities and personal experiences.*
	Can write a series of simple phrases and sentences about their family, living conditions, educational background, present or most recent job. *Can write short, simple imaginary biographies and simple poems about people.*
A1	*Can write simple phrases and sentences about themselves and imaginary people, where they live and what they do.*

	REPORTS AND ESSAYS
C2	*Can produce clear, smoothly flowing, complex reports, articles or essays which present a case, or give critical appreciation of proposals or literary works.* *Can provide an appropriate and effective logical structure which helps the reader to find significant points.*
C1	*Can write clear, well-structured expositions of complex subjects, underlining the relevant salient issues.* *Can expand and support points of view at some length with subsidiary points, reasons and relevant examples.*
B2	*Can write an essay or report which develops an argument systematically with appropriate highlighting of significant points and relevant supporting detail.* *Can evaluate different ideas or solutions to a problem.*
	Can write an essay or report which develops an argument, giving reasons in support of or against a particular point of view and explaining the advantages and disadvantages of various options. *Can synthesise information and arguments from a number of sources.*
B1	*Can write short, simple essays on topics of interest.* *Can summarise, report and give his/her opinion about accumulated factual information on familiar routine and non-routine matters within his/her field with some confidence.*
	Can write very brief reports to a standard conventionalised format, which pass on routine factual information and state reasons for actions.
A2	*No descriptor available*
A1	*No descriptor available*

> *Users of the Framework may wish to consider and where appropriate state:*
>
> - *for what purposes the learner will need/be equipped/be required to engage in which writing activities.*

4.4.1.3 **Production strategies involve mobilising resources, balancing between different competences – exploiting strengths and underplaying weaknesses – in order to match the available potential to the nature of the task.** Internal resources will be activated, possibly involving conscious preparation (*Rehearsing*), possibly calculating the effect of different styles, discourse structures or formulations (*Considering audience*), possibly looking things up or obtaining assistance when dealing with a deficit (*Locating resources*). When adequate resources have *not* been mobilised or located the language user may find it advisable to go for a more modest version of the task and, for example, write a postcard rather than a letter; on the other hand, having located appropriate support, he or she may choose to do the reverse – scaling up the task *(Task adjustment)*. In a similar way, without sufficient resources the learner/user may have to compromise what he or she would really like to express in order to match the linguistic means available; conversely, additional linguistic support, perhaps available later during re-drafting, may enable him or her to be more ambitious in forming and expressing his or her thoughts (*Message adjustment*).

Ways of scaling down ambitions to fit resources in order to ensure success in a more limited area have been described as *Avoidance strategies*; scaling up and finding ways to cope have been described as *Achievement strategies*. In using achievement strategies the language user adopts a positive approach with what resources he or she has: approximating and overgeneralising with simpler language, paraphrasing or describing aspects of what he or she wants to say, even 'foreignising' L1 (first language) expressions (*Compensating*); using highly accessible pre-fabricated language he or she feels sure of – 'islands of reliability' – to create stepping stones through what for the user is a novel situation or concept he or she wants to express (*Building on previous knowledge*), or just having a go with what he or she can half remember and thinks *might* work (*Trying out*). Whether or not the language user is aware of compensating, skating over thin ice or using language tentatively, feedback in terms of facial expression, gesture and subsequent moves in the conversation offer him or her the opportunity to monitor the success of the communication (*Monitoring success*). In addition, particularly in non-interactive activities (e.g. giving a presentation, writing a report) the language user may consciously monitor linguistically as well as communicatively, spot slips and 'favourite' mistakes and correct them (*Self-correction*).

- Planning   Rehearsing;
              Locating resources;
              Considering audience;
              Task adjustment;
              Message adjustment.

- Execution   Compensating;
              Building on previous knowledge;
              Trying out.
- Evaluation   Monitoring success.
- Repair   Self-correction.

Illustrative scales are provided for:

- Planning;
- Compensating;
- Monitoring and repair.

	PLANNING
C2	*As B2*
C1	*As B2*
B2	*Can plan what is to be said and the means to say it, considering the effect on the recipient/s.*
B1	*Can rehearse and try out new combinations and expressions, inviting feedback.*
	Can work out how to communicate the main point(s) he/she wants to get across, exploiting any resources available and limiting the message to what he/she can recall or find the means to express.
A2	*Can recall and rehearse an appropriate set of phrases from his/her repertoire.*
A1	*No descriptor available*

	COMPENSATING
C2	*Can substitute an equivalent term for a word he/she can't recall so smoothly that it is scarcely noticeable.*
C1	*As B2+*
B2	*Can use circumlocution and paraphrase to cover gaps in vocabulary and structure.*
B1	*Can define the features of something concrete for which he/she can't remember the word.* *Can convey meaning by qualifying a word meaning something similar (e.g. a truck for people = bus).*
	Can use a simple word meaning something similar to the concept he/she wants to convey and invites 'correction'. *Can foreignise a mother tongue word and ask for confirmation.*
A2	*Can use an inadequate word from his/her repertoire and use gesture to clarify what he/she wants to say.*
	Can identify what he/she means by pointing to it (e.g. 'I'd like this, please').
A1	*No descriptor available*

	MONITORING AND REPAIR
C2	*Can backtrack and restructure around a difficulty so smoothly the interlocutor is hardly aware of it.*
C1	*Can backtrack when he/she encounters a difficulty and reformulate what he/she wants to say without fully interrupting the flow of speech.*
B2	*Can correct slips and errors if he/she becomes conscious of them or if they have led to misunderstandings.* *Can make a note of 'favourite mistakes' and consciously monitor speech for it/them.*
B1	*Can correct mix-ups with tenses or expressions that lead to misunderstandings provided the interlocutor indicates there is a problem.*
	Can ask for confirmation that a form used is correct. *Can start again using a different tactic when communication breaks down.*
A2	*No descriptor available*
A1	*No descriptor available*

4.4.2   Receptive activities and strategies

These include listening and reading activities.

4.4.2.1   In *aural reception (listening)* activities the language user as listener receives and processes a spoken input produced by one or more speakers. Listening activities include:

- listening to public announcements (information, instructions, warnings, etc.);
- listening to media (radio, TV, recordings, cinema);
- listening as a member of a live audience (theatre, public meetings, public lectures, entertainments, etc.);
- listening to overheard conversations, etc.

In each case the user may be listening:

- for gist;
- for specific information;
- for detailed understanding;
- for implications, etc.

Illustrative scales are provided for:

- Overall listening comprehension;
- Understanding interaction between native speakers;
- Listening as a member of a live audience;
- Listening to announcements and instructions;
- Listening to audio media and recordings.

	OVERALL LISTENING COMPREHENSION
C2	*Has no difficulty in understanding any kind of spoken language, whether live or broadcast, delivered at fast native speed.*
C1	*Can understand enough to follow extended speech on abstract and complex topics beyond his/her own field, though he/she may need to confirm occasional details, especially if the accent is unfamiliar.* *Can recognise a wide range of idiomatic expressions and colloquialisms, appreciating register shifts.* *Can follow extended speech even when it is not clearly structured and when relationships are only implied and not signalled explicitly.*
B2	*Can understand standard spoken language, live or broadcast, on both familiar and unfamiliar topics normally encountered in personal, social, academic or vocational life. Only extreme background noise, inadequate discourse structure and/or idiomatic usage influences the ability to understand.* *Can understand the main ideas of propositionally and linguistically complex speech on both concrete and abstract topics delivered in a standard dialect, including technical discussions in his/her field of specialisation.* *Can follow extended speech and complex lines of argument provided the topic is reasonably familiar, and the direction of the talk is sign-posted by explicit markers.*
B1	*Can understand straightforward factual information about common everyday or job related topics, identifying both general messages and specific details, provided speech is clearly articulated in a generally familiar accent.* *Can understand the main points of clear standard speech on familiar matters regularly encountered in work, school, leisure etc., including short narratives.*
A2	*Can understand enough to be able to meet needs of a concrete type provided speech is clearly and slowly articulated.* *Can understand phrases and expressions related to areas of most immediate priority (e.g. very basic personal and family information, shopping, local geography, employment) provided speech is clearly and slowly articulated.*
A1	*Can follow speech which is very slow and carefully articulated, with long pauses for him/her to assimilate meaning.*

	UNDERSTANDING CONVERSATION BETWEEN NATIVE SPEAKERS
C2	*As C1*
C1	*Can easily follow complex interactions between third parties in group discussion and debate, even on abstract, complex unfamiliar topics.*
B2	*Can keep up with an animated conversation between native speakers.* *Can with some effort catch much of what is said around him/her, but may find it difficult to participate effectively in discussion with several native speakers who do not modify their language in any way.*
B1	*Can generally follow the main points of extended discussion around him/her, provided speech is clearly articulated in standard dialect.*
A2	*Can generally identify the topic of discussion around him/her, when it is conducted slowly and clearly.*
A1	*No descriptor available*

	LISTENING AS A MEMBER OF A LIVE AUDIENCE
C2	*Can follow specialised lectures and presentations employing a high degree of colloquialism, regional usage or unfamiliar terminology.*
C1	*Can follow most lectures, discussions and debates with relative ease.*
B2	*Can follow the essentials of lectures, talks and reports and other forms of academic/professional presentation which are propositionally and linguistically complex.*
B1	*Can follow a lecture or talk within his/her own field, provided the subject matter is familiar and the presentation straightforward and clearly structured.*
	Can follow in outline straightforward short talks on familiar topics provided these are delivered in clearly articulated standard speech.
A2	*No descriptor available*
A1	*No descriptor available*

	LISTENING TO ANNOUNCEMENTS AND INSTRUCTIONS
C2	*As C1*
C1	*Can extract specific information from poor quality, audibly distorted public announcements, e.g. in a station, sports stadium etc.* *Can understand complex technical information, such as operating instructions, specifications for familiar products and services.*
B2	*Can understand announcements and messages on concrete and abstract topics spoken in standard dialect at normal speed.*
B1	*Can understand simple technical information, such as operating instructions for everyday equipment.* *Can follow detailed directions.*
A2	*Can catch the main point in short, clear, simple messages and announcements.* *Can understand simple directions relating to how to get from X to Y, by foot or public transport.*
A1	*Can understand instructions addressed carefully and slowly to him/her and follow short, simple directions.*

	LISTENING TO AUDIO MEDIA AND RECORDINGS
C2	*As C1*
C1	*Can understand a wide range of recorded and broadcast audio material, including some non-standard usage, and identify finer points of detail including implicit attitudes and relationships between speakers.*
B2	*Can understand recordings in standard dialect likely to be encountered in social, professional or academic life and identify speaker viewpoints and attitudes as well as the information content.*
	Can understand most radio documentaries and most other recorded or broadcast audio material delivered in standard dialect and can identify the speaker's mood, tone etc.
B1	*Can understand the information content of the majority of recorded or broadcast audio material on topics of personal interest delivered in clear standard speech.*
	Can understand the main points of radio news bulletins and simpler recorded material about familiar subjects delivered relatively slowly and clearly.
A2	*Can understand and extract the essential information from short, recorded passages dealing with predictable everyday matters which are delivered slowly and clearly.*
A1	*No descriptor available*

Users of the Framework may wish to consider and where appropriate state:

- *to what range of inputs the learner will need/be equipped/be required to listen;*
- *for what purposes the learner will listen to the input;*
- *in what mode of listening the learner will engage.*

4.4.2.2 In **visual reception (reading)** activities the user as reader receives and processes as input written texts produced by one or more writers. Examples of reading activities include:

- reading for general orientation;
- reading for information, e.g. using reference works;
- reading and following instructions;
- reading for pleasure.

The language user may read:

- for gist;
- for specific information;
- for detailed understanding;
- for implications, etc.

Illustrative scales are provided for:

- Overall reading comprehension;
- Reading correspondence;

- Reading for orientation;
- Reading for information and argument;
- Reading instructions.

	OVERALL READING COMPREHENSION
C2	*Can understand and interpret critically virtually all forms of the written language including abstract, structurally complex, or highly colloquial literary and non-literary writings.* *Can understand a wide range of long and complex texts, appreciating subtle distinctions of style and implicit as well as explicit meaning.*
C1	*Can understand in detail lengthy, complex texts, whether or not they relate to his/her own area of speciality, provided he/she can reread difficult sections.*
B2	*Can read with a large degree of independence, adapting style and speed of reading to different texts and purposes, and using appropriate reference sources selectively. Has a broad active reading vocabulary, but may experience some difficulty with low frequency idioms.*
B1	*Can read straightforward factual texts on subjects related to his/her field and interest with a satisfactory level of comprehension.*
A2	*Can understand short, simple texts on familiar matters of a concrete type which consist of high frequency everyday or job-related language.*
	Can understand short, simple texts containing the highest frequency vocabulary, including a proportion of shared international vocabulary items.
A1	*Can understand very short, simple texts a single phrase at a time, picking up familiar names, words and basic phrases and rereading as required.*

	READING CORRESPONDENCE
C2	*As C1*
C1	*Can understand any correspondence given the occasional use of a dictionary.*
B2	*Can read correspondence relating to his/her field of interest and readily grasp the essential meaning.*
B1	*Can understand the description of events, feelings and wishes in personal letters well enough to correspond regularly with a pen friend.*
A2	*Can understand basic types of standard routine letters and faxes (enquiries, orders, letters of confirmation etc.) on familiar topics.*
	Can understand short simple personal letters.
A1	*Can understand short, simple messages on postcards.*

	READING FOR ORIENTATION
C2	*As B2*
C1	*As B2*
B2	*Can scan quickly through long and complex texts, locating relevant details.* *Can quickly identify the content and relevance of news items, articles and reports on a wide range of professional topics, deciding whether closer study is worthwhile.*
B1	*Can scan longer texts in order to locate desired information, and gather information from different parts of a text, or from different texts in order to fulfil a specific task.*
	Can find and understand relevant information in everyday material, such as letters, brochures and short official documents.
A2	*Can find specific, predictable information in simple everyday material such as advertisements, prospectuses, menus, reference lists and timetables.* *Can locate specific information in lists and isolate the information required (e.g. use the 'Yellow Pages' to find a service or tradesman).* *Can understand everyday signs and notices: in public places, such as streets, restaurants, railway stations; in workplaces, such as directions, instructions, hazard warnings.*
A1	*Can recognise familiar names, words and very basic phrases on simple notices in the most common everyday situations.*

	READING FOR INFORMATION AND ARGUMENT
C2	*As C1*
C1	*Can understand in detail a wide range of lengthy, complex texts likely to be encountered in social, professional or academic life, identifying finer points of detail including attitudes and implied as well as stated opinions.*
B2	*Can obtain information, ideas and opinions from highly specialised sources within his/her field.* *Can understand specialised articles outside his/her field, provided he/she can use a dictionary occasionally to confirm his/her interpretation of terminology.*
	Can understand articles and reports concerned with contemporary problems in which the writers adopt particular stances or viewpoints.
B1	*Can identify the main conclusions in clearly signalled argumentative texts.* *Can recognise the line of argument in the treatment of the issue presented, though not necessarily in detail.*
	Can recognise significant points in straightforward newspaper articles on familiar subjects.
A2	*Can identify specific information in simpler written material he/she encounters such as letters, brochures and short newspaper articles describing events.*
A1	*Can get an idea of the content of simpler informational material and short simple descriptions, especially if there is visual support.*

	READING INSTRUCTIONS
C2	*As C1*
C1	*Can understand in detail lengthy, complex instructions on a new machine or procedure, whether or not the instructions relate to his/her own area of speciality, provided he/she can reread difficult sections.*
B2	*Can understand lengthy, complex instructions in his field, including details on conditions and warnings, provided he/she can reread difficult sections.*
B1	*Can understand clearly written, straightforward instructions for a piece of equipment.*
A2	*Can understand regulations, for example safety, when expressed in simple language.*
A2	*Can understand simple instructions on equipment encountered in everyday life – such as a public telephone.*
A1	*Can follow short, simple written directions (e.g. to go from X to Y).*

Users of the Framework may wish to consider and where appropriate state:

- *for what purposes the learner will need, or wish/be equipped/be required to read;*
- *in which modes the learner will need or wish/be equipped/be required to read.*

4.4.2.3 In ~~*audio-visual reception*~~ the user ~~simultaneously receives an auditory and a~~ ~~visual input.~~ Such activities include:

- following a text as it is read aloud;
- watching TV, video, or a film with subtitles;
- using new technologies (multi-media, CD ROM, etc.).

An illustrative scale is provided for watching TV and film:

	WATCHING TV AND FILM
C2	*As C1*
C1	*Can follow films employing a considerable degree of slang and idiomatic usage.*
B2	*Can understand most TV news and current affairs programmes.* *Can understand documentaries, live interviews, talk shows, plays and the majority of films in standard dialect.*
B1	*Can understand a large part of many TV programmes on topics of personal interest such as interviews, short lectures, and news reports when the delivery is relatively slow and clear.*
B1	*Can follow many films in which visuals and action carry much of the storyline, and which are delivered clearly in straightforward language.* *Can catch the main points in TV programmes on familiar topics when the delivery is relatively slow and clear.*
A2	*Can identify the main point of TV news items reporting events, accidents etc. where the visual supports the commentary.*
A2	*Can follow changes of topic of factual TV news items, and form an idea of the main content.*
A1	*No descriptor available*

4.4.2.4 **Reception strategies** involve identifying the context and knowledge of the world relevant to it, activating in the process what are thought to be appropriate *schemata*. These in turn set up expectations about the organisation and content of what is to come (*Framing*). During the process of receptive activity cues identified in the total context (linguistic and non-linguistic) and the expectations in relation to that context set up by the relevant schemata are used to build up a representation of the meaning being expressed and a hypothesis as to the communicative intention behind it. Through a process of successive approximation, apparent and possible gaps in the message are filled in order to flesh out the representation of meaning, and the significance of the message and of its constituent parts are worked out (*Inferring*). The gaps filled through inference may be caused by linguistic restrictions, difficult receptive conditions, lack of associated knowledge, or by assumed familiarity, obliqueness, understatement or phonetic reduction on the part of the speaker/writer. The viability of the current model arrived at through this process is checked against the evidence of the incoming co-textual and contextual cues to see if they 'fit' the activated schema – the way one is interpreting the situation (*Hypothesis testing*). An identified mismatch leads to a return to step one (*Framing*) in the search for an alternative schema which would better explain the incoming cues (*Revising Hypotheses*).

- Planning: Framing (selecting mental set, activating schemata, setting up expectations).
- Execution: Identifying cues and inferring from them.
- Evaluation: Hypothesis testing: matching cues to schemata.
- Repair: Revising hypotheses.

An illustrative scale is provided:

	IDENTIFYING CUES AND INFERRING (Spoken & Written)
C2	*As C1*
C1	*Is skilled at using contextual, grammatical and lexical cues to infer attitude, mood and intentions and anticipate what will come next.*
B2	*Can use a variety of strategies to achieve comprehension, including listening for main points; checking comprehension by using contextual clues.*
B1	*Can identify unfamiliar words from the context on topics related to his/her field and interests.* *Can extrapolate the meaning of occasional unknown words from the context and deduce sentence meaning provided the topic discussed is familiar.*
A2	*Can use an idea of the overall meaning of short texts and utterances on everyday topics of a concrete type to derive the probable meaning of unknown words from the context.*
A1	*No descriptor available*

4.4.3   *Interactive activities and strategies*

4.4.3.1   *Spoken interaction*

In interactive activities the language user acts alternately as speaker and listener with one or more interlocutors so as to construct conjointly, through the negotiation of meaning following the co-operative principle, conversational discourse.

Reception and production strategies are employed constantly during interaction. There are also classes of cognitive and collaborative strategies (also called discourse strategies and co-operation strategies) concerned with managing co-operation and interaction such as turntaking and turngiving, framing the issue and establishing a line of approach, proposing and evaluating solutions, recapping and summarising the point reached, and mediating in a conflict.

Examples of interactive activities include:

- transactions
- casual conversation
- informal discussion
- formal discussion
- debate
- interview
- negotiation
- co-planning
- practical goal-oriented co-operation

Illustrative scales are provided for:

- Overall spoken interaction
- Understanding a native speaker interlocutor
- Conversation
- Informal discussion
- Formal discussion and meetings
- Goal-oriented co-operation
- Transactions to obtain goods and services
- Information exchange
- Interviewing and being interviewed

	OVERALL SPOKEN INTERACTION
C2	*Has a good command of idiomatic expressions and colloquialisms with awareness of connotative levels of meaning. Can convey finer shades of meaning precisely by using, with reasonable accuracy, a wide range of modification devices. Can backtrack and restructure around a difficulty so smoothly the interlocutor is hardly aware of it.*
C1	*Can express him/herself fluently and spontaneously, almost effortlessly. Has a good command of a broad lexical repertoire allowing gaps to be readily overcome with circumlocutions. There is little obvious searching for expressions or avoidance strategies; only a conceptually difficult subject can hinder a natural, smooth flow of language.*
B2	*Can use the language fluently, accurately and effectively on a wide range of general, academic, vocational or leisure topics, marking clearly the relationships between ideas. Can communicate spontaneously with good grammatical control without much sign of having to restrict what he/she wants to say, adopting a level of formality appropriate to the circumstances.*
	Can interact with a degree of fluency and spontaneity that makes regular interaction, and sustained relationships with native speakers quite possible without imposing strain on either party. Can highlight the personal significance of events and experiences, account for and sustain views clearly by providing relevant explanations and arguments.
B1	*Can communicate with some confidence on familiar routine and non-routine matters related to his/her interests and professional field. Can exchange, check and confirm information, deal with less routine situations and explain why something is a problem. Can express thoughts on more abstract, cultural topics such as films, books, music etc.*
	Can exploit a wide range of simple language to deal with most situations likely to arise whilst travelling. Can enter unprepared into conversation on familiar topics, express personal opinions and exchange information on topics that are familiar, of personal interest or pertinent to everyday life (e.g. family, hobbies, work, travel and current events).
A2	*Can interact with reasonable ease in structured situations and short conversations, provided the other person helps if necessary. Can manage simple, routine exchanges without undue effort; can ask and answer questions and exchange ideas and information on familiar topics in predictable everyday situations.*
	Can communicate in simple and routine tasks requiring a simple and direct exchange of information on familiar and routine matters to do with work and free time. Can handle very short social exchanges but is rarely able to understand enough to keep conversation going of his/her own accord.
A1	*Can interact in a simple way but communication is totally dependent on repetition at a slower rate of speech, rephrasing and repair. Can ask and answer simple questions, initiate and respond to simple statements in areas of immediate need or on very familiar topics.*

	UNDERSTANDING A NATIVE SPEAKER INTERLOCUTOR
C2	*Can understand any native speaker interlocutor, even on abstract and complex topics of a specialist nature beyond his/her own field, given an opportunity to adjust to a non-standard accent or dialect.*
C1	*Can understand in detail speech on abstract and complex topics of a specialist nature beyond his/her own field, though he/she may need to confirm occasional details, especially if the accent is unfamiliar.*
B2	*Can understand in detail what is said to him/her in the standard spoken language even in a noisy environment.*
B1	*Can follow clearly articulated speech directed at him/her in everyday conversation, though will sometimes have to ask for repetition of particular words and phrases.*
A2	*Can understand enough to manage simple, routine exchanges without undue effort.* *Can generally understand clear, standard speech on familiar matters directed at him/her, provided he/she can ask for repetition or reformulation from time to time.*
	Can understand what is said clearly, slowly and directly to him/her in simple everyday conversation; can be made to understand, if the speaker can take the trouble.
A1	*Can understand everyday expressions aimed at the satisfaction of simple needs of a concrete type, delivered directly to him/her in clear, slow and repeated speech by a sympathetic speaker.* *Can understand questions and instructions addressed carefully and slowly to him/her and follow short, simple directions.*

	CONVERSATION
C2	*Can converse comfortably and appropriately, unhampered by any linguistic limitations in conducting a full social and personal life.*
C1	*Can use language flexibly and effectively for social purposes, including emotional, allusive and joking usage.*
B2	*Can engage in extended conversation on most general topics in a clearly participatory fashion, even in a noisy environment.* *Can sustain relationships with native speakers without unintentionally amusing or irritating them or requiring them to behave other than they would with a native speaker.* *Can convey degrees of emotion and highlight the personal significance of events and experiences.*
B1	*Can enter unprepared into conversations on familiar topics.* *Can follow clearly articulated speech directed at him/her in everyday conversation, though will sometimes have to ask for repetition of particular words and phrases.* *Can maintain a conversation or discussion but may sometimes be difficult to follow when trying to say exactly what he/she would like to.* *Can express and respond to feelings such as surprise, happiness, sadness, interest and indifference.*
A2	*Can establish social contact: greetings and farewells; introductions; giving thanks.* *Can generally understand clear, standard speech on familiar matters directed at him/her, provided he/she can ask for repetition or reformulation from time to time.* *Can participate in short conversations in routine contexts on topics of interest.* *Can express how he/she feels in simple terms, and express thanks.* *Can handle very short social exchanges but is rarely able to understand enough to keep conversation going of his/her own accord, though he/she can be made to understand if the speaker will take the trouble.* *Can use simple everyday polite forms of greeting and address.* *Can make and respond to invitations, suggestions and apologies.* *Can say what he/she likes and dislikes.*
A1	*Can make an introduction and use basic greeting and leave-taking expressions.* *Can ask how people are and react to news.* *Can understand everyday expressions aimed at the satisfaction of simple needs of a concrete type, delivered directly to him/her in clear, slow and repeated speech by a sympathetic speaker.*

	INFORMAL DISCUSSION (WITH FRIENDS)
C2	*As C1*
C1	Can easily follow and contribute to complex interactions between third parties in group discussion even on abstract, complex unfamiliar topics.
B2	Can keep up with an animated discussion between native speakers. Can express his/her ideas and opinions with precision, and present and respond to complex lines of argument convincingly.
	Can take an active part in informal discussion in familiar contexts, commenting, putting point of view clearly, evaluating alternative proposals and making and responding to hypotheses. Can with some effort catch much of what is said around him/her in discussion, but may find it difficult to participate effectively in discussion with several native speakers who do not modify their language in any way. Can account for and sustain his/her opinions in discussion by providing relevant explanations, arguments and comments.
B1	Can follow much of what is said around him/her on general topics provided interlocutors avoid very idiomatic usage and articulate clearly. Can express his/her thoughts about abstract or cultural topics such as music, films. Can explain why something is a problem. Can give brief comments on the views of others. Can compare and contrast alternatives, discussing what to do, where to go, who or which to choose, etc.
	Can generally follow the main points in an informal discussion with friends provided speech is clearly articulated in standard dialect. Can give or seek personal views and opinions in discussing topics of interest. Can make his/her opinions and reactions understood as regards solutions to problems or practical questions of where to go, what to do, how to organise an event (e.g. an outing). Can express belief, opinion, agreement and disagreement politely.
A2	Can generally identify the topic of discussion around him/her when it is conducted slowly and clearly. Can discuss what to do in the evening, at the weekend. Can make and respond to suggestions. Can agree and disagree with others.
	Can discuss everyday practical issues in a simple way when addressed clearly, slowly and directly. Can discuss what to do, where to go and make arrangements to meet.
A1	*No descriptors available*

	FORMAL DISCUSSION AND MEETINGS
C2	Can hold his/her own in formal discussion of complex issues, putting an articulate and persuasive argument, at no disadvantage to native speakers.
C1	Can easily keep up with the debate, even on abstract, complex unfamiliar topics. Can argue a formal position convincingly, responding to questions and comments and answering complex lines of counter argument fluently, spontaneously and appropriately.
B2	Can keep up with an animated discussion, identifying accurately arguments supporting and opposing points of view. Can express his/her ideas and opinions with precision, present and respond to complex lines of argument convincingly.
	Can participate actively in routine and non-routine formal discussion. Can follow the discussion on matters related to his/her field, understand in detail the points given prominence by the speaker. Can contribute, account for and sustain his/her opinion, evaluate alternative proposals and make and respond to hypotheses.
B1	Can follow much of what is said that is related to his/her field, provided interlocutors avoid very idiomatic usage and articulate clearly. Can put over a point of view clearly, but has difficulty engaging in debate. Can take part in routine formal discussion of familiar subjects which is conducted in clearly articulated speech in the standard dialect and which involves the exchange of factual information, receiving instructions or the discussion of solutions to practical problems.
A2	Can generally follow changes of topic in formal discussion related to his/her field which is conducted slowly and clearly. Can exchange relevant information and give his/her opinion on practical problems when asked directly, provided he/she receives some help with formulation and can ask for repetition of key points if necessary.
	Can say what he/she thinks about things when addressed directly in a formal meeting, provided he/she can ask for repetition of key points if necessary.
A1	*No descriptor available*

Note: The descriptors on this sub-scale have not been empirically calibrated with the measurement model.

	GOAL-ORIENTED CO-OPERATION (e.g. Repairing a car, discussing a document, organising an event)
C2	*As B2*
C1	*As B2*
B2	*Can understand detailed instructions reliably.* *Can help along the progress of the work by inviting others to join in, say what they think, etc.* *Can outline an issue or a problem clearly, speculating about causes or consequences, and weighing advantages and disadvantages of different approaches.*
B1	*Can follow what is said, though he/she may occasionally have to ask for repetition or clarification if the other people's talk is rapid or extended.* *Can explain why something is a problem, discuss what to do next, compare and contrast alternatives.* *Can give brief comments on the views of others.* *Can generally follow what is said and, when necessary, can repeat back part of what someone has said to confirm mutual understanding.* *Can make his/her opinions and reactions understood as regards possible solutions or the question of what to do next, giving brief reasons and explanations.* *Can invite others to give their views on how to proceed.*
A2	*Can understand enough to manage simple, routine tasks without undue effort, asking very simply for repetition when he/she does not understand.* *Can discuss what to do next, making and responding to suggestions, asking for and giving directions.* *Can indicate when he/she is following and can be made to understand what is necessary, if the speaker takes the trouble.* *Can communicate in simple and routine tasks using simple phrases to ask for and provide things, to get simple information and to discuss what to do next.*
A1	*Can understand questions and instructions addressed carefully and slowly to him/her and follow short, simple directions.* *Can ask people for things, and give people things.*

	TRANSACTIONS TO OBTAIN GOODS AND SERVICES
C2	*As B2*
C1	*As B2*
B2	*Can cope linguistically to negotiate a solution to a dispute like an undeserved traffic ticket, financial responsibility for damage in a flat, for blame regarding an accident.* *Can outline a case for compensation, using persuasive language to demand satisfaction and state clearly the limits to any concession he/she is prepared to make.*
	Can explain a problem which has arisen and make it clear that the provider of the service/customer must make a concession.
B1	*Can deal with most transactions likely to arise whilst travelling, arranging travel or accommodation, or dealing with authorities during a foreign visit.* *Can cope with less routine situations in shops, post offices, banks, e.g. returning an unsatisfactory purchase. Can make a complaint.* *Can deal with most situations likely to arise when making travel arrangements through an agent or when actually travelling, e.g. asking passenger where to get off for an unfamiliar destination.*
A2	*Can deal with common aspects of everyday living such as travel, lodgings, eating and shopping.* *Can get all the information needed from a tourist office, as long as it is of a straightforward, non-specialised nature.*
	Can ask for and provide everyday goods and services. *Can get simple information about travel, use public transport: buses, trains, and taxis, ask and give directions, and buy tickets.* *Can ask about things and make simple transactions in shops, post offices or banks.* *Can give and receive information about quantities, numbers, prices, etc.* ✓ *Can make simple purchases by stating what is wanted and asking the price.* *Can order a meal.*
A1	*Can ask people for things and give people things.* *Can handle numbers, quantities, cost and time.*

	INFORMATION EXCHANGE
C2	*As B2*
C1	*As B2*
B2	*Can understand and exchange complex information and advice on the full range of matters related to his/her occupational role.*
	Can pass on detailed information reliably. *Can give a clear, detailed description of how to carry out a procedure.* *Can synthesise and report information and arguments from a number of sources.*
B1	*Can exchange, check and confirm accumulated factual information on familiar routine and non-routine matters within his/her field with some confidence.* *Can describe how to do something, giving detailed instructions.* *Can summarise and give his or her opinion about a short story, article, talk, discussion, interview, or documentary and answer further questions of detail.*
	Can find out and pass on straightforward factual information. *Can ask for and follow detailed directions.* *Can obtain more detailed information.*
A2	*Can understand enough to manage simple, routine exchanges without undue effort.* *Can deal with practical everyday demands: finding out and passing on straightforward factual information.* *Can ask and answer questions about habits and routines.* *Can ask and answer questions about pastimes and past activities.* *Can give and follow simple directions and instructions, e.g. explain how to get somewhere.*
	Can communicate in simple and routine tasks requiring a simple and direct exchange of information. *Can exchange limited information on familiar and routine operational matters.* *Can ask and answer questions about what they do at work and in free time.* *Can ask for and give directions referring to a map or plan.* *Can ask for and provide personal information.*
A1	*Can understand questions and instructions addressed carefully and slowly to him/her and follow short, simple directions.* *Can ask and answer simple questions, initiate and respond to simple statements in areas of immediate need or on very familiar topics.* *Can ask and answer questions about themselves and other people, where they live, people they know, things they have.* *Can indicate time by such phrases as next week, last Friday, in November, three o'clock.*

	INTERVIEWING AND BEING INTERVIEWED
C2	*Can keep up his/her side of the dialogue extremely well, structuring the talk and interacting authoritatively with complete fluency as interviewer or interviewee, at no disadvantage to a native speaker.*
C1	*Can participate fully in an interview, as either interviewer or interviewee, expanding and developing the point being discussed fluently without any support, and handling interjections well.*
B2	*Can carry out an effective, fluent interview, departing spontaneously from prepared questions, following up and probing interesting replies.*
	Can take initiatives in an interview, expand and develop ideas with little help or prodding from an interviewer.
B1	*Can provide concrete information required in an interview/consultation (e.g. describe symptoms to a doctor) but does so with limited precision.* *Can carry out a prepared interview, checking and confirming information, though he/she may occasionally have to ask for repetition if the other person's response is rapid or extended.*
	Can take some initiatives in an interview/consultation (e.g. to bring up a new subject) but is very dependent on interviewer in the interaction. *Can use a prepared questionnaire to carry out a structured interview, with some spontaneous follow up questions.*
A2	*Can make him/herself understood in an interview and communicate ideas and information on familiar topics, provided he/she can ask for clarification occasionally, and is given some help to express what he/she wants to.*
	Can answer simple questions and respond to simple statements in an interview.
A1	*Can reply in an interview to simple direct questions spoken very slowly and clearly in direct non-idiomatic speech about personal details.*

4.4.3.2   Written interaction

Interaction through the medium of written language includes such activities as:

* passing and exchanging notes, memos, etc. when spoken interaction is impossible and inappropriate;
* correspondence by letter, fax, e-mail, etc.;
* negotiating the text of agreements, contracts, communiqués, etc. by reformulating and exchanging drafts, amendments, proof corrections, etc.;
* participating in on-line or off-line computer conferences.

4.4.3.3   Face-to-face interaction may of course involve a mixture of media: spoken, written, audio-visual, paralinguistic (see section 4.4.5.2) and paratextual (see 4.4.5.3).

4.4.3.4   With the increasing sophistication of computer software, interactive man-machine communication is coming to play an ever more important part in the public, occupational, educational and even personal domains.

Illustrative scales are provided for:

- overall written interaction
- correspondence
- notes, messages and forms

	OVERALL WRITTEN INTERACTION
C2	As C1
C1	*Can express him/herself with clarity and precision, relating to the addressee flexibly and effectively.*
B2	*Can express news and views effectively in writing, and relate to those of others.*
B1	*Can convey information and ideas on abstract as well as concrete topics, check information and ask about or explain problems with reasonable precision.* *Can write personal letters and notes asking for or conveying simple information of immediate relevance, getting across the point he/she feels to be important.*
A2	*Can write short, simple formulaic notes relating to matters in areas of immediate need.*
A1	*Can ask for or pass on personal details in written form.*

	CORRESPONDENCE
C2	As C1
C1	*Can express him/herself with clarity and precision in personal correspondence, using language flexibly and effectively, including emotional, allusive and joking usage.*
B2	*Can write letters conveying degrees of emotion and highlighting the personal significance of events and experiences and commenting on the correspondent's news and views.*
B1	*Can write personal letters giving news and expressing thoughts about abstract or cultural topics such as music, films.* *Can write personal letters describing experiences, feelings and events in some detail.*
A2	*Can write very simple personal letters expressing thanks and apology.*
A1	*Can write a short simple postcard.*

	NOTES, MESSAGES & FORMS
C2	*As B1*
C1	*As B1*
B2	*As B1*
B1	*Can take messages communicating enquiries, explaining problems.* *Can write notes conveying simple information of immediate relevance to friends, service people, teachers and others who feature in his/her everyday life, getting across comprehensibly the points he/she feels are important.*
A2	*Can take a short, simple message provided he/she can ask for repetition and reformulation.* *Can write short, simple notes and messages relating to matters in areas of immediate need.*
A1	*Can write numbers and dates, own name, nationality, address, age, date of birth or arrival in the country, etc. such as on a hotel registration form.*

Users of the Framework may wish to consider and where appropriate state:

- *in which kinds of communicative interaction the learner will need/be equipped/be required to engage;*
- *which roles the learner will need/be equipped/be required to play in the interaction.*

4.4.3.5 Interaction strategies

Interaction encompasses both receptive and productive activity as well as activity unique to the construction of joint discourse and therefore all reception strategies and all production strategies mentioned above are also involved in interaction. However, the fact that spoken interaction entails the collective creation of meaning by the establishment of some degree of common mental context, defining what can be taken as given, working out where people are coming from, converging towards each other or defining and maintaining a comfortable distance, usually in real time, means that in addition to receptive and productive strategies there is a class of strategies exclusive to interaction concerned with the management of this process. In addition, the fact that interaction is primarily face to face tends to provide far greater redundancy both in textual, linguistic terms and with regard to paralinguistic features, contextual cues, all of which can be made more or less elaborate, more or less explicit to the extent that the constant monitoring of the process by the participants indicates that this is appropriate.

Planning for spoken interaction involves the activation of schemata or a 'praxeogram' (i.e. a diagram representing the structure of a communicative interaction) of the exchanges possible and probable in the forthcoming activity (*Framing*) and consideration of the communicative distance from other interlocutors (*Identifying information/opinion gap; Judging what can be taken as given*) in order to decide on options and prepare possible moves in those exchanges (*Planning moves*). During the activity itself, language users adopt turntaking strategies in order to obtain the discourse initiative (*Taking the floor*), to cement the collaboration in the task and keep the discussion on course (*Co-operating:*

interpersonal), to help mutual understanding and maintain a focused approach to the task at hand (*Co-operating: ideational*), and so that they themselves can ask for assistance in formulating something (*Asking for Help*). As with Planning, Evaluation takes place at a communicative level: judging the 'fit' between the schemata thought to apply, and what is actually happening (*Monitoring: schemata, praxeogram*) and the extent to which things are going the way one wants them to go (*Monitoring: effect, success*); miscomprehension or intolerable ambiguity leads to requests for clarification which may be on a communicative or linguistic level (*Asking for, giving clarification*), and to active intervention to re-establish communication and clear up misunderstandings when necessary (*Communication Repair*).

Planning
- framing (selecting praxeogram)
- identifying information/opinion gap (felicity conditions)
- judging what can be presupposed
- planning moves

Execution
- taking the floor
- co-operating (interpersonal)
- co-operating (ideational)
- dealing with the unexpected
- asking for help

Evaluation
- monitoring (schema, praxeogram)
- monitoring (effect, success)

Repair
- asking for clarification
- giving clarification
- communication repair

Illustrative scales are provided for:

- taking the floor;
- co-operating;
- asking for clarification.

	TAKING THE FLOOR (TURNTAKING)
C2	*As C1*
C1	*Can select a suitable phrase from a readily available range of discourse functions to preface his/her remarks appropriately in order to get the floor, or to gain time and keep the floor whilst thinking.*
B2	*Can intervene appropriately in discussion, exploiting appropriate language to do so.* *Can initiate, maintain and end discourse appropriately with effective turntaking.* *Can initiate discourse, take his/her turn when appropriate and end conversation when he/she needs to, though he/she may not always do this elegantly.* *Can use stock phrases (e.g. 'That's a difficult question to answer') to gain time and keep the turn whilst formulating what to say.*
B1	*Can intervene in a discussion on a familiar topic, using a suitable phrase to get the floor.*
	Can initiate, maintain and close simple, face-to-face conversation on topics that are familiar or of personal interest.
A2	*Can use simple techniques to start, maintain, or end a short conversation.* *Can initiate, maintain and close simple, face-to-face conversation.*
	Can ask for attention.
A1	*No descriptor available*

	CO-OPERATING
C2	*As C1*
C1	*Can relate own contribution skilfully to those of other speakers.*
B2	*Can give feedback on and follow up statements and inferences and so help the development of the discussion.* *Can help the discussion along on familiar ground, confirming comprehension, inviting others in, etc.*
B1	*Can exploit a basic repertoire of language and strategies to help keep a conversation or discussion going.* *Can summarise the point reached in a discussion and so help focus the talk.*
	Can repeat back part of what someone has said to confirm mutual understanding and help keep the development of ideas on course. Can invite others into the discussion.
A2	*Can indicate when he/she is following.*
A1	*No descriptor available*

	ASKING FOR CLARIFICATION
C2	*As B2*
C1	*As B2*
B2	*Can ask follow-up questions to check that he/she has understood what a speaker intended to say, and get clarification of ambiguous points.*
B1	*Can ask someone to clarify or elaborate what they have just said.*
A2	*Can ask very simply for repetition when he/she does not understand.* *Can ask for clarification about key words or phrases not understood using stock phrases.* *Can say he/she didn't follow.*
A1	*No descriptor available*

4.4.4 Mediating activities and strategies

In **mediating activities**, the language user is not concerned to express his/her own meanings, but simply to act as an intermediary between interlocutors who are unable to understand each other directly – normally (but not exclusively) speakers of different languages. Examples of mediating activities include spoken interpretation and written translation as well as summarising and paraphrasing texts in the same language, when the language of the original text is not understandable to the intended recipient e.g.:

4.4.4.1   oral mediation:
- simultaneous interpretation (conferences, meetings, formal speeches, etc.);
- consecutive interpretation (speeches of welcome, guided tours, etc.);
- informal interpretation:
  - of foreign visitors in own country
  - of native speakers when abroad
  - in social and transactional situations for friends, family, clients, foreign guests, etc.
  - of signs, menus, notices, etc.

4.4.4.2   written mediation:
- exact translation (e.g. of contracts, legal and scientific texts, etc.);
- literary translation (novels, drama, poetry, libretti, etc.);
- summarising gist (newspaper and magazine articles, etc.) within L2 or between L1 and L2;
- paraphrasing (specialised texts for lay persons, etc.).

4.4.4.3   **Mediation strategies** reflect ways of coping with the demands of using finite resources to process information and establish equivalent meaning. The process may

involve some pre-planning to organise and maximise resources (*Developing background knowledge; Locating supports; Preparing a glossary*) as well as consideration of how to tackle the task at hand (*Considering the interlocutors' needs; Selecting the size of interpretation unit*). During the process of interpretation, glossing, or translation, the mediator needs to look ahead at what is coming next whilst formulating what has just been said, generally juggling with two different 'chunks' or interpretation units simultaneously (*Previewing*). He or she needs to note ways of expressing things to extend his or her glossary (*Noting possibilities, equivalences*), and to construct islands of reliability, (prefabricated chunks) which free up processing capacity for previewing. On the other hand he or she also needs to use techniques to skate over uncertainty and avoid breakdown – whilst maintaining previewing (*Bridging gaps*). Evaluation takes place at a communicative level (*Checking congruence*) and at a linguistic level (*Checking consistency of usage*) and, certainly with written translation, leads to repair through consultation of reference works and people knowledgeable in the field concerned (*refining by consulting dictionaries, thesaurus; consulting experts, sources*).

- Planning   Developing background knowledge;
  Locating supports;
  Preparing a glossary;
  Considering interlocutors' needs;
  Selecting unit of interpretation.
- Execution   Previewing: processing input and formulating the last chunk simultaneously in real time;
  Noting possibilities, equivalences;
  Bridging gaps.
- Evaluation   Checking congruence of two versions;
  Checking consistency of usage.
- Repair   Refining by consulting dictionaries, thesaurus;
  Consulting experts, sources.

No illustrative scales are yet available.

Users of the Framework may wish to consider and where appropriate state:

- *the mediating activities in which the learner will need/be equipped/be required to engage.*

4.4.5 *Non-verbal communication*

4.4.5.1 **Practical actions** accompanying language activities (normally face-to-face oral activities) include:

- *pointing,* e.g. by finger, hand, glance, nod. These actions are used with deictics for the identification of objects, persons, etc., such as, 'Can I have that one? No, not that one, that one';
- *demonstration,* accompanying deictics and simple present verbs and pro-verbs, such as, 'I take this and fix it here, like this. Now you do the same!';

- *clearly observable actions*, which can be assumed as known in narrative, comment, orders, etc., such as, 'Don't do that!', 'Well done there!', 'Oh no, he's dropped it!'. In all these cases, the utterance is uninterpretable unless the action is perceived.

Users of the Framework may wish to consider and where appropriate state:

- *how skilled learners will need/be equipped/be required to be in matching actions to words and* vice-versa;
- *in which situations they will need/be equipped/be required to do so.*

Overarticulatn for the sake of parallelism; just plain silly!

4.4.5.2 *Paralinguistics* includes:

Body language. Paralinguistic body language differs from practical actions accompanied by language in that it carries conventionalised meanings, which may well differ from one culture to another. For example, the following are used in many European countries:

- gesture (e.g. shaken fist for 'protest');
- facial expression (e.g. smile or scowl);
- posture (e.g. slump for 'despair' or sitting forward for 'keen interest');
- eye contact (e.g. a conspiratorial wink or a disbelieving stare);
- body contact (e.g. kiss or handshake);
- proxemics (e.g. standing close or aloof).

use *of extra-linguistic speech-sounds.* Such sounds (or syllables) are paralinguistic in that they carry conventionalised meanings but lie outside the regular phonological system of a language, for example, (in English):

'sh'	requesting silence
's-s-s'	expressing public disapproval
'ugh'	expressing disgust
'humph'	expressing disgruntlement
'tut, tut'	expressing polite disapproval

prosodic qualities. The use of these qualities is paralinguistic if they carry conventionalised meanings (e.g. related to attitudes and states of mind), but fall outside the regular phonological system in which prosodic features of length, tone, stress may play a part, for example:

voice quality	(gruff, breathy, piercing, etc.)
pitch	(growling, whining, screaming, etc.)
loudness	(whispering, murmuring, shouting, etc.)
length	(e.g. ve-e-e-ery good!)

Many paralinguistic effects are produced by combinations of pitch, length, loudness and voice quality.

Paralinguistic communication should be carefully distinguished from developed *sign languages*, which fall outside the present scope of CEF, though experts in that field may find many of its concepts and categories relevant to their concerns.

Users of the Framework may wish to consider and where appropriate state:

- which target paralinguistic behaviours the learner will need/be equipped/be required to a) recognise and understand b) use.

4.4.5.3 **Paratextual features**: a similarly 'paralinguistic' role is played in relation to written texts by such devices as:

- illustrations (photographs, drawings, etc.)
- charts, tables, diagrams, figures, etc.
- typographic features (fonts, pitch, spacing, underlining, layout, etc.)

Users of the Framework may wish to consider and where appropriate state:

- which paratextual features the learner will need/be equipped/be required to a) recognise and respond to and b) use.

4.5 Communicative language processes

To act as a speaker, writer, listener or reader, the learner must be able to carry out a sequence of skilled actions.

To speak, the learner must be able to:

- *plan* and *organise* a message (cognitive skills);
- *formulate* a linguistic utterance (linguistic skills);
- *articulate* the utterance (phonetic skills).

To write, the learner must be able to:

- *organise* and *formulate* the message (cognitive and linguistic skills);
- *hand-write* or *type* the text (manual skills) or otherwise transfer the text to writing.

To listen, the learner must be able to:

- *perceive* the utterance (auditory phonetic skills);
- *identify* the linguistic message (linguistic skills);
- *understand* the message (semantic skills);
- *interpret* the message (cognitive skills).

To read, the reader must be able to:

- *perceive* the written text (visual skills);
- *recognise* the script (orthographic skills);
- *identify* the message (linguistic skills);
- *understand* the message (semantic skills);
- *interpret* the message (cognitive skills).

The observable stages of these processes are well understood. Others – events in the central nervous system – are not. The following analysis is intended only to identify some parts of the process relevant to the development of language proficiency.

4.5.1 Planning

The selection, interrelation and co-ordination of components of general and communicative language competences (see Chapter 5) to be brought to bear on the communicative event in order to accomplish the user/learner's communicative intentions.

4.5.2 Execution

4.5.2.1 Production
The production process involves two components:

The *formulation* component takes the output from the planning component and assembles it into linguistic form. This involves lexical, grammatical, phonological (and in the case of writing, orthographic) processes which are distinguishable and appear (e.g. in cases of dysphasia) to have some degree of independence but whose exact interrelation is not fully understood.

The *articulation* component organises the motor innervation of the vocal apparatus to convert the output of the phonological processes into co-ordinated movements of the speech organs to produce a train of speech waves constituting the spoken utterance, or alternatively the motor innervation of the musculature of the hand to produce hand-written or typewritten text.

4.5.2.2 Reception
The **receptive process** involves four steps which, while they take place in linear sequence (bottom-up), are constantly updated and reinterpreted (top-down) in the light of real world knowledge, schematic expectations and new textual understanding in a subconscious interactive process.

- the perception of speech and writing: sound/character and word recognition (cursive and print);
- the identification of the text, complete or partial, as relevant;
- the semantic and cognitive **understanding** of the text as a linguistic entity;
- the interpretation of the message in context.

The skills involved include:
*   perceptual skills;
*   memory;
*   decoding skills;
*   inferencing;
*   predicting;
*   imagination;
*   rapid scanning;
*   referring back and forth.

Comprehension, especially of written texts, can be assisted by the proper use of aids, including reference materials such as:
*   dictionaries (monolingual and bilingual);
*   thesauruses;
*   pronunciation dictionaries;
*   electronic dictionaries, grammars, spell-checkers and other aids;
*   reference grammars.

4.5.2.3   Interaction

The processes involved in *spoken interaction* differ from a simple succession of speaking and listening activities in a number of ways:

*   productive and receptive **processes overlap**. Whilst the interlocutor's utterance, still incomplete, is being processed, the planning of the user's response is initiated – on the basis of a hypothesis as to its nature, meaning and interpretation.
*   **discourse is cumulative**. As an interaction proceeds, the participants converge in their readings of a situation, develop expectations and focus on relevant issues. These processes are reflected in the form of the utterances produced.

In *written interaction* (e.g. a correspondence by letter, fax, e-mail, etc.) the processes of reception and production remain distinct (though electronic interaction, e.g. via the Internet, is becoming ever closer to 'real time' interaction). The effects of cumulative discourse are similar to those for spoken interaction.

4.5.3   *Monitoring*

The strategic component deals with updating of mental activities and competences in the course of communication. This applies equally to the productive and receptive processes. It should be noted that an important factor in the control of the productive processes is the *feedback* the speaker/writer receives at each stage: formulation, articulation and acoustic.

   In a wider sense, the strategic component is also concerned with the monitoring of the communicative process as it proceeds, and with ways of managing the process accordingly, e.g.:

- dealing with the unexpected, such as changes of domain, theme schema, etc.;
- dealing with communication breakdown in interaction or production as a result of such factors as memory lapses;
- inadequate communicative competence for the task in hand by using compensating strategies like restructuring, circumlocution, substitution, asking for help;
- misunderstandings and misinterpretation (by asking for clarification);
- slips of the tongue, mishearings (by using repair strategies).

Users of the Framework may wish to consider and where appropriate state:

- *to what degree which skills are required for the satisfactory accomplishment of the communicative tasks the learner is expected to undertake;*
- *which skills can be presupposed and which will need to be developed;*
- *which reference aids the learner will need/be equipped/be required to use effectively.*

4.6 Texts

As explained in Chapter 2, 'text' is used to cover any piece of language, whether a spoken utterance or a piece of writing, which users/learners receive, produce or exchange. There can thus be no act of communication through language without a text; language activities and processes are all analysed and classified in terms of the relation of the user/learner and any interlocutor(s) to the text whether viewed as a finished product, an artefact, or as an objective or as a product in process of elaboration. These activities and processes are dealt with in some detail in section 4.4 and 4.5. Texts have many different functions in social life and result in corresponding differences in form and substance. Different *media* are used for different purposes. Differences of medium and purpose and function lead to corresponding differences not only in the context of messages, but also in their organisation and presentation. Accordingly, texts may be classified into different text types belonging to different *genres*. See also Section 5.2.3.2 (macrofunctions).

4.6.1 Texts and media

Every text is carried by a particular medium, normally by sound waves or written artefacts. Subcategories can be established according to physical properties of the medium which affect the processes of production and reception, e.g. for speech, direct close-up speech as against public address or telephone, or for writing print as against cursive writing, or different scripts. To communicate using a particular medium, users/learners must have the necessary sensory/motor equipment. In the case of speech, they must be able to hear well under the given conditions and have fine control of the organs of phonation and articulation. In the case of normal writing, they must be able to see with the necessary visual acuity and have control of their hands. They must then have the knowledge and skills described elsewhere, on the one hand to identify, understand and interpret the text or on the other to organise, formulate and produce it. This will be true for any text, whatever its nature.

The above must not discourage people who have learning difficulties or sensory/motor disabilities from learning or using foreign languages. Devices ranging from simple hearing aids to eye-operated computer speech synthesisers have been developed to overcome even the most severe sensory and motor difficulties, whilst the use of appropriate methods and strategies have enabled young people with learning difficulties to achieve worthwhile foreign language learning objectives with remarkable success. Lip-reading, the exploitation of residual hearing and phonetic training have enabled the severely deaf to achieve a high level of speech communication in a second or foreign language. Given the necessary determination and encouragement, human beings have an extraordinary capacity to overcome obstacles to communication and the production and understanding of texts.

In principle, any text can be carried by any medium. However, in practice medium and text are more closely related. Scripts do not generally carry the full meaningful phonetic information carried by speech. Alphabetic scripts do not generally carry prosodic information systematically (e.g. stress, intonation, pausing, stylistic reduction, etc.). Consonantal and logographic scripts carry less. Paralinguistic features are usually unrepresented in any script, though they may of course be referred to in the text of a novel, play, etc. In compensation, paratextual features are employed in writing, which are tied to the spatial medium and not available to speech. Moreover, the nature of the medium exercises a strong pressure on the nature of the text and vice-versa. As extreme examples, a stone inscription is difficult and expensive to produce and is very durable and immovable. An air-letter is cheap and easy to use, easily transported, but light and fragile. Electronic communication using a VDU need not produce a permanent artefact at all. The texts they typically carry are correspondingly contrasted: in the one case, a carefully composed, frugal text preserving monumental information for future generations and inducing reverence for the place and person(s) celebrated, and in the other, a hastily scribbled personal note of topical but ephemeral interest to the correspondents. A similar ambiguity of classification thus arises between text-types and media to that between text-types and activities. Books, magazines and newspapers are, from their physical nature and appearance, different media. From the nature and structure of their contents they are different text-types. Medium and text-type are closely related and both are derivative from the function they perform.

4.6.2 Media include:

- voice (*viva voce*);
- telephone, videophone, teleconference;
- public address systems;
- radio broadcasts;
- TV;
- cinema films;
- computer (e-mail, CD Rom, etc.);
- videotape, -cassette, -disc;
- audiotape, -cassette, -disc;
- print;
- manuscript;
- etc.

94

> *Users of the Framework may wish to consider and where appropriate state:*
>
> • *which media the learner will need/be equipped/be required to handle a) receptively b) productively c) interactively d) in mediation.*

4.6.3   *Text-types include:*

Spoken, e.g.:
public announcements and instructions;
public speeches, lectures, presentations, sermons;
rituals (ceremonies, formal religious services);
entertainment (drama, shows, readings, songs);
sports commentaries (football, cricket, boxing, horse-racing, etc.);
news broadcasts;
public debates and discussion;
inter-personal dialogues and conversations;
telephone conversations;
job interviews.

Written, e.g.:
books, fiction and non-fiction, including literary journals;
magazines;
newspapers;
instruction manuals (DIY, cookbooks, etc.);
textbooks;
comic strips;
brochures, prospectuses;
leaflets;
advertising material;
public signs and notices;
supermarket, shop, market stall signs;
packaging and labelling on goods;
tickets, etc.;
forms and questionnaires;
dictionaries (monolingual and bilingual), thesauri;
business and professional letters, faxes;
personal letters;
essays and exercises;
memoranda, reports and papers;
notes and messages, etc.;
databases (news, literature, general information, etc.).

The following scales, based upon those developed in the Swiss projects described in Appendix B, give examples of activities involving a written text output produced in response to, respectively, a spoken or written input. Only the higher levels of these activities can enable a learner to meet the requirements of university studies or professional training, though some ability to deal with simple input text and to produce a written response is feasible at more modest levels.

	NOTE-TAKING (LECTURES, SEMINARS, ETC.)
C2	*Is aware of the implications and allusions of what is said and can make notes on them as well as on the actual words used by the speaker.*
C1	*Can take detailed notes during a lecture on topics in his/her field of interest, recording the information so accurately and so close to the original that the notes could also be useful to other people.*
B2	*Can understand a clearly structured lecture on a familiar subject, and can take notes on points which strike him/her as important, even though he/she tends to concentrate on the words themselves and therefore to miss some information.*
B1	*Can take notes during a lecture which are precise enough for his/her own use at a later date, provided the topic is within his/her field of interest and the talk is clear and well-structured.* *Can take notes as a list of key points during a straightforward lecture, provided the topic is familiar, and the talk is both formulated in simple language and delivered in clearly articulated standard speech.*
A2	*No descriptor available*
A1	*No descriptor available*

	PROCESSING TEXT
C2	*Can summarise information from different sources, reconstructing arguments and accounts in a coherent presentation of the overall result.*
C1	*Can summarise long, demanding texts.*
B2	*Can summarise a wide range of factual and imaginative texts, commenting on and discussing contrasting points of view and the main themes.* *Can summarise extracts from news items, interviews or documentaries containing opinions, argument and discussion.* *Can summarise the plot and sequence of events in a film or play.*
B1	*Can collate short pieces of information from several sources and summarise them for somebody else.* *Can paraphrase short written passages in a simple fashion, using the original text wording and ordering.*
A2	*Can pick out and reproduce key words and phrases or short sentences from a short text within the learner's limited competence and experience.* *Can copy out short texts in printed or clearly handwritten format.*
A1	*Can copy out single words and short texts presented in standard printed format.*

Users of the Framework may wish to consider and where appropriate state:

- *with which text types the learner will need/be equipped/be required to deal a) receptively, b) productively, c) interactively, d) in mediation.*

Sections 4.6.1 to 4.6.3 confine themselves to text types and the media which carry them. Matters often dealt with under 'genre' are treated in this Framework in 5.2.3 'pragmatic competences'.

Users of the Framework may wish to consider and where appropriate state:

- *whether and, if so, how, the differences in the medium and in the psycholinguistic processes involved in speaking, listening, reading and writing in productive, receptive and interactive activities are taken into account a) in the selection, adaptation or composition of the spoken and written texts presented to learners, b) in the way that the learners are expected to handle the texts, and c) in the evaluation of the texts which learners produce;*
- *whether and, if so, how learners and teachers are made critically aware of the textual characteristics of a) classroom discourse b) testing and examination rubrics and answers, and c) instructional and reference materials;*
- *whether and, if so, how learners are brought to make the texts they produce more appropriate to: a) their communicative purposes, b) the contexts of use (domains, situations, recipients, constraints), c) the media employed.*

4.6.4   Texts and activities

The output of the process of language production is a text, which once it is uttered or written becomes an artefact carried by a particular medium and independent of its producer. The text then functions as the input to the process of language reception. Written artefacts are concrete objects, whether carved in stone, handwritten, typed, printed or electronically generated. They allow communication to take place despite the complete separation of producer and receiver in space and/or time – a property on which human society largely depends. In face-to-face oral interaction the medium is acoustic, sound waves which are normally ephemeral and irrecoverable. Indeed, few speakers are able to reproduce in exact detail a text they have just uttered in the course of conversation. Once it has served its communicative purposes it is discarded from memory – if indeed it has ever lodged there as a complete entity. However, as a result of modern technology, sound waves can be recorded and broadcast or stored in another medium and later reconverted into speech-waves. In this way, the temporo-spatial separation of producer and receiver is made possible. Furthermore, recordings of spontaneous discourse and conversation can be transcribed and analysed at leisure as texts. There is necessarily a close correlation between the categories proposed for the description of language activities and the texts resulting from those activities. Indeed the same word may be used for both. 'Translation' may denote either the act of translating or the text produced. Similarly, 'conversation', 'debate' or 'interview' may denote the communicative interaction of the participants, but equally the sequence of their exchanged utterances, which constitutes a text of a particular type belonging to a corresponding genre.

All the activities of production, reception, interaction and mediation take place in time. The real-time nature of speech is apparent, both in the activities of speaking and listening and in the medium itself. 'Before' and 'after' in a spoken text are to be taken quite literally. In a written text, which is usually (excluding 'scrolled' texts) a static spatial artefact, this is not necessarily so. In production, a written text can be edited, passages inserted or deleted. We cannot tell in what order the elements have been produced, though they are presented in a linear order as a string of symbols. Receptively, the reader's eye is free to move over the text in any way, possibly following the linear sequence in strict order, as a child learning to read will generally do. Skilled, mature readers are much more likely to scan a text for highly information-bearing elements in order to establish an overall structure of meaning and then return to read more closely – and if need be to re-read a number of times – such words, phrases, sentences and paragraphs as are of particular relevance to their needs and purposes. An author or editor may well use paratextual features (see section 4.4.5.3) to steer this process and, indeed, plan the text in accordance with the way in which it is expected to be read by the audience for which it is intended. Similarly, a spoken text may be carefully planned in advance so as to appear to be spontaneous, yet to ensure that an essential message is effectively conveyed under the different conditions that constrain the reception of speech. Process and product are indissolubly linked.

The text is central to any act of linguistic communication, the external, objective link between producer and receiver, whether they are communicating face to face or at a distance. The diagrams below show in a schematic form the relation between the user/learner, on whom the Framework is focused, the interlocutor(s), activities and texts.

1. *Production.* The user/learner produces a spoken or written text, received, often at a distance, by one or more listeners or readers, who are not called upon to reply.

1.1. *Speaking*

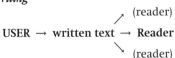

                  ↗ (listener)

USER → sound waves → **Listener**

                  ↘ (listener)

1.2. *Writing*

                ↗ (reader)

USER → written text → **Reader**

               ↘ (reader)

2. *Reception.* The user/learner receives a text from one or more speakers or writers, again often at a distance, and is not called upon to reply.

2.1. *Listening*

(speaker) ↘

Speaker → sound waves → USER

(speaker) ↗

2.2. *Reading*

(writer) ↘

Writer → written text → USER

(writer) ↗

3. *Interaction*. The user/learner enters into a face-to-face dialogue with an interlocutor. The text of the dialogue consists of utterances respectively produced and received by each party in alternation.

USER	↔	discourse	↔	Interlocutor
USER	→	Text 1.	→	interlocutor
USER	←	Text 2.	←	interlocutor
USER	→	Text 3.	→	interlocutor
USER	←	Text 4.	←	interlocutor
etc.				

4. *Mediation* covers two activities.

4.1. *Translation*. The user/learner receives a text from a speaker or writer, who is not present, in one language or code (Lx) and produces a parallel text in a different language or code (Ly) to be received by another person as listener or reader at a distance.

Writer (Lx) → **text** (in Lx) → **USER** → **text** (in Ly) → **Reader** (Ly)

4.2. *Interpretation*. The user/learner acts as an intermediary in a face-to-face interaction between two interlocutors who do not share the same language or code, receiving a text in one language (Lx) and producing a corresponding text in the other (Ly).

Interlocutor (Lx)	↔ discourse (Lx)	↔	USER ↔	discourse (Ly)	↔ Interlocutor (Ly)
Interlocutor (Lx)	→ Text (Lx1)	→	USER →	Text (Ly1)	→ Interlocutor (Ly)
Interlocutor (Lx)	← Text (Lx2)	←	USER ←	Text (Ly2)	← Interlocutor (Ly)
Interlucutor (Lx)	→ Text (Lx3)	→	USER →	Text (Ly3)	→ Interlocutor (Ly)
Interlocutor (Lx)	← Text (Lx4)	←	USER ←	Text (Ly4)	← Interlocutor (Ly)
etc.					

In addition to interaction and mediation activities as defined above, there are many activities in which the user/learner is required to produce a textual response to a textual stimulus. The textual stimulus may be an oral question, a set of written instructions (e.g. an examination rubric), a discursive text, authentic or composed, etc. or some combination of these. The required textual response may be anything from a single word to a three-hour essay. Both input and output texts may be spoken or written and in L1 or L2. The relation between the two texts may be meaning-preserving or not. Accordingly, even if we overlook the part which may be played in the teaching/learning of modern languages by activities in which the learner produces an L1 text in response to an L1 stimulus (as may often be the case with regard to the sociocultural component), some 24 activity types may be distinguished. For example, the following cases (Table 6) in which both input and output are in the target language.

Whilst such text-to-text activities have a place in everyday language use, they are particularly frequent in language learning/teaching and testing. The more mechanical meaning-preserving activities (repetition, dictation, reading aloud, phonetic transcription) are currently out of favour in communication-oriented language teaching owing to their artificiality and what are seen as undesirable backwash effects. A case can perhaps be made for them as testing devices for the technical reason that performance depends

Table 6. *Text-to-text activities*

Input text		Output text			
Medium	*Language*	*Medium*	*Language preserving*	*Meaning preserving*	*Activity type (examples)*
spoken	L2	spoken	L2	Yes	repetition
spoken	L2	written	L2	Yes	dictation
spoken	L2	spoken	L2	No	oral question/ answer
spoken	L2	written	L2	No	written answers to oral L2 questions
written	L2	spoken	L2	Yes	reading aloud
written	L2	written	L2	Yes	copying, transcription
written	L2	spoken	L2	No	spoken response to written L2 rubric
written	L2	written	L2	No	writing in response to written L2 rubric

closely on the ability to use linguistic competences to reduce the information content of the text. In any case, the advantage of examining all possible combinations of categories in taxonomic sets is not only that it enables experience to be ordered, but also that it reveals gaps and suggests new possibilities.

5 The user/learner's competences

In order to carry out the tasks and activities required to deal with the communicative situations in which they are involved, users and learners draw upon a number of competences developed in the course of their previous experience. In return, participation in communicative events (including, of course, those events specifically designed to promote language learning) results in the further development of the learner's competences, for both immediate and long-term use.

All human competences contribute in one way or another to the language user's ability to communicate and may be regarded as aspects of communicative competence. It may however be useful to distinguish those less closely related to language from linguistic competences more narrowly defined.

5.1 General competences

5.1.1 *Declarative knowledge* (savoir)

5.1.1.1 Knowledge of the world
Mature human beings have a highly developed and finely articulated model of the world and its workings, closely correlated with the vocabulary and grammar of their mother tongue. Indeed, both develop in relation to each other. The question, '*What is that?*' may ask for the name of a newly observed phenomenon or for the meaning (referent) of a new word. The basic features of this model are fully developed during early childhood, but it is further developed through education and experience during adolescence and indeed throughout adult life. Communication depends on the congruence of the models of the world and of language which have been internalised by the persons taking part. One aim of scientific endeavour is to discover the structure and workings of the universe and to provide a standardised terminology to describe and refer to them. Ordinary language has developed in a more organic way and the relation between the categories of form and meaning varies somewhat from one language to another, though within fairly narrow limits imposed by the actual nature of reality. Divergence is wider in the social sphere than in relation to the physical environment, though there, too, languages differentiate natural phenomena very much in relation to their significance for the life of the community. Second and foreign language teaching is often able to assume that learners have already acquired a knowledge of the world sufficient for the purpose. This is, however, not by any means always the case (see 2.1.1).

Knowledge of the world (whether it derives from experience, education or from information sources, etc.) embraces:

- The locations, institutions and organisations, persons, objects, events, processes and operations in different domains as exemplified in Table 5 (section 4.1.2). Of considerable importance to the learner of a particular language is factual knowledge concerning the country or countries in which the language is spoken, such as its major geographical, environmental, demographic, economic and political features.
- Classes of entities (concrete/abstract, animate/inanimate, etc.) and their properties and relations (temporo-spatial, associative, analytic, logical, cause/effect, etc.) as set out, for instance, in *Threshold Level 1990*, Chapter 6.

Users of the Framework may wish to consider and where appropriate state:

- *what knowledge of the world the language learner will be assumed/required to possess;*
- *what new knowledge of the world, particularly in respect of the country in which the language is spoken the learner will need/be equipped to acquire in the course of language learning.*

5.1.1.2 Sociocultural knowledge

Strictly speaking, knowledge of the society and culture of the community or communities in which a language is spoken is one aspect of knowledge of the world. It is, however, of sufficient importance to the language learner to merit special attention, especially since unlike many other aspects of knowledge it is likely to lie outside the learner's previous experience and may well be distorted by stereotypes.

The features distinctively characteristic of a particular European society and its culture may relate, for example, to:

1. *Everyday living*, e.g.:
   - food and drink, meal times, table manners;
   - public holidays;
   - working hours and practices;
   - leisure activities (hobbies, sports, reading habits, media).

2. *Living conditions*, e.g.:
   - living standards (with regional, class and ethnic variations);
   - housing conditions;
   - welfare arrangements.

3. *Interpersonal relations* (including relations of power and solidarity) e.g. with respect to:
   - class structure of society and relations between classes;
   - relations between sexes (gender, intimacy);
   - family structures and relations;
   - relations between generations;
   - relations in work situations;
   - relations between public and police, officials, etc.;

- race and community relations;
- relations among political and religious groupings.

4. *Values, beliefs and attitudes* in relation to such factors as:
    - social class;
    - occupational groups (academic, management, public service, skilled and manual workforces);
    - wealth (income and inherited);
    - regional cultures;
    - security;
    - institutions;
    - tradition and social change;
    - history, especially iconic historical personages and events;
    - minorities (ethnic, religious);
    - national identity;
    - foreign countries, states, peoples;
    - politics;
    - arts (music, visual arts, literature, drama, popular music and song);
    - religion;
    - humour.

5. *Body language* (see section 4.4.5). Knowledge of the conventions governing such behaviour form part of the user/learner's sociocultural competence.

6. *Social conventions*, e.g. with regard to giving and receiving hospitality, such as:
    - punctuality;
    - presents;
    - dress;
    - refreshments, drinks, meals;
    - behavioural and conversational conventions and taboos;
    - length of stay;
    - leave-taking.

7. *Ritual behaviour* in such areas as:
    - religious observances and rites;
    - birth, marriage, death;
    - audience and spectator behaviour at public performances and ceremonies;
    - celebrations, festivals, dances, discos, etc.

5.1.1.3 Intercultural awareness

Knowledge, awareness and understanding of the relation (similarities and distinctive differences) between the 'world of origin' and the 'world of the target community' produce an intercultural awareness. It is, of course, important to note that intercultural awareness includes an awareness of regional and social diversity in both worlds. It is also enriched by awareness of a wider range of cultures than those carried by the learner's L1 and L2. This wider awareness helps to place both in context. In addition to objective knowledge, intercultural awareness covers an awareness of how each community appears from the perspective of the other, often in the form of national stereotypes.

Users of the Framework may wish to consider and where appropriate state:

- *what prior sociocultural experience and knowledge the learner is assumed/required to have;*
- *what new experience and knowledge of social life in his/her community as well as in the target community the learner will need to acquire in order to meet the requirements of L2 communication;*
- *what awareness of the relation between home and target cultures the learner will need so as to develop an appropriate intercultural competence.*

5.1.2 Skills and know-how (savoir-faire)

5.1.2.1 Practical skills and know-how include:

- *Social skills*: the ability to act in accordance with the types of convention set out in 5.1.1.2 above and to perform the expected routines, in so far as it is considered appropriate for outsiders and particularly foreigners to do so.

- *Living skills*: the ability to carry out effectively the routine actions required for daily life (bathing, dressing, walking, cooking, eating, etc.); maintenance and repair of household equipment, etc.

- *Vocational and professional skills*: the ability to perform specialised actions (mental and physical) required to carry out the duties of (self-)employment.

- *Leisure skills*: the ability to carry out effectively the actions required for leisure activities, e.g.:
    - arts (painting, sculpture, playing musical instruments, etc.);
    - crafts (knitting, embroidery, weaving, basketry, carpentry, etc.);
    - sports (team games, athletics, jogging, climbing, swimming, etc.);
    - hobbies (photography, gardening, etc.).

Users of the Framework may wish to consider and where appropriate state:

- *what practical skills and know-how the learner will need/be required to possess in order to communicate effectively in an area of concern.*

5.1.2.2 Intercultural skills and know-how
These include:

- the ability to bring the culture of origin and the foreign culture into relation with each other;
- cultural sensitivity and the ability to identify and use a variety of strategies for contact with those from other cultures;

- the capacity to fulfil the role of cultural intermediary between one's own culture and the foreign culture and to deal effectively with intercultural misunderstanding and conflict situations;
- the ability to overcome stereotyped relationships.

Users of the Framework may wish to consider and where appropriate state:

- *what cultural intermediary roles and functions the learner will need/be equipped/be required to fulfil;*
- *what features of the home and target culture the learner will need/be enabled/required to distinguish;*
- *what provision is expected to be made for the learner to experience the target culture;*
- *what opportunities the learner will have of acting as a cultural intermediary.*

5.1.3 'Existential' competence (savoir-être)

The communicative activity of users/learners is affected not only by their knowledge, understanding and skills, but also by selfhood factors connected with their individual personalities, characterised by the attitudes, motivations, values, beliefs, cognitive styles and personality types which contribute to their personal identity. These include:

1. *attitudes,* such as the user/learner's degree of:
   - openness towards, and interest in, new experiences, other persons, ideas, peoples, societies and cultures;
   - willingness to relativise one's own cultural viewpoint and cultural value-system;
   - willingness and ability to distance oneself from conventional attitudes to cultural difference.

2. *motivations*:
   - intrinsic/extrinsic;
   - instrumental/integrative;
   - communicative drive, the human need to communicate.

3. *values,* e.g. ethical and moral.

4. *beliefs,* e.g. religious, ideological, philosophical.

5. *cognitive styles,* e.g.:
   - convergent/divergent;
   - holistic/analytic/synthetic.

6. *personality factors,* e.g.:
   - loquacity/taciturnity;
   - enterprise/timidity;
   - optimism/pessimism;
   - introversion/extroversion;
   - proactivity/reactivity;

- intropunitive/extrapunitive/impunitive personality (guilt);
- (freedom from) fear or embarrassment;
- rigidity/flexibility;
- open-mindedness/closed-mindedness;
- spontaneity/self-monitoring;
- intelligence;
- meticulousness/carelessness;
- memorising ability;
- industry/laziness;
- ambition/(lack of) ambition;
- (lack of) self-awareness;
- (lack of) self-reliance;
- (lack of) self-confidence;
- (lack of) self-esteem.

Attitudes and personality factors greatly affect not only the language users'/learners' roles in communicative acts but also their ability to learn. The development of an 'intercultural personality' involving both attitudes and awareness is seen by many as an important educational goal in its own right. Important ethical and pedagogic issues are raised, such as:

- the extent to which personality development can be an explicit educational objective;
- how cultural relativism is to be reconciled with ethical and moral integrity;
- which personality factors a) facilitate b) impede foreign or second language learning and acquisition;
- how learners can be helped to exploit strengths and overcome weaknesses;
- how the diversity of personalities can be reconciled with the constraints imposed on and by educational systems.

Users of the Framework may wish to consider and where appropriate state:

- *whether, and if so which personality features learners will need/be encouraged/equipped/ required to develop/display;*
- *whether, and if so in what ways, learner characteristics are taken into account in provisions for language learning, teaching and assessment.*

5.1.4 Ability to learn (savoir-apprendre)

In its most general sense, *savoir-apprendre* is the ability to observe and participate in new experiences and to incorporate new knowledge into existing knowledge, modifying the latter where necessary. Language learning abilities are developed in the course of the experience of learning. They enable the learner to deal more effectively and independently with new language learning challenges, to see what options exist and to make better use of opportunities. Ability to learn has several components, such as language and communication awareness; general phonetic skills; study skills; and heuristic skills.

5.1.4.1 Language and communication awareness

Sensitivity to language and language use, involving knowledge and understanding of the principles according to which languages are organised and used, enables new experience to be assimilated into an ordered framework and welcomed as an enrichment. The associated new language may then be more readily learnt and used, rather than resisted as a threat to the learner's already established linguistic system, which is often believed to be normal and 'natural'.

5.1.4.2 General phonetic awareness and skills

Many learners, particularly mature students, will find their ability to pronounce new languages facilitated by:

- an ability to distinguish and produce unfamiliar sounds and prosodic patterns;
- an ability to perceive and catenate unfamiliar sound sequences;
- an ability, as a listener, to resolve (i.e. divide into distinct and significant parts) a continuous stream of sound into a meaningful structured string of phonological elements;
- an understanding/mastery of the processes of sound perception and production applicable to new language learning.

These general phonetic skills are distinct from the ability to pronounce a particular language.

> *Users of the Framework may wish to consider and where appropriate state:*
>
> - *what steps if any are taken to develop the learner's language and communication awareness;*
> - *what auditory discrimination and articulatory skills the learner will need/be assumed/ equipped/required to possess.*

5.1.4.3 Study skills

These include:

- ability to make effective use of the learning opportunities created by teaching situations, e.g.:
    - to maintain attention to the presented information;
    - to grasp the intention of the task set;
    - to co-operate effectively in pair and group work;
    - to make rapid and frequent active use of the language learnt;
    - ability to use available materials for independent learning;

- ability to organise and use materials for self-directed learning;
- ability to learn effectively (both linguistically and socioculturally) from direct observation of and participation in communication events by the cultivation of perceptual, analytical and heuristic skills;
- awareness of one's own strengths and weaknesses as a learner;
- ability to identify one's own needs and goals;
- ability to organise one's own strategies and procedures to pursue these goals, in accordance with one's own characteristics and resources.

5.1.4.4   Heuristic skills

These include:

- the ability of the learner to come to terms with new experience (new language, new people, new ways of behaving, etc.) and to bring other competences to bear (e.g. by observing, grasping the significance of what is observed, analysing, inferencing, memorising, etc.) in the specific learning situation;
- the ability of the learner (particularly in using target language reference sources) to find, understand and if necessary convey new information;
- the ability to use new technologies (e.g. by searching for information in databases, hypertexts, etc.).

Users of the Framework may wish to consider and where appropriate state:

- *what study skills learners are encouraged/enabled to use and develop;*
- *what heuristic abilities learners are encouraged/enabled to use and develop;*
- *what provision is made for learners to become increasingly independent in their learning and use of language.*

5.2   Communicative language competences

For the realisation of communicative intentions, users/learners bring to bear their general capacities as detailed above together with a more specifically language-related communicative competence. Communicative competence in this narrower sense has the following components:

- linguistic competences;
- sociolinguistic competences;
- pragmatic competences.

5.2.1   Linguistic competences

No complete, exhaustive description of any language as a formal system for the expression of meaning has ever been produced. Language systems are of great complexity and the language of a large, diversified, advanced society is never completely mastered by any of its users. Nor could it be, since every language is in continuous evolution in response to the exigencies of its use in communication. Most nation states have attempted to establish a standard form of the language, though never in exhaustive detail. For its presentation, the model of linguistic description in use for teaching the corpus is still the same model as was employed for the long-dead classical languages. This 'traditional' model was, however, repudiated over 100 years ago by most professional linguists, who insisted that languages should be described as they exist in use rather than as some authority thinks they should be and that the traditional model, having been developed for languages of a particular type, was inappropriate for the description of language systems with a very different organisation. However, none of the many proposals for alternative models has gained general acceptance. Indeed, the possibility of one universal model of description for all languages has been denied. Recent work on linguistic universals has not as yet produced results which can be used directly to facilitate language learning, teaching and assessment. Most descriptive linguists are now content to codify practice, relating form and meaning, using terminology which diverges from traditional practice only where it is necessary to deal with phenomena outside the range of traditional models of description. This is the approach adopted in Section 4.2. It attempts to identify and classify the main components of linguistic competence defined as knowledge of, and ability to use, the formal resources from which well-formed, meaningful messages may be assembled and formulated. The scheme that follows aims only to offer as classificatory tools some parameters and categories which may be found useful for the description of linguistic content and as a basis for reflection. Those practitioners who prefer to use a different frame of reference are free, here as elsewhere, to do so. They should then identify the theory, tradition or practice they are following. Here, we distinguish:

5.2.1.1 lexical competence;
5.2.1.2 grammatical competence;
5.2.1.3 semantic competence;
5.2.1.4 phonological competence;
5.2.1.5 Orthographic competence;
5.2.1.6 Orthoepic competence.

Progress in the development of a learner's ability to use linguistic resources can be scaled and is presented in that form below as appropriate.

	GENERAL LINGUISTIC RANGE
C2	*Can exploit a comprehensive and reliable mastery of a very wide range of language to formulate thoughts precisely, give emphasis, differentiate and eliminate ambiguity . . . No signs of having to restrict what he/she wants to say.*
C1	*Can select an appropriate formulation from a broad range of language to express him/herself clearly, without having to restrict what he/she wants to say.*
B2	*Can express him/herself clearly and without much sign of having to restrict what he/she wants to say.*
	Has a sufficient range of language to be able to give clear descriptions, express viewpoints and develop arguments without much conspicuous searching for words, using some complex sentence forms to do so.
B1	*Has a sufficient range of language to describe unpredictable situations, explain the main points in an idea or problem with reasonable precision and express thoughts on abstract or cultural topics such as music and films.*
	Has enough language to get by, with sufficient vocabulary to express him/herself with some hesitation and circumlocutions on topics such as family, hobbies and interests, work, travel, and current events, but lexical limitations cause repetition and even difficulty with formulation at times.
A2	*Has a repertoire of basic language which enables him/her to deal with everyday situations with predictable content, though he/she will generally have to compromise the message and search for words.*
	Can produce brief everyday expressions in order to satisfy simple needs of a concrete type: personal details, daily routines, wants and needs, requests for information. *Can use basic sentence patterns and communicate with memorised phrases, groups of a few words and formulae about themselves and other people, what they do, places, possessions etc.* *Has a limited repertoire of short memorised phrases covering predictable survival situations; frequent breakdowns and misunderstandings occur in non-routine situations.*
A1	*Has a very basic range of simple expressions about personal details and needs of a concrete type.*

5.2.1.1 ***Lexical competence***, knowledge of, and ability to use, the vocabulary of a language, consists of lexical elements and grammatical elements.

Lexical elements include:

a) *Fixed expressions*, consisting of several words, which are used and learnt as wholes. Fixed expressions include:

- *sentential formulae*, including:

  direct exponents of language functions (see section 5.2.3.2) such as greetings, e.g.
    How do you do? Good morning! etc.
  proverbs, etc. (see section 5.2.2.3)
  relict archaisms, e.g. *Be off with you!*

- *phrasal idioms*, often:

  semantically opaque, frozen metaphors, e.g.:
  He *kicked the bucket* (i.e. he died).
  It's *a long shot* (= unlikely to succeed).

He *drove hell for leather* (i.e. very fast).
intensifiers. Their use is often contextually and stylistically restricted, e.g. *as white as snow* (= 'pure'), as against *as white as a sheet* (= 'pallid').

- *fixed frames*, learnt and used as unanalysed wholes, into which words or phrases are inserted to form meaningful sentences, e.g.: *'Please may I have . . .'*.

- other fixed phrases, such as:

  phrasal verbs, e.g. *to put up with, to make do (with)*;
  compound prepositions, e.g. *in front of.*

- fixed collocations, consisting of words regularly used together, e.g. *to make a speech/mistake.*

b) *Single word forms.* A particular single word form may have several distinct meanings (polysemy), e.g. *tank*, a liquid container or an armoured armed vehicle. Single word forms include members of the open word classes: noun, verb, adjective, adverb, though these may include closed lexical sets (e.g. days of the week, months of the year, weights and measures, etc.). Other lexical sets may also be established for grammatical and semantic purposes (see below).

Grammatical elements belong to closed word classes, e.g. (in English):

articles	(a, the)
quantifiers	(some, all, many, etc.)
demonstratives	(this, that, these, those)
personal pronouns	(I, we, he, she, it, they, me, you, etc.)
question words and	
relatives	(who, what, which, where, how, etc.)
possessives	(my, your, his, her, its, etc.)
prepositions	(in, at, by, with, of, etc.)
auxiliary verbs	(be, do, have, modals)
conjunctions	(and, but, if, although)
particles	(e.g. in German: ja, wohl, aber, doch, etc.)

Illustrative scales are available for the range of vocabulary knowledge, and the ability to control that knowledge.

	VOCABULARY RANGE
C2	*Has a good command of a very broad lexical repertoire including idiomatic expressions and colloquialisms; shows awareness of connotative levels of meaning.*
C1	*Has a good command of a broad lexical repertoire allowing gaps to be readily overcome with circumlocutions; little obvious searching for expressions or avoidance strategies. Good command of idiomatic expressions and colloquialisms.*
B2	*Has a good range of vocabulary for matters connected to his/her field and most general topics. Can vary formulation to avoid frequent repetition, but lexical gaps can still cause hesitation and circumlocution.*
B1	*Has a sufficient vocabulary to express him/herself with some circumlocutions on most topics pertinent to his/her everyday life such as family, hobbies and interests, work, travel, and current events.*
A2	*Has sufficient vocabulary to conduct routine, everyday transactions involving familiar situations and topics.* *Has a sufficient vocabulary for the expression of basic communicative needs.* *Has a sufficient vocabulary for coping with simple survival needs.*
A1	*Has a basic vocabulary repertoire of isolated words and phrases related to particular concrete situations.*

	VOCABULARY CONTROL
C2	*Consistently correct and appropriate use of vocabulary.*
C1	*Occasional minor slips, but no significant vocabulary errors.*
B2	*Lexical accuracy is generally high, though some confusion and incorrect word choice does occur without hindering communication.*
B1	*Shows good control of elementary vocabulary but major errors still occur when expressing more complex thoughts or handling unfamiliar topics and situations.*
A2	*Can control a narrow repertoire dealing with concrete everyday needs.*
A1	*No descriptor available*

Users of the Framework may wish to consider and where appropriate state:

- *which lexical elements (fixed expressions and single word forms) the learner will need/be equipped/be required to recognise and/or use;*
- *how they are selected and ordered.*

5.2.1.2 Grammatical competence

Grammatical competence may be defined as knowledge of, and ability to use, the grammatical resources of a language.

Formally, the grammar of a language may be seen as the set of principles governing the assembly of elements into meaningful labelled and bracketed strings (sentences). Grammatical competence is the ability to understand and express meaning by producing and recognising well-formed phrases and sentences in accordance with these principles (as opposed to memorising and reproducing them as fixed formulae). The grammar of any language in this sense is highly complex and so far defies definitive or exhaustive treatment. There are a number of competing theories and models for the organisation of words into sentences. It is not the function of the Framework to judge between them or to advocate the use of any one, but rather to encourage users to state which they have chosen to follow and what consequences their choice has for their practice. Here we limit ourselves to identifying some parameters and categories which have been widely used in grammatical description.

The description of grammatical organisation involves the specification of:

- *elements*, e.g.:   morphs
  morphemes-roots and affixes
  words

- *categories*, e.g.:   number, case, gender
  concrete/abstract, countable/uncountable
  (in)transitive, active/passive voice
  past/present/future tense
  progressive, (im)perfect aspect

- *classes*, e.g.:   conjugations
  declensions
  open word classes: nouns, verbs, adjectives, adverbs, closed word
      classes (grammatical elements – see section 5.2.1.1)

- *structures*, e.g.:   compound and complex words
  phrases: (noun phrase, verb phrase, etc.)
  clauses: (main, subordinate, co-ordinate)
  sentences: (simple, compound, complex)

- *processes* (descriptive), e.g.:
  nominalisation
  affixation
  suppletion
  gradation
  transposition
  transformation

- *relations*, e.g.:   government
  concord
  valency

An illustrative scale is available for grammatical accuracy. This scale should be seen in relation to the scale for general linguistic range shown at the beginning of this section. It is not considered possible to produce a scale for progression in respect of grammatical structure which would be applicable across all languages.

	GRAMMATICAL ACCURACY
C2	*Maintains consistent grammatical control of complex language, even while attention is otherwise engaged (e.g. in forward planning, in monitoring others' reactions).*
C1	*Consistently maintains a high degree of grammatical accuracy; errors are rare and difficult to spot.*
B2	*Good grammatical control; occasional 'slips' or non-systematic errors and minor flaws in sentence structure may still occur, but they are rare and can often be corrected in retrospect.*
	Shows a relatively high degree of grammatical control. Does not make mistakes which lead to misunderstanding.
B1	*Communicates with reasonable accuracy in familiar contexts; generally good control though with noticeable mother tongue influence. Errors occur, but it is clear what he/she is trying to express.*
	Uses reasonably accurately a repertoire of frequently used 'routines' and patterns associated with more predictable situations.
A2	*Uses some simple structures correctly, but still systematically makes basic mistakes – for example tends to mix up tenses and forget to mark agreement; nevertheless, it is usually clear what he/she is trying to say.*
A1	*Shows only limited control of a few simple grammatical structures and sentence patterns in a learnt repertoire.*

Users of the Framework may wish to consider and where appropriate state:

- *on which theory of grammar they have based their work;*
- *which grammatical elements, categories, classes, structures, processes and relations are learners, etc. equipped/required to handle.*

A distinction is traditionally drawn between morphology and syntax.

Morphology deals with the internal organisation of words. Words may be analysed into morphemes, classed as:

- roots, or stems;
- affixes (prefixes, suffixes, infixes), including:
  word-forming affixes (e.g. re-, un-, -ly, -ness);
  inflexional affixes (e.g. s, -ed, -ing).

Word-formation:

Words may be classified into:

- simple words (root only, e.g. six, tree, break);
- complex words (root + affixes, e.g. unbrokenly, sixes);
- compound words (containing more than one root, e.g. sixpence, breakdown, oak-tree, evening dress).

Morphology also deals with other ways of modifying word forms, e.g.:

• vowel alteration	(sing/sang/sung, mouse/mice)
• consonant modification	(lend/lent)
• irregular forms	(bring/brought, catch/caught)
• suppletion	(go/went)
• zero forms	(sheep/sheep, cut/cut/cut)

Morphophonology deals with the phonetically conditioned variation of morphemes (e.g. English s/z/iz in walk<u>s</u>, lie<u>s</u>, rise<u>s</u>; t/d/id in laugh<u>ed</u>, cri<u>ed</u>, shout<u>ed</u>), and their morphologically conditioned phonetic variation (e.g. i:/e in creep/crept, mean/meant, weep/wept).

Users of the Framework may wish to consider and where appropriate state:

• *what morphological elements and processes the learner will need/be equipped/required to handle.*

Syntax deals with the organisation of words into sentences in terms of the categories, elements, classes, structures, processes and relations involved, often presented in the form of a set of rules. The syntax of the language of a mature native speaker is highly complex and largely unconscious. The ability to organise sentences to convey meaning is a central aspect of communicative competence.

Users of the Framework may wish to consider and where appropriate state:

• *what grammatical elements, categories, classes, structures, processes and relations learners will need/be equipped/required to handle.*

5.2.1.3 Semantic competence
deals with the learner's awareness and control of the organisation of meaning.
Lexical semantics deals with questions of word meaning, e.g.:
• relation of word to general context:
  reference;
  connotation;
  exponence of general specific notions;
• interlexical relations, such as:
  synonymy/antonymy;
  hyponymy;
  collocation;
  part-whole relations;
  componential analysis;
  translation equivalence.

Grammatical semantics deals with the meaning of grammatical elements, categories, structures and processes (see section 5.2.1.2).

Pragmatic semantics deals with logical relations such as entailment, presupposition, implicature, etc.

Users of the Framework may wish to consider and where appropriate state:

- *what kinds of semantic relation learners are equipped/required to build up/demonstrate.*

Questions of meaning are of course central to communication and are treated *passim* in this Framework (see particularly section 5.1.1.1).

Linguistic competence is treated here in a formal sense. From the point of view of theoretical or descriptive linguistics, a language is a highly complex symbolic system. When an attempt is made, as here, to separate out the many different components of communicative competence, knowledge (largely unconscious) of and ability to handle formal structure is legitimately identifiable as one of those components. How much, if indeed any, of this formal analysis should enter into language learning or teaching is a different matter. The functional/notional approach adopted in the Council of Europe publications *Waystage 1990, Threshold Level 1990* and *Vantage Level* offers an alternative to the treatment of linguistic competence in Section 5.2.1–3. Instead of starting from language forms and their meanings, it starts from a systematic classification of communicative functions and of notions, divided into general and specific, and secondarily deals with forms, lexical and grammatical, as their exponents. The approaches are complementary ways of dealing with the 'double articulation' of language. Languages are based on an organisation of form and an organisation of meaning. The two kinds of organisation cut across each other in a largely arbitrary fashion. A description based on the organisation of the forms of expression atomises meaning, and that based on the organisation of meaning atomises form. Which is to be preferred by the user will depend on the purpose for which the description is produced. The success of the Threshold Level approach indicates that many practitioners find it more advantageous to go from meaning to form rather than the more traditional practice of organising progression in purely formal terms. On the other hand, some may prefer to use a 'communicative grammar', as for example, in *Un niveau-seuil.* What is clear is that a language learner has to acquire both forms and meanings.

5.2.1.4 Phonological competence

involves a knowledge of, and skill in the perception and production of:
- the sound-units (*phonemes*) of the language and their realisation in particular contexts (*allophones*);
- the phonetic features which distinguish phonemes (*distinctive features*, e.g. voicing, rounding, nasality, plosion);
- the phonetic composition of words (*syllable structure*, the sequence of phonemes, word stress, word tones);
- sentence phonetics (*prosody*)
  - sentence stress and rhythm
  - intonation;

- phonetic reduction
  - vowel reduction
  - strong and weak forms
  - assimilation
  - elision.

	PHONOLOGICAL CONTROL
C2	*As C1*
C1	*Can vary intonation and place sentence stress correctly in order to express finer shades of meaning.*
B2	*Has acquired a clear, natural, pronunciation and intonation.*
B1	*Pronunciation is clearly intelligible even if a foreign accent is sometimes evident and occasional mispronunciations occur.*
A2	*Pronunciation is generally clear enough to be understood despite a noticeable foreign accent, but conversational partners will need to ask for repetition from time to time.*
A1	*Pronunciation of a very limited repertoire of learnt words and phrases can be understood with some effort by native speakers used to dealing with speakers of his/her language group.*

Users of the Framework may wish to consider and where appropriate state:

- *what new phonological skills are required of the learner;*
- *what is the relative importance of sounds and prosody;*
- *whether phonetic accuracy and fluency are an early learning objective or developed as a longer term objective.*

5.2.1.5 Orthographic competence

involves a knowledge of and skill in the perception and production of the symbols of which written texts are composed. The writing systems of all European languages are based on the alphabetic principle, though those of some other languages follow an ideographic (logographic) principle (e.g. Chinese) or a consonantal principle (e.g. Arabic). For alphabetic systems, learners should know and be able to perceive and produce:

- the form of letters in printed and cursive forms in both upper and lower case
- the proper spelling of words, including recognised contracted forms
- punctuation marks and their conventions of use
- typographical conventions and varieties of font, etc.
- logographic signs in common use (e.g. @, &, $, etc.)

5.2.1.6 Orthoepic competence

Conversely, users required to read aloud a prepared text, or to use in speech words first encountered in their written form, need to be able to produce a correct pronunciation from the written form. This may involve:

- knowledge of spelling conventions
- ability to consult a dictionary and a knowledge of the conventions used there for the representation of pronunciation
- knowledge of the implications of written forms, particularly punctuation marks, for phrasing and intonation
- ability to resolve ambiguity (homonyms, syntactic ambiguities, etc.) in the light of the context

	ORTHOGRAPHIC CONTROL
C2	*Writing is orthographically free of error.*
C1	*Layout, paragraphing and punctuation are consistent and helpful.* *Spelling is accurate, apart from occasional slips of the pen.*
B2	*Can produce clearly intelligible continuous writing which follows standard layout and paragraphing conventions.* *Spelling and punctuation are reasonably accurate but may show signs of mother tongue influence.*
B1	*Can produce continuous writing which is generally intelligible throughout.* *Spelling, punctuation and layout are accurate enough to be followed most of the time.*
A2	*Can copy short sentences on everyday subjects – e.g. directions how to get somewhere.* *Can write with reasonable phonetic accuracy (but not necessarily fully standard spelling) short words that are in his/her oral vocabulary.*
A1	*Can copy familiar words and short phrases e.g. simple signs or instructions, names of everyday objects, names of shops and set phrases used regularly.* *Can spell his/her address, nationality and other personal details.*

Users of the Framework may wish to consider and where appropriate state:

- *the orthographic and orthoepic needs of learners in relation to their use of spoken and written varieties of language, and their need to convert text from spoken to written form and vice versa.*

5.2.2 *Sociolinguistic competence*

Sociolinguistic competence is concerned with the knowledge and skills required to deal with the social dimension of language use. As was remarked with regard to sociocultural competence, since language is a sociocultural phenomenon, much of what is contained in the Framework, particularly in respect of the sociocultural, is of relevance to sociolinguistic competence. The matters treated here are those specifically relating to language use and not dealt with elsewhere: linguistic markers of social relations; politeness conventions; expressions of folk-wisdom; register differences; and dialect and accent.

5.2.2.1   Linguistic markers of social relations

These are of course widely divergent in different languages and cultures, depending on such factors as a) relative status, b) closeness of relation, c) register of discourse, etc. The examples given below for English are not universally applicable and may or may not have equivalence in other languages.

- use and choice of greetings:
    on arrival, e.g. *Hello! Good morning!*
    introductions, e.g. *How do you do?*
    leave-taking, e.g. *Good-bye . . . See you later*

- use and choice of address forms:
    frozen, e.g. *My Lord, Your Grace*
    formal, e.g. *Sir, Madam, Miss, Dr, Professor* (+ surname)
    informal, e.g. first name only, such as *John! Susan!*
                    no address form
    familiar, e.g. *dear, darling;* (popular) *mate, love*
    peremptory, e.g. surname only, such as *Smith! You (there)!*
    ritual insult, e.g. *you stupid idiot!* (often affectionate)

- conventions for turntaking

- use and choice of expletives (e.g. *Dear, dear!, My God!, Bloody Hell!,* etc.)

5.2.2.2   Politeness conventions

Politeness conventions provide one of the most important reasons for departing from the straightforward application of the 'co-operative principle' (see section 5.2.3.1). They vary from one culture to another and are a frequent source of inter-ethnic misunderstanding, especially when polite expressions are literally interpreted.

1. *'positive' politeness*, e.g.:
   - showing interest in a person's well being;
   - sharing experiences and concerns, 'troubles talk';
   - expressing admiration, affection, gratitude;
   - offering gifts, promising future favours, hospitality;

2. *'negative' politeness*, e.g.:
   - avoiding face-threatening behaviour (dogmatism, direct orders, etc.);
   - expressing regret, apologising for face-threatening behaviour (correction, contra-diction, prohibitions, etc.);
   - using hedges, etc. (e.g. ' I think', tag questions, etc.);

3. appropriate use of 'please', 'thank you', etc.;

4. *impoliteness* (deliberate flouting of politeness conventions), e.g.:
   - bluntness, frankness;
   - expressing contempt, dislike;

- strong complaint and reprimand;
- venting anger, impatience;
- asserting superiority.

5.2.2.3 Expressions of folk wisdom

These fixed formulae, which both incorporate and reinforce common attitudes, make a significant contribution to popular culture. They are frequently used, or perhaps more often referred to or played upon, for instance in newspaper headlines. A knowledge of this accumulated folk wisdom, expressed in language assumed to be known to all, is a significant component of the linguistic aspect of sociocultural competence.

- proverbs, e.g. *a stitch in time saves nine*
- idioms, e.g. *a sprat to catch a mackerel*
- familiar quotations, e.g. *a man's a man for a' that*
- expressions of:
    belief, such as – weathersaws, e.g. *Fine before seven, rain by eleven*
    attitudes, such as – clichés, e.g. *It takes all sorts to make a world*
    values, e.g. *It's not cricket.*

Graffiti, T-shirt slogans, TV catch phrases, work-place cards and posters now often have this function.

5.2.2.4 Register differences

The term 'register' is used to refer to systematic differences between varieties of language used in different contexts. This is a very broad concept, which could cover what is here dealt with under 'tasks' (section 4.3), 'text-types' (4.6.4) and 'macrofunctions'(5.2.3.2). In this section we deal with differences in level of formality:

- frozen, e.g. *Pray silence for His Worship the Mayor!*
- formal, e.g. *May we now come to order, please.*
- neutral, e.g. *Shall we begin?*
- informal, e.g. *Right. What about making a start?*
- familiar, e.g. *O.K. Let's get going.*
- intimate, e.g. *Ready dear?*

In early learning (say up to level B1), a relatively neutral register is appropriate, unless there are compelling reasons otherwise. It is this register that native speakers are likely to use towards and expect from foreigners and strangers generally. Acquaintance with more formal or more familiar registers is likely to come over a period of time, perhaps through the reading of different text-types, particularly novels, at first as a receptive competence. Some caution should be exercised in using more formal or more familiar registers, since their inappropriate use may well lead to misinterpretation and ridicule.

5.2.2.5   Dialect and accent

Sociolinguistic competence also includes the ability to recognise the linguistic markers of, for example:

*   social class
*   regional provenance
*   national origin
*   ethnicity
*   occupational group

Such markers include:

*   lexicon, e.g. Scottish *wee* for 'small'
*   grammar, e.g. Cockney *I ain't seen nothing* for 'I haven't seen anything'
*   phonology, e.g. New York *boid* for 'bird'

*   vocal characteristics (rhythm, loudness, etc.)
*   paralinguistics
*   body language

No European language communities are entirely homogenous. Different regions have their peculiarities in language and culture. These are usually most marked in those who live purely local lives and therefore correlate with social class, occupation and educational level. Recognition of such dialectal features therefore gives significant clues as to the interlocutor's characteristics. Stereotyping plays a large role in this process. It can be reduced by the development of intercultural skills (see section 5.1.2.2). Learners will in the course of time also come into contact with speakers of various provenances. Before themselves adopting dialect forms they should be aware of their social connotations and of the need for coherence and consistency.

The scaling of items for aspects of sociolinguistic competence proved problematic (see Appendix B). Items successfully scaled are shown in the illustrative scale below. As can be seen, the bottom part of the scale concerns only markers of social relations and politeness conventions. From Level B2, users are then found able to express themselves adequately in language which is sociolinguistically appropriate to the situations and persons involved, and begin to acquire an ability to cope with variation of speech, plus a greater degree of control over register and idiom.

	SOCIOLINGUISTIC APPROPRIATENESS
C2	*Has a good command of idiomatic expressions and colloquialisms with awareness of connotative levels of meaning.* *Appreciates fully the sociolinguistic and sociocultural implications of language used by native speakers and can react accordingly.* *Can mediate effectively between speakers of the target language and that of his/her community of origin taking account of sociocultural and sociolinguistic differences.*
C1	*Can recognise a wide range of idiomatic expressions and colloquialisms, appreciating register shifts; may, however, need to confirm occasional details, especially if the accent is unfamiliar.* *Can follow films employing a considerable degree of slang and idiomatic usage.* *Can use language flexibly and effectively for social purposes, including emotional, allusive and joking usage.*
B2	*Can express him or herself confidently, clearly and politely in a formal or informal register, appropriate to the situation and person(s) concerned.* *Can with some effort keep up with and contribute to group discussions even when speech is fast and colloquial.* *Can sustain relationships with native speakers without unintentionally amusing or irritating them or requiring them to behave other than they would with a native speaker.* *Can express him or herself appropriately in situations and avoid crass errors of formulation.*
B1	*Can perform and respond to a wide range of language functions, using their most common exponents in a neutral register.* *Is aware of the salient politeness conventions and acts appropriately.* *Is aware of, and looks out for signs of, the most significant differences between the customs, usages, attitudes, values and beliefs prevalent in the community concerned and those of his or her own.*
A2	*Can perform and respond to basic language functions, such as information exchange and requests and express opinions and attitudes in a simple way.* *Can socialise simply but effectively using the simplest common expressions and following basic routines.* *Can handle very short social exchanges, using everyday polite forms of greeting and address. Can make and respond to invitations, suggestions, apologies, etc.*
A1	*Can establish basic social contact by using the simplest everyday polite forms of: greetings and farewells; introductions; saying please, thank you, sorry, etc.*

Users of the Framework may wish to consider and where appropriate state:

- *what range of greetings, address forms and expletives learners should need/be equipped/be required to a) recognise b) evaluate sociologically c) use themselves;*
- *which politeness conventions learners should need/be equipped/be required to a) recognise and understand b) use themselves;*
- *which forms of impoliteness learners should need/be equipped/be required to a) recognise and understand b) use themselves and in which situations to do so;*
- *which proverbs, clichés and folk idioms learners should need/be equipped/be required to a) recognise and understand b) use themselves;*
- *which registers learners should need/be equipped/be required to a) recognise b) use;*
- *which social groups in the target community and, perhaps, in the international community the learner should need/be equipped/be required to recognise by their use of language.*

5.2.3 Pragmatic competences

Pragmatic competences are concerned with the user/learner's knowledge of the principles according to which messages are:

a) organised, structured and arranged ('discourse competence');
b) used to perform communicative functions ('functional competence');
c) sequenced according to interactional and transactional schemata ('design competence').

5.2.3.1 **Discourse competence** is the ability of a user/learner to arrange sentences in sequence so as to produce coherent stretches of language. It includes knowledge of and ability to control the ordering of sentences in terms of:

- topic/focus;
- given/new;
- 'natural' sequencing: e.g. temporal:
     - *He fell over and I hit him,* as against
     - *I hit him and he fell over.*
- cause/effect (invertible) – *prices are rising – people want higher wages.*
- ability to structure and manage discourse in terms of:
  thematic organisation;
  coherence and cohesion;
  logical ordering;
  style and register;
  rhetorical effectiveness;
  the *'co-operative principle'* (Grice 1975): 'make your contribution such as is required, at the stage at which it occurs, by the accepted purpose or direction of the talk exchange in which you are engaged, by observing the following maxims:
     - quality (try to make your contribution one that is true);
     - quantity (make your contribution as informative as necessary, but not more);
     - relevance (do not say what is not relevant);
     - manner (be brief and orderly, avoid obscurity and ambiguity)'.

Departure from these criteria for straightforward and efficient communication should be for a specific purpose rather than because of inability to meet them.

- *Text design*: knowledge of the design conventions in the community concerning, e.g.:
  how information is structured in realising the various macrofunctions (description, narrative, exposition, etc.);
  how stories, anecdotes, jokes, etc. are told;
  how a case is built up (in law, debate, etc.);
  how written texts (essays, formal letters, etc.) are laid out, signposted and sequenced.

A good deal of mother tongue education is devoted to building a young person's discourse skills. In learning a foreign language, a learner is likely to start with short turns, usually of single sentence length. At higher levels of proficiency, the development of discourse competence, the components of which are indicated in the section, becomes of increasing importance.

Illustrative scales are available for the following aspects of discourse competence:

- Flexibility to circumstances;
- Turntaking (also presented under interaction strategies);
- Thematic development;
- Coherence and cohesion.

	FLEXIBILITY
C2	*Shows great flexibility reformulating ideas in differing linguistic forms to give emphasis, to differentiate according to the situation, interlocutor, etc. and to eliminate ambiguity.*
C1	*As B2+*
B2	*Can adjust what he/she says and the means of expressing it to the situation and the recipient and adopt a level of formality appropriate to the circumstances.*
	Can adjust to the changes of direction, style and emphasis normally found in conversation. *Can vary formulation of what he/she wants to say.*
B1	*Can adapt his/her expression to deal with less routine, even difficult, situations.*
	Can exploit a wide range of simple language flexibly to express much of what he/she wants.
A2	*Can adapt well rehearsed memorised simple phrases to particular circumstances through limited lexical substitution.*
	Can expand learned phrases through simple recombinations of their elements.
A1	*No descriptor available*

	TURNTAKING
C2	*As C1*
C1	*Can select a suitable phrase from a readily available range of discourse functions to preface his/her remarks appropriately in order to get the floor, or to gain time and keep the floor whilst thinking.*
B2	*Can intervene appropriately in discussion, exploiting appropriate language to do so.* *Can initiate, maintain and end discourse appropriately with effective turntaking.* *Can initiate discourse, take his/her turn when appropriate and end conversation when he/she needs to, though he/she may not always do this elegantly.* *Can use stock phrases (e.g. 'That's a difficult question to answer') to gain time and keep the turn whilst formulating what to say.*
B1	*Can intervene in a discussion on a familiar topic, using a suitable phrase to get the floor.*
	Can initiate, maintain and close simple face-to-face conversation on topics that are familiar or of personal interest.
A2	*Can use simple techniques to start, maintain, or end a short conversation.* *Can initiate, maintain and close simple, face-to-face conversation.*
	Can ask for attention.
A1	*No descriptor available*

	THEMATIC DEVELOPMENT
C2	*As C1*
C1	*Can give elaborate descriptions and narratives, integrating sub-themes, developing particular points and rounding off with an appropriate conclusion.*
B2	*Can develop a clear description or narrative, expanding and supporting his/her main points with relevant supporting detail and examples.*
B1	*Can reasonably fluently relate a straightforward narrative or description as a linear sequence of points.*
A2	*Can tell a story or describe something in a simple list of points.*
A1	*No descriptor available*

	COHERENCE AND COHESION
C2	*Can create coherent and cohesive text making full and appropriate use of a variety of organisational patterns and a wide range of cohesive devices.*
C1	*Can produce clear, smoothly flowing, well-structured speech, showing controlled use of organisational patterns, connectors and cohesive devices.*
B2	*Can use a variety of linking words efficiently to mark clearly the relationships between ideas.* *Can use a limited number of cohesive devices to link his/her utterances into clear, coherent discourse, though there may be some 'jumpiness' in a long contribution.*
B1	*Can link a series of shorter, discrete simple elements into a connected, linear sequence of points.*
A2	*Can use the most frequently occurring connectors to link simple sentences in order to tell a story or describe something as a simple list of points.* *Can link groups of words with simple connectors like 'and', 'but' and 'because'.*
A1	*Can link words or groups of words with very basic linear connectors like 'and' or 'then'.*

5.2.3.2 Functional competence

This component is concerned with the use of spoken discourse and written texts in communication for particular functional purposes (see section 4.2). Conversational competence is not simply a matter of knowing which particular functions (microfunctions) are expressed by which language forms. Participants are engaged in an interaction, in which each initiative leads to a response and moves the interaction further on, according to its purpose, through a succession of stages from opening exchanges to its final conclusion. Competent speakers have an understanding of the process and skills in operating it. A macrofunction is characterised by its interactional structure. More complex situations may well have an internal structure involving sequences of macrofunctions, which in many cases are ordered according to formal or informal patterns of social interaction (schemata).

1. *Microfunctions* are categories for the functional use of single (usually short) utterances, usually as turns in an interaction. Microfunctions are categorised in some detail (but not exhaustively) in *Threshold Level 1990*, Chapter 5:

1.1 imparting and seeking factual information:
- identifying
- reporting
- correcting
- asking
- answering

1.2 expressing and finding out attitudes:
- factual (agreement/disagreement)
- knowledge (knowledge/ignorance, remembering, forgetting, probability, certainty)
- modality (obligations, necessity, ability, permission)
- volition (wants, desires, intentions, preference)
- emotions (pleasure/displeasure, likes/dislikes, satisfaction, interest, surprise, hope, disappointment, fear, worry, gratitude)
- moral (apologies, approval, regret, sympathy)

1.3 suasion:
- suggestions, requests, warnings, advice, encouragement, asking help, invitations, offers

1.4 socialising:
- attracting attention, addressing, greetings, introductions, toasting, leave-taking

1.5 structuring discourse:
- (28 microfunctions, opening, turntaking, closing, etc.)

1.6 communication repair
- (16 microfunctions)

2. *Macrofunctions* are categories for the functional use of spoken discourse or written text consisting of a (sometimes extended) sequence of sentences, e.g.:

- description
- narration
- commentary
- exposition
- exegesis
- explanation
- demonstration
- instruction
- argumentation
- persuasion
  etc.

3. *Interaction schemata*

Functional competence also includes knowledge of and ability to use the schemata (patterns of social interaction) which underlie communication, such as verbal exchange patterns. The interactive communicative activities set out in section 4.4.3 involve structured sequences of actions by the parties in turns. At their simplest, they form pairs such as:

question:	answer
statement:	agreement/disagreement
request/offer/apology:	acceptance/non-acceptance
greeting/toast:	response

Triplets, in which the first speaker acknowledges or responds to the interlocutor's reply, are common. Pairs and triplets are usually embedded in longer transactions and interactions. For instance, in more complex goal-oriented co-operative transactions, language is used as necessary to:

- form the working group and establish relations among participants;
- establish common knowledge of the relevant features of the current situation and arrive at a common reading;
- identify what could and ought to be changed;
- establish common agreement on goals and on the action required to meet them;
- agree roles in carrying out the action;
- manage the practical actions involved by e.g.:
  identifying and dealing with problems which arise;
  co-ordinating and sequencing contributions;
  mutual encouragement;
  recognising the achievement of sub-goals;
- recognise the final achievement of the task;
- evaluate the transaction;
- complete and terminate the transaction.

The total process can be represented schematically. An example is the general schema offered for the purchase of goods or services in *Threshold Level 1990*, Chapter 8:

General Schema for purchase of goods or services
1. Moving to place of transaction
   1.1 Finding the way to the shop, store, supermarket, restaurant, station, hotel, etc.
   1.2 Finding the way to the counter, department, table, ticket office, reception, etc.
2. Establishing contact
   2.1 Exchanging greetings with the shopkeeper/assistant/waiter/receptionist, etc.
      2.1.1 assistant greets
      2.1.2 customer greets
3. Selecting goods/services
   3.1 identifying category of goods/services required
      3.1.1 seeking information
      3.1.2 giving information
   3.2 identifying options
   3.3 discussing pros and cons of options (e.g. quality, price, colour, size of goods)
      3.3.1 seeking information
      3.3.2 giving information

    3.3.3 seeking advice
    3.3.4 giving advice
    3.3.5 asking for preference
    3.3.6 expressing preference, etc.
   3.4 identifying particular goods required
   3.5 examining goods
   3.6 agreeing to purchase
 4. Exchanging goods for payment
   4.1 agreeing prices of items
   4.2 agreeing addition of total
   4.3 receiving/handing over payment
   4.4 receiving/handing over goods (and receipt)
   4.5 exchanging thanks
    4.5.1 assistant thanks
    4.5.2 customer thanks
 5. Leave-taking
   5.1 expressing (mutual) satisfaction
    5.1.1 assistant expresses satisfaction
    5.1.2 customer expresses satisfaction
   5.2 exchanging interpersonal comment (e.g. weather, local gossip)
   5.3 exchanging parting greetings
    5.3.1 assistant greets
    5.3.2 customer greets

NB It should be noted that, as with similar schemata, the availability of this schema to shoppers and shop assistants does not mean that on every occasion this form is used. Especially under modern conditions, language is often used more sparingly, particularly to deal with problems that arise in an otherwise depersonalised and semi-automated transaction, or to humanise it (see section 4.1.1).

It is not feasible to develop illustrative scales for all the areas of competence implied when one talks of functional ability. Certain microfunctional activities are in fact scaled in the illustrative scales for interactive and productive communicative activities.

Two generic qualitative factors which determine the functional success of the learner/user are:

a) *fluency*, the ability to articulate, to keep going, and to cope when one lands in a dead end
b) *propositional precision*, the ability to formulate thoughts and propositions so as to make one's meaning clear.

Illustrative scales are available for these two qualitative aspects:

	SPOKEN FLUENCY
C2	*Can express him/herself at length with a natural, effortless, unhesitating flow. Pauses only to reflect on precisely the right words to express his/her thoughts or to find an appropriate example or explanation.*
C1	*Can express him/herself fluently and spontaneously, almost effortlessly. Only a conceptually difficult subject can hinder a natural, smooth flow of language.*
B2	*Can communicate spontaneously, often showing remarkable fluency and ease of expression in even longer complex stretches of speech.* *Can produce stretches of language with a fairly even tempo; although he/she can be hesitant as he/she searches for patterns and expressions, there are few noticeably long pauses.* *Can interact with a degree of fluency and spontaneity that makes regular interaction with native speakers quite possible without imposing strain on either party.*
B1	*Can express him/herself with relative ease. Despite some problems with formulation resulting in pauses and 'cul-de-sacs', he/she is able to keep going effectively without help.* *Can keep going comprehensibly, even though pausing for grammatical and lexical planning and repair is very evident, especially in longer stretches of free production.*
A2	*Can make him/herself understood in short contributions, even though pauses, false starts and reformulation are very evident.* *Can construct phrases on familiar topics with sufficient ease to handle short exchanges, despite very noticeable hesitation and false starts.*
A1	*Can manage very short, isolated, mainly pre-packaged utterances, with much pausing to search for expressions, to articulate less familiar words, and to repair communication.*

	PROPOSITIONAL PRECISION
C2	*Can convey finer shades of meaning precisely by using, with reasonable accuracy, a wide range of qualifying devices (e.g. adverbs expressing degree, clauses expressing limitations).* *Can give emphasis, differentiate and eliminate ambiguity.*
C1	*Can qualify opinions and statements precisely in relation to degrees of, for example, certainty/uncertainty, belief/doubt, likelihood, etc.*
B2	*Can pass on detailed information reliably.*
B1	*Can explain the main points in an idea or problem with reasonable precision.* *Can convey simple, straightforward information of immediate relevance, getting across which point he/she feels is most important.* *Can express the main point he/she wants to make comprehensibly.*
A2	*Can communicate what he/she wants to say in a simple and direct exchange of limited information on familiar and routine matters, but in other situations he/she generally has to compromise the message.*
A1	*No descriptor available*

Users of the Framework may wish to consider and where appropriate state:

- *what discourse features the learner is equipped/required to control;*
- *which macrofunctions the learner is equipped/required to produce;*
- *which microfunctions the learner is equipped/required to produce;*
- *what interaction schemata are needed by/required of the learner;*
- *which he/she is assumed to control and which are to be taught;*
- *according to what principles macro- and microfunctions are selected and ordered;*
- *how* qualitative *progress in the pragmatic component can be characterised.*

6 Language learning and teaching

In the body of this chapter we ask:

In what ways does the learner come to be able to carry out the tasks, activities and processes and build up the competences necessary for communication?
How can teachers, assisted by their various support services, facilitate these processes?
How can education authorities and other decision-makers best plan curricula for modern languages?

First, however, we should give some further consideration to learning objectives.

6.1   What is it that learners have to learn or acquire?

6.1.1   Statements of the aims and objectives of language learning and teaching should be based on an appreciation of the needs of learners and of society, on the tasks, activities and processes that the learners need to carry out in order to satisfy those needs, and on the competences and strategies they need to develop/build up in order to do so. Accordingly, Chapters 4 and 5 attempt to set out what a fully competent user of a language is able to do and what knowledge, skills and attitudes make these activities possible. They do as comprehensively as possible since we cannot know which activities will be of importance to a particular learner. They indicate that, in order to participate with full effectiveness in communicative events, learners must have learnt or acquired:

* the necessary competences, as detailed in Chapter 5;
* the ability to put these competences into action, as detailed in Chapter 4;
* the ability to employ the strategies necessary to bring the competences into action.

6.1.2   For the purposes of representing or steering the progress of language learners, it is useful to describe their abilities at a series of successive levels. Such scales have been offered where appropriate in Chapters 4 and 5. When charting the progress of students through the earlier stages of their general education, at a time when their future career needs cannot be foreseen, or indeed whenever an overall assessment has to be made of a learner's language proficiency, it may be most useful and practical to combine a number of these categories into a single summary characterisation of language ability, as, for instance, in Table 1 presented in Chapter 3.

Greater flexibility is afforded by a scheme, such as that in Table 2 in Chapter 3, intended for the purposes of learner self-assessment, in which the various language activities are scaled separately, though each again holistically. This presentation allows a profile to be established in cases where skills development is uneven. Even greater flexibility is of course provided by the detailed and separate scaling of sub-categories as in Chapters 4 and 5. Whilst all the abilities set out in those chapters have to be deployed by a language user to deal effectively with the full range of communicative events, not all learners will wish, or need, to acquire them all in a non-native language. For instance, some learners will have no requirement for written language. Others may be concerned only with the understanding of written texts. However, there is no strict implication that such learners should confine themselves to the spoken and written forms of the language respectively.

It may be, according to the learner's cognitive style, that the memorisation of spoken forms is greatly facilitated by association with the corresponding written forms. Vice versa, the perception of written forms may be facilitated, or even necessitated, by associating them with the corresponding oral utterances. If this is so, the sense modality not required for use – and consequently not stated as an *objective* – may nevertheless be involved in language learning as a *means* to an end. It is a matter for decision (conscious or not) which competence, tasks, activities and strategies should be given a role in the development of a particular learner as objective or means.

It is also not a logical necessity for a competence, task, activity or strategy which is identified as an objective as being necessary to the satisfaction of the learner's communicative needs, to be included in a learning programme. For instance, much of what is included as 'knowledge of the world' may be assumed as prior knowledge, already within the learner's general competence as a result of previous experience of life or instruction given in the mother tongue. The problem may then be simply finding the proper exponence in L2 for a notional category in L1. It will be a matter for decision what new knowledge must be learnt and what can be assumed. A problem arises when a particular conceptual field is differently organised in L1 and L2, as is frequently the case, so that correspondence of word-meanings is partial or inexact. How serious is the mismatch? To what misunderstandings may it lead? Accordingly, what priority should it be given at a particular stage of learning? At what level should mastery of the distinction be required or attended to? Can the problem be left to sort itself out with experience?

Similar issues arise with respect to pronunciation. Many phonemes can be transferred from L1 to L2 unproblematically. In some cases the sounds used in particular contexts may be noticeably different. Other phonemes in L2 may not be present in L1. If they are not acquired or learnt, some loss of information is entailed and misunderstandings may occur. How frequent and significant are they likely to be? What priority should they be given? Here, the question of the age or the stage of learning at which they are best learnt is complicated by the fact that habituation is strongest at the phonetic level. To raise phonetic errors into consciousness and unlearn the automatised behaviours only once a close approximation to native norms becomes fully appropriate, may be much more expensive (in time and effort) than it would have been in the initial phase of learning, especially at an early age.

Such considerations mean that the appropriate objectives for a particular stage of learning for a particular learner, or class of learner at a particular age, cannot necessarily be derived by a straightforward across-the-board reading of the scales proposed for each parameter. Decisions have to be made in each case.

6.1.3 *Plurilingual competence and pluricultural competence*

The fact that the Framework does not confine itself to providing 'overview' scaling of communicative abilities, but breaks down global categories into their components and provides scaling for them, is of particular importance when considering the development of plurilingual and pluricultural competences.

6.1.3.1 An uneven and changing competence

Plurilingual and pluricultural competence is generally uneven in one or more ways:

- Learners generally attain greater proficiency in one language than in the others;
- The profile of competences in one language is different from that in others (for example, excellent speaking competence in two languages, but good writing competence in only one of them);
- The pluricultural profile differs from the plurilingual profile (for example: good knowledge of the culture of a community but a poor knowledge of its language, or poor knowledge of a community whose dominant language is nevertheless well mastered).

Such imbalances are entirely normal. If the concept of plurilingualism and pluriculturalism is extended to take into account the situation of all those who in their native language and culture are exposed to different dialects and to the cultural variation inherent in any complex society, it is clear that here again imbalances (or, if preferred, different types of balance) are the norm.

This imbalance is also linked to the changing nature of plurilingual and pluricultural competence. Whereas the traditional view of 'monolingual' communicative competence in the 'mother tongue' suggests it is quickly stabilised, a plurilingual and pluricultural competence presents a transitory profile and a changing configuration. Depending on the career path, family history, travel experience, reading and hobbies of the individual in question, significant changes take place in his/her linguistic and cultural biography, altering the forms of imbalance in his/her plurilingualism, and rendering more complex his/her experience of the plurality of cultures. This does not by any means imply instability, uncertainty or lack of balance on the part of the person in question, but rather contributes, in the majority of cases, to improved awareness of identity.

6.1.3.2 Differentiated competence allowing for language switching

Because of this imbalance, one of the features of a plurilingual and pluricultural competence is that in applying this competence, the individual in question draws upon both his/her general and language skills and knowledge (see Chapters 4 and 5) in different ways. For example the *strategies* used in carrying out *tasks* involving language use may vary according to the language in question. *Savoir-être* (existential competence demonstrating openness, conviviality and good will (e.g. by the use of gestures, mime, proxemics) may, in the case of a language in which the individual has poorly mastered the linguistic component, make up for this deficiency in the course of interaction with a native speaker, whereas in a language he or she knows better, this same individual may adopt a more distant or reserved attitude. The *task* may also be redefined, the linguistic message reshaped or redistributed, according to the resources available for expression or the individual's perception of these resources.

A further characteristic of plurilingual and pluricultural competence is that it does not consist of the simple addition of monolingual competences but permits combinations and alternations of different kinds. It is possible to code switch during the message, to resort to bilingual forms of speech. A single, richer repertoire of this kind thus allows choice concerning strategies for task accomplishment, drawing where appropriate on an interlinguistic variation and language switching.

6.1.3.3   Development of awareness and the process of use and learning

Plurilingual and pluricultural competence also promotes the development of linguistic and communication awareness, and even metacognitive strategies which enable the social agent to become more aware of and control his or her own 'spontaneous' ways of handling tasks and in particular their linguistic dimension. In addition, this experience of plurilingualism and pluriculturalism:

* exploits pre-existing *sociolinguistic and pragmatic competences* which in turn develops them further;
* leads to a better perception of what is general and what is specific concerning the linguistic organisation of different languages (form of metalinguistic, interlinguistic or so to speak 'hyperlinguistic' awareness);
* by its nature refines knowledge of how to learn and the capacity to enter into relations with others and new situations.

It may, therefore, to some degree accelerate subsequent learning in the linguistic and cultural areas. This is the case even if plurilingual and pluricultural competence is 'uneven' and if proficiency in a particular language remains 'partial'.

It can be claimed, moreover, that while the knowledge of one foreign language and culture does not always lead to going beyond what may be ethnocentric in relation to the 'native' language and culture, and may even have the opposite effect (it is not uncommon for the learning of **one** language and contact with **one** foreign culture to reinforce stereotypes and preconceived ideas rather than reduce them), a knowledge of several languages is more likely to achieve this, while at the same time enriching the potential for learning.

In this context the promotion of respect for the diversity of languages and of learning more than one foreign language in school is significant. It is not simply a linguistic policy choice at an important point in the history of Europe, for example, nor even – however important this may be – a matter of increasing future opportunities for young people competent in more than two languages. It is also a matter of helping learners:

* to construct their linguistic and cultural identity through integrating into it a diversified experience of otherness;
* to develop their ability to learn through this same diversified experience of relating to several languages and cultures.

6.1.3.4   Partial competence and plurilingual and pluricultural competence

It is in this perspective also that the concept of *partial competence* in a particular language is meaningful: it is not a matter of being satisfied, for reasons of principle or pragmatism, with the development of a limited or compartmentalised mastery of a foreign language by a learner, but rather of seeing this proficiency, imperfect at a given moment, as forming part of a plurilingual competence which it enriches. It should also be pointed out that this 'partial' competence, which is part of a *multiple* competence, is at the same time a *functional* competence with respect to a specific limited objective.

The partial competence in a given language may concern receptive *language activities* (for example with the emphasis on oral or written comprehension); it may concern a particular *domain* and specific *tasks* (for example, to allow a post office clerk to give information on the most usual post office operations to foreign clients speaking a particular language). But it may also involve *general competences* (for example non-linguistic *knowledge* about the characteristics of other languages and cultures and their communities), so long as there is a functional role to this complementary development of one or other dimension of the specified competences. In other words, in the framework of reference proposed here, the notion of partial competence is to be viewed in relation to the different components of the model (see Chapter 3) and variation in objectives.

6.1.4   Variation in objectives in relation to the Framework

Curriculum design in language learning (no doubt even more so than in other disciplines and other types of learning) implies choices between kinds and levels of objectives. The present proposal for a framework of reference takes particular account of this situation. Each of the major components of the model presented may provide a focus for learning objectives and become a specific entry point for the use of the Framework.

6.1.4.1   Types of objectives in relation to the Framework

Teaching/learning objectives may in fact be conceived:

a) In terms of the development of the learner's general competences (see section 5.1) and thus be a matter of *declarative knowledge (savoir), skills and know-how (savoir-faire), personality traits, attitudes, etc. (savoir-être)* or *ability to learn*, or more particularly one or other of these dimensions. In some cases, the learning of a foreign language aims above all at imparting declarative knowledge to the learner (for example, of the grammar or literature or certain cultural characteristics of the foreign country). In other instances, language learning will be seen as a way for the learner to develop his or her personality (for example greater assurance or self-confidence, greater willingness to speak in a group) or to develop his or her knowledge of how to learn (greater openness to what is new, awareness of otherness, curiosity about the unknown). There is every reason to consider that these particular objectives relating at any given time to a specific sector or type of competence, or the development of a partial competence, can in an across-the-board way contribute to the establishment or reinforcement of a plurilingual and pluricultural competence. In other terms, the pursuit of a partial objective may be part of an overall learning project.

b) In terms of the extension and diversification of communicative language competence (see section 5.2) and is then concerned with the *linguistic component*, or the *pragmatic component* or the *sociolinguistic component*, or all of these. The main aim of learning a foreign language may be mastery of the linguistic component of a language (knowledge of its phonetic system, its vocabulary and syntax) without any concern for sociolinguistic finesse or pragmatic effectiveness. In other instances the objective may be primarily of a pragmatic nature and seek to develop a capacity to act in the foreign language with the limited linguistic resources available and without any particular concern for the sociolinguistic aspect. The options are of course never so exclusive as this and harmonious progress in the different components is generally aimed at, but there is no shortage of examples, past and present, of a particular concentration on one or other of the components of communicative competence. Communicative language competence, considered as a plurilingual and pluricultural competence, being a whole (i.e. including varieties of the native language and varieties of one or more foreign languages), it is equally possible to claim that, at certain times and in certain contexts, the main objective of teaching a foreign language (even though not made apparent) was refinement of knowledge and mastery of the native language (e.g. by resorting to translation, work on registers and the appropriateness of vocabulary in translating into the native language, forms of comparative stylistics and semantics).

c) In terms of the better performance in one or more specific language activities (see section 4.4) and is then a matter of *reception, production, interaction* or *mediation*. It may be that the main stated objective of learning a foreign language is to have effective results in receptive activities (reading or listening) or mediation (translating or interpreting) or face-to-face interaction. Here again, it goes without saying that such polarisation can never be total or be pursued independently of any other aim. However, in defining objectives it is possible to attach significantly greater importance to one aspect above others, and this major focus, if it is consistent, will affect the entire process: choice of content and learning tasks, deciding on and structuring progression and possible remedial action, selection of type of texts, etc.

It will be seen that generally speaking the notion of *partial competence* has been primarily introduced and used in respect of some of these choices (e.g. insistence on learning that emphasises in its objectives receptive activities and written and/or oral comprehension). But what is proposed here is an extension of this use:

- on the one hand by intimating that other partial competence-related objectives may be identified (as has been referred to in *a* or *b* or *d*) in relation to the reference framework;
- on the other hand by pointing out that this same reference framework allows for any so-called 'partial' competence to be incorporated within a more general series of communicative and learning competences.

d) In terms of optimal functional operation in a given domain (see section 4.1.1) and thus concerns the *public domain*, the *occupational domain*, the *educational domain* or the *personal domain*. The main aim of learning a foreign language may be to perform a job better, or to help with studies or to facilitate life in a foreign country. As with the other

136

major components of the model proposed, such aims are explicitly reflected in course descriptions, in proposals and requests for language services, and learning/teaching materials. It is in this area that it has been possible to speak of 'specific objectives', 'specialised courses', 'vocational language', 'preparation for a period of residence abroad', 'linguistic reception of migrant workers'. This does not mean that consideration given to the specific needs of a particular target group which has to adapt its plurilingual and pluricultural competence to a particular social field of activity must always require an educational approach appropriate to this aim. But, as with the other components, formulating an objective under this heading and with this focus normally has consequences for other aspects and stages of curriculum design and the provision of teaching and learning.

It should be noted that this type of objective involving functional adaptation for a given domain also corresponds to situations of bilingual education, immersion (as understood by the experiments carried out in Canada) and schooling where the language of tuition is different from that spoken in the family environment (e.g. an education exclusively in French in some multilingual former colonies in Africa). From this point of view, and this is not incompatible with the main thrust of this analysis, these situations of immersion, whatever the linguistic results they may lead to, are aimed at developing partial competences: those relating to the educational domain and the acquisition of knowledge other than linguistic. It will be recalled that in many experiments of total immersion at a young age in Canada, despite the fact that the language of education was French, initially no specific provision was made in the timetable for teaching French to the English-speaking children concerned.

e) In terms of the enrichment or diversification of strategies or in terms of the fulfilment of tasks (see sections 4.5 and Chapter 7) and thus relates to the management of actions linked to the learning and use of one or more languages, and the discovery or experience of other cultures.

In many learning experiences it may seem preferable, at one time or another, to focus attention on the development of strategies that will enable one or other type of task having a linguistic dimension to be carried out. Accordingly, the objective is to improve the strategies traditionally used by the learner by rendering them more sophisticated, more extensive and more conscious, by seeking to adapt them to tasks for which they had not originally been used. Whether these are communication or learning strategies, if one takes the view that they enable an individual to mobilise his or her own competences in order to implement and possibly improve or extend them, it is worthwhile ensuring that such strategies are indeed cultivated as an objective, even though they may not form an end in themselves.

Tasks are normally focused within a given domain and considered as objectives to be achieved in relation to that domain, fitting in with point *d* above. But there are cases where the learning objective is limited to the more or less stereotyped carrying out of certain tasks that may involve limited linguistic elements in one or more foreign languages: an often quoted example is that of a switchboard operator where the 'plurilingual' performance expected, based on a decision taken locally in a given company, is limited to the production of a few fixed formulations relating to routine operations. Such examples are more a case of semi-automated behaviour than partial competences but there can be no denying that the carrying out of well-defined repetitive tasks in such cases can also constitute the primary focus of a learning objective.

More generally, formulating objectives in terms of tasks has the advantage, for the learner too, of identifying in practical terms what the expected results are, and can also play a short-term motivating role throughout the learning process. To quote a simple example, telling children that the activity they are about to undertake will enable them to play 'Happy Families' in the foreign language (the objective being the possible carrying out of a 'task') can also be a motivating way of learning the vocabulary for the various family members (part of the linguistic component of a broader communicative objective). In this sense, too, the so-called project-based approach, global simulations and various role-playing games establish what are basically transitory objectives defined in terms of tasks to be carried out but the major interest of which as far as learning is concerned resides either in the language resources and activities that such a task (or sequence of tasks) requires or in the strategies employed or applied. In other terms, although in the rationale adopted for the conception of the framework of reference plurilingual and pluricultural competence becomes apparent and is developed through the carrying out of tasks, in the approach to learning adapted, these tasks are only presented as apparent objectives or as a step towards the achievement of other objectives.

6.1.4.2 The complementarity of partial objectives

Defining language teaching/learning objectives in this manner, in terms of the major components of a general reference model, or of each of the sub-components of these, is not a mere stylistic exercise. It illustrates the possible diversity of learning aims and the variety to be found in the provision of teaching. Obviously, a great many types of provision, in and out of school, cover several of these objectives at the same time. And equally obviously (but it is worth repeating) pursuing a specifically designated objective also means, with respect to the coherence of the model illustrated here, that the achievement of the stated objective will lead to other results which were not specifically aimed at or which were not the main concern.

If, for example, it is presumed that the objective is essentially concerned with a domain, and is focused on the demands of a given job, for example that of waiter in a restaurant, then to achieve this objective language activities will be developed which are concerned with oral interaction; in relation to communicative competence attention will be focused on certain lexical fields of the linguistic component (presentation and description of dishes, for example), and certain sociolinguistic norms (forms of address to use with customers, possible request for assistance from a third party, etc.); and there will no doubt be an insistence on certain aspects of *savoir-être* (discretion, politeness, smiling affably, patience, etc.), or on knowledge concerned with the cuisine and eating habits of the particular foreign culture. It is possible to develop other examples in which other components would be chosen as the main objective, but this particular example will no doubt suffice to complete what was said above concerning the concept of *partial competence* (see the comments made on the relativisation of what may be understood by partial knowledge of a language).

6.2 The processes of language learning

6.2.1 Acquisition or learning?

The terms 'language acquisition' and 'language learning' are currently used in a number of different ways. Many use them interchangeably. Others use one or the other as the general term, using the other in a more restricted sense. Thus 'language acquisition' may be used either as the general term or confined:

a)   to interpretations of the language of non-native speakers in terms of current theories of universal grammar (e.g. parameter setting). This work is almost always a branch of theoretical psycholinguistics of little or no direct concern to practitioners, especially since grammar is considered to be far removed from accessibility to consciousness.

b)   to untutored knowledge and ability to use a non-native language resulting either from direct exposure to text or from direct participation in communicative events.

'Language learning' may be used as the general term, or confined to the process whereby language ability is gained as the result of a planned process, especially by formal study in an institutional setting.

At the present time it does not seem possible to impose a standardised terminology, especially since there is no obvious super-ordinate term covering 'learning' and 'acquisition' in their restricted senses.

> *Users of the Framework are asked to consider and if possible state in which sense they use the terms and to avoid using them in ways counter to current specific usage.*
>
> *They may also wish to consider and where appropriate state:*
>
> * *how opportunities for language acquisition in the sense of (b) above can be provided and exploited.*

6.2.2 How do learners learn?

6.2.2.1   There is at present no sufficiently strong research-based consensus on how learners learn for the Framework to base itself on any one learning theory. Some theorists believe that the human information-processing abilities are strong enough for it to be sufficient for a human being to be exposed to sufficient understandable language for him/her to acquire the language and be able to use it both for understanding and for production. They believe the 'acquisition' process to be inaccessible to observation or intuition and that it cannot be facilitated by conscious manipulation, whether by teaching or by study methods. For them, the most important thing a teacher can do is provide the richest possible linguistic environment in which learning can take place without formal teaching.

6.2.2.2   Others believe that in addition to exposure to comprehensible input, active participation in communicative interaction is a necessary and sufficient condition for language development. They, too, consider that explicit teaching or study of the language is irrelevant. At the other extreme, some believe that students who have learnt the necessary rules of grammar and learnt a vocabulary will be able to understand and use the language in the light of their previous experience and common sense without any need to rehearse. Between these polar extremes, most 'mainstream' learners, teachers and their support services will follow more eclectic practices, recognising that learners do not necessarily learn what teachers teach and that they require substantial contextualised and intelligible language input as well as opportunities to use the language interactively, but that learning is facilitated, especially under artificial classroom conditions, by a combination of conscious learning and sufficient practice to reduce or eliminate the conscious attention paid to low-level physical skills of speaking and writing as well as to morphological and syntactic accuracy, thus freeing the mind for higher-level strategies of communication. Some (many fewer than previously) believe that this aim may be achieved by drilling to the point of over learning.

6.2.2.3   There is of course considerable variation among learners of different ages, types and backgrounds as to which of these elements they respond to most fruitfully, and among teachers, course-writers, etc. as to the balance of elements provided in courses according to the importance they attach to production vs. reception, accuracy vs. fluency, etc.

> *Users of the Framework may wish to consider and where appropriate state the assumptions concerning language learning on which their work is based and their methodological consequences.*

6.3   What can each kind of Framework user do to facilitate language learning?

The language teaching profession forms a 'partnership for learning' made up of many specialists in addition to the teachers and learners most immediately concerned at the point of learning. This section considers the respective roles of each of the parties.

6.3.1   Those concerned with examinations and qualifications will have to consider which learning parameters are relevant to the qualifications concerned, and the level required. They will have to make concrete decisions on which particular tasks and activities to include, which themes to handle, which formulae, idioms and lexical items to require candidates to recognise or recall, what sociocultural knowledge and skills to test, etc. They may not need to be concerned with the processes by which the language proficiency tested has been learnt or acquired, except in so far as their own testing procedures may have a positive or negative 'wash back' effect on language learning.

6.3.2 Authorities, when drawing up curricular guidelines or formulating syllabuses, may concentrate on the specification of learning objectives. In doing so, they may specify only higher-level objectives in terms of tasks, themes, competence, etc. They are not obliged, though they may wish to do so, to specify in detail the vocabulary, grammar and functional/notional repertoires which will enable learners to perform the tasks and treat the themes. They are not obliged, but may wish, to lay down guidelines or make suggestions as to the classroom methods to be employed and the stages through which learners are expected to progress.

6.3.3 Textbook writers and course designers are not obliged, though they may well wish to do so, to formulate their objectives in terms of the tasks they wish to equip learners to perform or the competence and strategies they are to develop. They are obliged to make concrete, detailed decisions on the selection and ordering of texts, activities, vocabulary and grammar to be presented to the learner. They are expected to provide detailed instructions for the classroom and/or individual tasks and activities to be undertaken by learners in response to the material presented. Their products greatly influence the learning/teaching process and must inevitably be based on strong assumptions (rarely stated and often unexamined, even unconscious) as to the nature of the learning process.

6.3.4 Teachers are generally called upon to respect any official guidelines, use textbooks and course materials (which they may or may not be in a position to analyse, evaluate, select and supplement), devise and administer tests and prepare pupils and students for qualifying examinations. They have to make minute-to-minute decisions about classroom activities, which they can prepare in outline beforehand, but must adjust flexibly in the light of pupil/student responses. They are expected to monitor the progress of pupils/students and find ways of recognising, analysing and overcoming their learning problems, as well as developing their individual learning abilities. It is necessary for them to understand learning processes in their great variety, though this understanding may well be an unconscious product of experience rather than a clearly formulated product of theoretical reflection, which is the proper contribution to the partnership for learning to be made by educational researchers and teacher trainers.

6.3.5 Learners are, of course, the persons ultimately concerned with language acquisition and learning processes. It is they who have to develop the competences and strategies (in so far as they have not already done so) and carry out the tasks, activities and processes needed to participate effectively in communicative events. However, relatively few learn proactively, taking initiatives to plan, structure and execute their own learning processes. Most learn reactively, following the instructions and carrying out the activities prescribed for them by teachers and by textbooks. However, once teaching stops, further learning *has* to be autonomous. Autonomous learning can be promoted if 'learning to learn' is regarded as an integral part of language learning, so that learners become increasingly aware of the way they learn, the options open to them and the options that best suit them. Even within the given institutional system they can then be brought increasingly to make choices in respect of objectives, materials and working methods in the light of their own needs, motivations, characteristics and resources. We hope that the Framework, together with the series of specialised user guides, will be of use not only to teachers and their support services, but also directly to learners in helping to make them, too, more aware of the options open to them and articulate concerning the choices they make.

6.4   Some methodological options for modern language learning and teaching

Up to this point, the Framework has been concerned with the construction of a comprehensive model of language use and the language user, drawing attention along the way to the relevance of the different components of the model to language learning, teaching and assessment. That relevance has been seen predominantly in terms of the content and objectives of language learning. These are briefly summarised in sections 6.1 and 6.2. However, a framework of reference for language learning, teaching and assessment must also deal with methodology, since its users will undoubtedly wish to reflect on and communicate their methodological decisions within a general framework. Chapter 6 sets out to provide such a framework.

It has, of course, to be emphasised that the same criteria apply to this chapter as to others. The approach to the methodology of learning and teaching has to be comprehensive, presenting all options in an explicit and transparent way and avoiding advocacy or dogmatism. It has been a fundamental methodological principle of the Council of Europe that the methods to be employed in language learning, teaching and research are those considered to be most effective in reaching the objectives agreed in the light of the needs of the individual learners in their social context. Effectiveness is contingent on the motivations and characteristics of the learners as well as the nature of the human and material resources which can be brought into play. Following this fundamental principle through necessarily results in a great diversity of objectives and an even greater diversity of methods and materials.

There are many ways in which modern languages are currently learnt and taught. For many years the Council of Europe has promoted an approach based on the communicative needs of learners and the use of materials and methods that will enable learners to satisfy these needs and which are appropriate to their characteristics as learners. However, as has been made clear in section 2.3.2 and *passim*, it is not the function of the Framework to promote one particular language teaching methodology, but instead to present options. A full exchange of information on these options and of experience with them must come from the field. At this stage it is possible only to indicate some of the options derived from existing practice and to ask users of the Framework to fill in gaps from their own knowledge and experience. A User Guide is available.

If there are practitioners who upon reflection are convinced that the objectives appropriate to the learners towards whom they have responsibilities are most effectively pursued by methods other than those advocated elsewhere by the Council of Europe, then we should like them to say so, to tell us and others of the methods they use and the objectives they pursue. This might lead to a wider understanding of the complex diversity of the world of language education, or to lively debate, which is always preferable to simple acceptance of a current orthodoxy merely because it is an orthodoxy.

6.4.1   General approaches

In general, how are learners expected to learn a second or foreign language (L2)? Is it in one or more of the following ways?

a)   by direct exposure to authentic use of language in L2 in one or more of the following ways:

>   face to face with native speaker(s);
>   overhearing conversation;
>   listening to radio, recordings, etc.;
>   watching and listening to TV, video, etc.;
>   reading unmodified, ungraded, authentic written texts (newspapers, magazines, stories, novels, public signs and notices, etc.);
>   using computer programmes, CD ROM, etc.;
>   participating in computer conferences on- or off-line;
>   participating in courses in other curriculum subjects which employ L2 as a medium of instruction;

b)   by direct exposure to specially selected (e.g. graded) spoken utterances and written texts in L2 ('intelligible input');

c)   by direct participation in authentic communicative interaction in L2, e.g. as a conversation partner with a competent interlocutor;

d)   by direct participation in specially devised and constructed tasks in L2 ('comprehensible output');

e)   autodidactically, by (guided) self-study, pursuing negotiated self-directed objectives and using available instructional media;

f)   by a combination of presentations, explanations, (drill) exercises and exploitation activities, but with L1 as the language of classroom management, explanation, etc.;

g)   by a combination of activities as in f), but using L2 only for *all* classroom purposes;

h)   by some combination of the above activities, starting perhaps with f), but progressively reducing the use of L1 and including more tasks and authentic texts, spoken and written, and an increasing self-study component;

i)   by combining the above with group and individual planning, implementation and evaluation of classroom activity with teacher support, negotiating interaction to satisfy different learner needs, etc.

Users of the Framework may wish to consider and state which approaches, in general, they follow, whether one of the above, or some other.

6.4.2 Consideration should be given to the relative *roles of teachers, learners and media*.

6.4.2.1 What different proportions of class time may be (expected to be) spent:

a) by the teacher expounding, explaining, etc. to the whole class?
b) in whole-class question/answer sessions (distinguishing between referential, display and test questions)?
c) in group or pair working?
d) in individual working?

6.4.2.2 *Teachers* should realise that their actions, reflecting their attitudes and abilities, are a most important part of the environment for language learning/acquisition. They present role-models which students may follow in their future use of the language and their practice as future teachers. What importance is attached to their:

a) teaching skills?
b) classroom management skills?
c) ability to engage in action research and to reflect on experience?
d) teaching styles?
e) understanding of and ability to handle testing, assessment and evaluation?
f) knowledge of and ability to teach sociocultural background information?
g) inter-cultural attitudes and skills?
h) knowledge of and ability to develop students' aesthetic appreciation of literature?
i) ability to deal with individualisation within classes containing diverse learner types and abilities?

How are the relevant qualities and abilities best developed?
During individual, pair or group working, should the teacher:

a) simply supervise and maintain order?
b) circulate to monitor work?
c) be available for individual counselling?
d) adopt the role of supervisor and facilitator, accepting and reacting to students' remarks on their learning and co-ordinating student activities, in addition to monitoring and counselling?

6.4.2.3 How far should *learners* be expected or required to:

a) follow all and only the teacher's instructions in a disciplined, orderly way, speaking only when called upon to do so?
b) participate actively in the learning process in co-operation with the teacher and other students to reach agreement on objectives and methods, accepting compromise, and engaging in peer teaching and peer assessment so as to progress steadily towards autonomy?

144

c) work independently with self-study materials including self-assessment?
d) compete with each other?

6.4.2.4   What use can and should be made of **instructional media** (audio and video cassettes, computers, etc.)?

a) none;
b) for whole-class demonstrations, repetitions, etc.;
c) in a language/video/computer laboratory mode;
d) in an individual self-instructional mode;
e) as a basis for group work (discussion, negotiation, co-operative and competitive games, etc.);
f) in international computer networking of schools, classes and individual students.

Users of the Framework may wish to consider and where appropriate state:

- *what are the relative roles and responsibilities of teachers and learners in the organisation, management, conduct and evaluation of the language-learning process;*
- *what use is made of instructional media.*

6.4.3   What part should be played by **texts** in language learning and teaching?

6.4.3.1   How may learners be expected or required to learn from spoken and written texts (see section 4.6)?

a) by simple exposure;

b) by simple exposure, but ensuring that new material is intelligible by inferencing from verbal context, visual support, etc.;

c) by exposure, with comprehension monitored and ensured by L2 question and answer, multiple choice, picture matching, etc.;

d) as c), but with one or more of the following:

comprehension tests in L1;
explanations in L1;
explanations (including any necessary *ad hoc* translation), in L2;
systematic pupil/student translation of text into L1;
pre-listening and/or group listening activities, pre-reading activities, etc.

6.4.3.2   How far should the written or spoken texts presented to learners be:

a) 'authentic', i.e. produced for communicative purposes with no language teaching intent, e.g.:

untreated authentic texts that the learner encounters in the course of direct experience of the language in use (daily newspapers, magazines, broadcasts, etc.);
authentic texts selected, graded and/or edited so as to be judged appropriate to the
learner's experience, interests and characteristics.

b)   specially composed for use in language teaching, e.g.:

texts composed to resemble authentic texts as (ii) above (e.g. specially written listening comprehension materials recorded by actors)
texts composed to give contextualised examples of the linguistic content to be
taught (e.g. in a particular course unit)
isolated sentences for exercise purposes (phonetic, grammatical, etc.)
textbook instruction, explanations etc., test and examination rubrics, teacher's
classroom language (instructions, explanations, classroom management etc.).
These may be regarded as special text-types. Are they 'learner-friendly'? What consideration is given to their content, formulation and presentation to ensure that
they are?

6.4.3.3   How far should learners have not only to *process*, but also to *produce* texts? These
may be:

a)   spoken:

written texts read aloud;
oral answers to exercise questions;
reproduction of memorised texts (plays, poems, etc.);
pair and group work exercises;
contributions to formal and informal discussion;
free conversation (in class or during pupil exchanges);
presentations.

b)   written:

dictated passages;
written exercises;
essays;
translations;
written reports;
project work;
letters to penfriends;
contributions to class links using fax or e-mail.

6.4.3.4   In receptive, productive and interactive modes, how far may learners be
expected and helped to differentiate text types and to develop different styles of listening, reading, speaking and writing as appropriate, acting both as individuals and as
members of groups (e.g. by sharing ideas and interpretations in the processes of comprehension and formulation)?

> *Users of the Framework may wish to consider and where appropriate state the place of texts (spoken and written) in their learning/teaching programme and exploitation activities: e.g.*
>
> • *according to what principles texts are selected, adapted or composed, ordered and presented;*
> • *whether texts are graded;*
> • *whether learners are a) expected b) helped to differentiate text types and to develop different listening and reading styles as appropriate to text type and to listen or read in detail or for gist, for specific points, etc.*

6.4.4 How far should learners be expected or required to learn from *tasks* and *activities* (see sections 4.3 and 4.4):

a) by simple participation in spontaneous activities?
b) by simple participation in tasks and activities planned as to type, goals, input, outcomes, participant roles and activities, etc.?
c) by participation not only in the task but in pre-planning as well as post-mortem analysis and evaluation?
d) as c) but also with explicit awareness-raising as to goals, the nature and structure of tasks, requirements of participant roles, etc.?

6.4.5 Should the development of the learner's ability to use *communicative strategies* (see section 4.4) be:

a) assumed to be transferable from the learner's L1 usage or facilitated;
b) by creating situation and setting tasks (e.g. role play and simulations) which require the operation of planning, execution, evaluation and repair strategies;
c) as b), but using awareness-raising techniques (e.g. recording and analysis of roleplays and simulations);
d) as b), but encouraging or requiring learners to focus on and follow explicit strategic procedures as the need arises.

> *Users of the Framework may wish to consider and where appropriate state the place of activities, tasks and strategies in their language learning/teaching programme.*

6.4.6 **General competences** (see section 5.1) may be developed in various ways.

6.4.6.1 With regard to knowledge of the world, learning a new language does not mean starting afresh. Much if not most of the knowledge that is needed can be taken for granted. However, it is not simply a question of learning new words for old ideas, though it is remarkable to what extent the framework of general and specific notions proposed in the Threshold Level has proved appropriate and adequate for twenty

European languages, even from different language families. Judgement is needed in deciding such questions as: Does the language to be taught or tested involve a knowledge of the world which in fact is beyond the learners' state of maturation, or outside their adult experience? If so, it cannot be taken for granted. The problem should not be avoided; in the case of the use of a non-native language as the medium of instruction in schools or universities (and indeed in mother tongue education itself) both the subject content and the language used are new. In the past many language textbooks, such as the *Orbis pictus* of the celebrated 17th century Czech educationist Comenius, have attempted to structure language learning in a way explicitly designed to give young people a structured world-view.

6.4.6.2   The position with regard to sociocultural knowledge and intercultural skills development is somewhat different. In some respects European peoples appear to share a common culture. In other respects there is considerable diversity, not simply between one nation and another but also between regions, classes, ethnic communities, genders and so on. Careful consideration has to be given to the representation of the target culture and the choice of the social group or groups to be focused on. Is there any place for the picturesque, generally archaic, folkloristic stereotypes of the sort found in children's picture books (Dutch clogs and windmills, English thatched cottages with roses round the door)? They capture the imagination and can be motivating particularly for younger children. They often correspond in some ways to the self-image of the country concerned and are preserved and promoted in festivals. If so, they can be presented in that light. They bear very little relation to the everyday lives of the vast majority of the population. A balance has to be struck in the light of the over-arching educational goal of developing the learners' pluricultural competence.

6.4.6.3   How then should the general, non-language-specific competences be treated in language courses?

a)   assumed to exist already, or be developed elsewhere (e.g. in other curricular subjects conducted in L1) sufficiently to be taken for granted in L2 teaching;
b)   treated *ad hoc* as and when problems arise;
c)   by selecting or constructing texts that illustrate new areas and items of knowledge
d)   by special courses or textbooks dealing with area studies (*Landeskunde, civilisation,* etc.) i) in L1, ii) in L2;
e)   through an intercultural component designed to raise awareness of the relevant experiential, cognitive and sociocultural backgrounds of learners and native speakers respectively;
f)   through role-play and simulations;
g)   through subject teaching using L2 as the medium of instruction;
h)   through direct contact with native speakers and authentic texts.

6.4.6.4   With regard to *existential competence*, the learner's personality features, motivations, attitudes, beliefs, etc. (see section 5.1.3) may be:

a) ignored as the learner's personal concern
b) taken into account in planning and monitoring the learning process
c) included as an objective of the learning programme

Users of the Framework may wish to consider and where appropriate state

- *which of the above (or other) means they use to develop general competences;*
- *what differences arise if practical skills are a) talked about as themes, b) exercised, c) demonstrated through actions accompanied by language or d) taught using the target language as the medium of instruction.*

6.4.6.5 With regard to ability to learn, learners may (be expected/required to) develop their *study skills* and *heuristic skills* and their acceptance of *responsibility for their own learning* (see section 5.1.4):

a) simply as 'spin-off' from language learning and teaching, without any special planning or provision;
b) by progressively transferring responsibility for learning from the teacher to the pupils/students and encouraging them to reflect on their learning and to share this experience with other learners;
c) by systematically raising the learners' awareness of the learning/teaching processes in which they are participating;
d) by engaging learners as participants in experimentation with different methodological options;
e) by getting learners to recognise their own cognitive style and to develop their own learning strategies accordingly.

Users of the Framework may wish to consider and where appropriate state the steps they take to promote the development of pupils/students as responsibly independent language learners and users.

6.4.7 The development of the learner's **linguistic competences** is a central, indispensable aspect of language learning. How may it best be facilitated in relation to vocabulary, grammar, pronunciation and orthography?

6.4.7.1 In which of the following ways should learners be expected or required to develop their **vocabulary**?

a) by simple exposure to words and fixed expressions used in authentic spoken and written texts?
b) by learner elicitation or dictionary, etc. look-up as needed for specific tasks and activities?

c) through inclusion in context, e.g. in course-book texts and subsequent recycling in exercises, exploitation activities, etc.?

d) by presenting words accompanied by visuals (pictures, gestures and miming, demonstrative actions, realia, etc.)?

e) by the memorisation of word-lists, etc. with translation equivalents?

f) by exploring semantic fields and constructing 'mind-maps', etc.?

g) by training in the use of monolingual and bilingual dictionaries, thesauruses and other works of reference?

h) by explanation and training in the application of lexical structure (e.g. word formation, compounding, collocations, phrasal verbs, idioms, etc.)?

i) by a more or less systematic study of the different distribution of semantic features in L1 and L2 (contrastive semantics)?

Users of the Framework may wish to consider and where appropriate state the ways in which vocabulary items (form and meaning) are presented to and learned by pupils and students.

6.4.7.2 *Size, range* and *control* of vocabulary are major parameters of language acquisition and hence for the assessment of a learner's language proficiency and for the planning of language learning and teaching.

Users of the Framework may wish to consider and where appropriate state:

- *what size of vocabulary (i.e. the number of words and fixed expressions) the learner will need/be equipped/be required to control;*
- *what range of vocabulary (i.e. the domains, themes etc. covered) the learner will need/be equipped/be required to control;*
- *what control over vocabulary the learner will need/be equipped/be required to exert;*
- *what distinction, if any, is made between learning for recognition and understanding, and learning for recall and productive use?;*
- *what use is made of inferencing techniques? How is their development promoted?*

6.4.7.3 Lexical selection

Constructors of testing and textbook materials are obliged to choose which words to include. Curriculum and syllabus designers are not obliged to do so, but may wish to provide guidelines in the interests of transparency and coherence in educational provision. There are a number of options:

- to select key words and phrases a) in thematic areas required for the achievement of communicative tasks relevant to learner needs, b) which embody cultural difference and/or significant values and beliefs shared by the social group(s) whose language is being learnt;

- to follow lexico-statistical principles selecting the highest frequency words in large general word-counts or those undertaken for restricted thematic areas;
- to select (authentic) spoken and written texts and learn/teach whatever words they contain;
- not to pre-plan vocabulary development, but to allow it to develop organically in response to learner demand when engaged in communicative tasks.

Users of the Framework may wish to consider and where appropriate state:

- *according to which principle(s) lexical selection has been made.*

6.4.7.4 Grammatical competence, the ability to organise sentences to convey meaning, is clearly central to communicative competence and most (though not all) of those concerned with language planning, teaching and testing pay close attention to the management of the process of learning to do so. This usually involves a selection, ordering and step-by-step presentation and drilling of new material, starting with short sentences consisting of a single clause with its constituent phrases represented by single words (e.g. *Jane is happy*) and finishing with multiclause complex sentences – their number, length and structure being of course unbounded. This does not preclude the early introduction of analytically complex material as a fixed formula (i.e. a vocabulary item) or as a fixed frame for lexical insertion (*please may I have a . . .*), or as the globally learnt words of a song (*In Dublin's fair city, where the girls are so pretty, I first set my eyes on sweet Molly Malone, as she wheeled her wheelbarrow through streets broad and narrow, crying 'Cockles and Mussels alive alive-oh'*).

6.4.7.5 Inherent complexity is not the only ordering principle to be considered.

1. The communicative yield of grammatical categories has to be taken into account, i.e. their role as exponents of general notions. For instance, should learners follow a progression which leaves them unable, after two years' study, to speak of past experience?
2. Contrastive factors are of great importance in assessing learning load and hence cost-effectiveness of competing orderings. For instance, subordinate clauses in German involve greater word-order problems for English and French learners than for Dutch learners. However, speakers of closely-related languages, e.g. Dutch/German, Czech/Slovak, may be prone to fall into mechanical word-for-word translation.
3. Authentic discourse and written texts may to some extent be graded for grammatical difficulty, but are likely to present a learner with new structures and perhaps categories, which adept learners may well acquire for active use before others nominally more basic.
4. The 'natural' acquisition order observed in L1 child language development might also perhaps be taken into account in planning L2 development.

The Framework cannot replace reference grammars or provide a strict ordering (though scaling may involve selection and hence some ordering in global terms) but provides a framework for the decisions of practitioners to be made known.

6.4.7.6   The sentence is generally regarded as the domain of grammatical description. However, some intersentential relations (e.g. anaphora: pronoun and pro-verb usage and the use of sentence adverbs) may be treated as part of linguistic rather than pragmatic competence (e.g. *We didn't expect John to fail. However, he did*).

Users of the Framework may wish to consider and where appropriate state:

- *the basis on which grammatical elements, categories, structures, processes and relations are selected and ordered;*
- *how their meaning is conveyed to learners;*
- *the role of contrastive grammar in language teaching and learning;*
- *the relative importance attached to range, fluency and accuracy in relation to the grammatical construction of sentences;*
- *the extent to which learners are to be made aware of the grammar of (a) the mother tongue (b) the target language (c) their contrastive relations.*

6.4.7.7   Learners may (be expected/required to) develop their **grammatical competence**:

a)   inductively, by exposure to new grammatical material in authentic texts as encountered;
b)   inductively, by incorporating new grammatical elements, categories, classes, structures, rules, etc. in texts specially composed to demonstrate their form, function and meaning;
c)   as b), but followed by explanations and formal exercises;
d)   by the presentation of formal paradigms, tables of forms, etc. followed by explanations using an appropriate metalanguage in L2 or L1 and formal exercises;
e)   by elicitation and, where necessary, reformulation of learners' hypotheses, etc.

6.4.7.8   If **formal exercises** are used, some or all of the following types may be employed:

a)   gap-filling
b)   sentence construction on a given model
c)   multiple choice
d)   category substitution exercises (e.g. singular/plural, present/past, active/passive, etc.)
e)   sentence merging (e.g. relativisation, adverbial and noun clauses, etc.)
f)   translation of example sentences from L1 to L2
g)   question and answer involving use of particular structures
h)   grammar-focused fluency exercises

> *Users of the Framework may wish to consider and where appropriate state:*
>
> - *how grammatical structure is a) analysed, ordered and presented to learners and (b) mastered by them.*
> - *how and according to what principles lexical, grammatical and pragmatic meaning in L2 is conveyed to/elicited from learners, e.g.:*
>   - *by translation from/into L1*
>   - *by L2 definition, explanation, etc.*
>   - *by induction from context.*

6.4.7.9 Pronunciation

How should learners be expected/required to develop their ability to **pronounce** a language?

a) simply by exposure to authentic spoken utterances;
b) by chorused imitation of i)   the teacher;
                             ii)   audio-recorded native speakers;
                             iii)   video-recorded native speakers;
c) by individualised language laboratory work;
d) by reading aloud phonetically weighted textual material;
e) by ear-training and phonetic drilling;
f) as d) and e) but with the use of phonetically transcribed texts;
g) by explicit phonetic training (see section 5.2.1.4);
h) by learning orthoepic conventions (i.e. how to pronounce written forms);
i) by some combination of the above.

6.4.7.10 Orthography

How should learners be expected/required to develop their ability to handle the writing system of a language?

a) by simple transfer from L1;
b) by exposure to authentic written texts:
                             i)   printed
                             ii)   typewritten
                             iii)   handwritten
c) by memorisation of the alphabet concerned with associated phonetic values (e.g. Roman, Cyrillic or Greek script where another is used for L1), together with diacritics and punctuation marks;
d) by practising cursive writing (including Cyrillic or 'Gothic' scripts, etc.) and noting the characteristic national handwriting conventions;
e) by memorising word-forms (individually or by applying spelling conventions) and punctuation conventions;
f) by the practice of dictation.

> *Users of the Framework may wish to consider and where appropriate state how the phonetic and orthographic forms of words, sentences, etc. are conveyed to and mastered by learners.*

6.4.8 Should the development of the learner's **sociolinguistic competence** (see section 5.2.2) be assumed to be transferable from the learner's experience of social life or facilitated:

a)   by exposure to authentic language used appropriately in its social setting?
b)   by selecting or constructing texts that exemplify sociolinguistic contrasts between the society of origin and the target society?
c)   by drawing attention to sociolinguistic contrasts as they are encountered, explaining and discussing them?
d)   by waiting for errors to be made, then marking, analysing and explaining them and giving the correct usage?
e)   as part of the explicit teaching of a sociocultural component in the study of a modern language?

6.4.9   Should the development of the learner's **pragmatic competences** (see section 5.2.3) be:

a)   assumed to be transferable from education and general experience in the mother tongue (L1)?

or facilitated:

b)   by progressively increasing the complexity of discourse structure and the functional range of the texts presented to the learner?
c)   by requiring the learner to produce texts of increasing complexity by translating texts of increasing complexity from L1 to L2?
d)   by setting tasks that require a wider functional range and adherence to verbal exchange patterns?
e)   by awareness-raising (analysis, explanation, terminology, etc.) in addition to practical activities?
f)   by explicit teaching and exercising of functions, verbal exchange patterns and discourse structure?

> *Users of the Framework may wish to consider and where appropriate state:*
>
> • *to what extent sociolinguistic and pragmatic competences can be assumed or left to develop naturally;*
> • *what methods and techniques should be employed to facilitate their development where it is felt to be necessary or advisable to do so.*

6.5   Errors and mistakes

Errors are due to an *'interlanguage'*, a simplified or distorted representation of the target competence. When the learner makes errors, his performance truly accords with his competence, which has developed characteristics different from those of L2 norms. *Mistakes*, on the other hand, occur in performance when a user/learner (as might be the case with a native speaker) does not bring his competences properly into action.

6.5.1   Different attitudes may be taken to learner errors, e.g.:

a)   errors and mistakes are evidence of failure to learn;
b)   errors and mistakes are evidence of inefficient teaching;
c)   errors and mistakes are evidence of the learner's willingness to communicate despite risks;
d)   errors are an inevitable, transient product of the learner's developing interlanguage.
e)   Mistakes are inevitable in **all** language use, including that of native speakers.

6.5.2   The action to be taken with regard to learner mistakes and errors may be:

a)   all errors and mistakes should be immediately corrected by the teacher;
b)   immediate peer-correction should be systematically encouraged to eradicate errors;
c)   all errors should be noted and corrected at a time when doing so does not interfere with communication (e.g. by separating the development of accuracy from the development of fluency);
d)   errors should not be simply corrected, but also analysed and explained at an appropriate time;
e)   mistakes which are mere slips should be passed over, but systematic errors should be eradicated;
f)   errors should be corrected only when they interfere with communication;
g)   errors should be accepted as 'transitional interlanguage' and ignored.

6.5.3   What use is made of the observation and analysis of learner errors:

a)   in planning future learning and teaching on an individual or group basis?
b)   in course planning and materials development?
c)   in the evaluation and assessment of learning and teaching, e.g.

are students assessed primarily in terms of their errors and mistakes in performing the tasks set?
if not, what other criteria of linguistic achievement are employed?
are errors and mistakes weighted and if so according to what criteria?
what relative importance is attached to errors and mistakes in:
pronunciation
spelling

vocabulary
morphology
syntax
usage
sociocultural content?

Users of the Framework may wish to consider and where appropriate state their attitude to and action in response to learner errors and mistakes and whether the same or different criteria apply to:

- *phonetic errors and mistakes;*
- *orthographic errors and mistakes;*
- *vocabulary errors and mistakes;*
- *morphological errors and mistakes;*
- *syntactic errors and mistakes;*
- *sociolinguistic and sociocultural errors and mistakes;*
- *pragmatic errors and mistakes.*

---

7 Tasks and their role in language teaching

7.1 Task description

Tasks are a feature of everyday life in the personal, public, educational or occupational domains. Task accomplishment by an individual involves the strategic activation of specific competences in order to carry out a set of purposeful actions in a particular domain with a clearly defined goal and a specific outcome (see section 4.1). Tasks can be extremely varied in nature, and may involve language activities to a greater or lesser extent, for example: creative (painting, story writing), skills based (repairing or assembling something), problem solving (jigsaw, crossword), routine transactions, interpreting a role in a play, taking part in a discussion, giving a presentation, planning a course of action, reading and replying to (an e-mail) message, etc. A task may be quite simple or extremely complex (e.g. studying a number of related diagrams and instructions and assembling an unfamiliar and intricate apparatus). A particular task may involve a greater or lesser number of steps or embedded sub-tasks and consequently the boundaries of any one task may be difficult to define.

Communication is an integral part of tasks where participants engage in interaction, production, reception or mediation, or a combination of two or more of these, for example: interacting with a public service official and completing a form; reading a report and discussing it with colleagues in order to arrive at a decision on a course of action; following written instructions while assembling something, and if an observer/helper is present, asking for help or describing/commenting on the process; preparing (in written form) and delivering a public lecture, interpreting informally for a visitor, etc.

Similar kinds of tasks are a central unit in many syllabuses, textbooks, classroom learning experiences and tests, although often in a modified form for learning or testing purposes. These 'real-life', 'target' or 'rehearsal' tasks are chosen on the basis of learners' needs outside the classroom, whether in the personal and public domains, or related to more specific occupational or educational needs.

Other kinds of classroom tasks are specifically 'pedagogic' in nature and have their basis in the social and interactive nature and immediacy of the classroom situation where learners engage in a 'willing suspension of disbelief' and accept the use of the target language rather than the easier and more natural mother tongue to carry out meaning-focused tasks. These pedagogic tasks are only indirectly related to real-life tasks and learner needs, and aim to develop communicative competence based on what is believed or known about learning processes in general and language acquisition in particular. Communicative pedagogic tasks (as opposed to exercises focusing specifically on decontextualised practice of forms) aim to actively involve learners in meaningful communication, are relevant (here and now in the formal learning context), are challenging but feasible (with task manipulation where appropriate), and have identifiable (and possibly less immediately evident) outcomes. Such tasks may involve 'metacommunicative' (sub)tasks, i.e. communication around task implementation and the language used in carrying out the task. This includes learner contributions to task selection, management, and evaluation, which in a language learning context may often become integral parts of the tasks themselves.

Classroom tasks, whether reflecting 'real-life' use or essentially 'pedagogic' in nature, are communicative to the extent that they require learners to comprehend, negotiate and express meaning in order to achieve a communicative goal. The emphasis in a communicative task is on successful task completion and consequently the primary focus is on meaning as learners realise their communicative intentions. However, in the case of tasks designed for language learning or teaching purposes, performance is concerned both with meaning and the way meanings are comprehended, expressed and negotiated. A changing balance needs to be established between attention to meaning and form, fluency and accuracy, in the overall selection and sequencing of tasks so that both task performance and language learning progress can be facilitated and appropriately acknowledged.

7.2 Task performance

In considering task performance in pedagogical contexts it is necessary to take into account both the learner's competences and the conditions and constraints specific to a particular task (which may be manipulated in order to modify the level of difficulty of classroom tasks), and the strategic interplay of learner competences and task parameters in carrying out a task.

7.2.1 Competences

Tasks of any kind require the activation of a range of appropriate general competences, for example: knowledge and experience of the world; sociocultural knowledge (concerning life in the target community and essential differences between practices, values and beliefs in that community and the learner's own society); skills such as intercultural skills (mediating between the two cultures), learning skills, and everyday practical skills and know-how (see section 5.1). In order to accomplish a communicative task, whether in a real-life or a learning/examination setting, the language user or learner draws also on communicative language competences (linguistic, sociolinguistic and pragmatic knowledge and skills – see section 5.2). In addition, individual personality and attitudinal characteristics affect the user or learner's task performance.

Successful task accomplishment may be facilitated by the prior activation of the learner's competences, for example, in the initial problem-posing or goal-setting phase of a task by providing or raising awareness of necessary linguistic elements, by drawing on prior knowledge and experience to activate appropriate schemata, and by encouraging task planning or rehearsal. In this way the processing load during task execution and monitoring is reduced and the learner's attention is freer to deal with any unexpected content and/or form-related problems that may arise, thereby increasing the likelihood of successful task completion in both quantitative and qualitative terms.

7.2.2   Conditions and constraints

In addition to user/learner competences and characteristics, performance is affected by certain task-related conditions and constraints which can vary from task to task, and the teacher or textbook writer can control a number of elements in order to adjust the level of task difficulty upwards or downwards.

Comprehension tasks may be designed so that the same input may be available to all learners but different outcomes may be envisaged quantitatively (amount of information required) or qualitatively (standard of performance expected). Alternatively, the input text may contain differing amounts of information or degrees of cognitive and/or organisational complexity, or different amounts of support (visuals, key words, prompts, charts, diagrams, etc.) may be made available to help learners. Input may be chosen for its relevance to the learner (motivation) or for reasons extrinsic to the learner. A text may be listened to or read as often as necessary or limits may be imposed. The type of response required can be quite simple (raise your hand) or demanding (create a new text). In the case of interaction and production tasks, performance conditions can be manipulated in order to make a task more or less demanding, for example by varying: the amount of time allowed for planning and for realisation; the duration of the interaction or production; the degree of (un)predictability, amount and kind of support provided, etc.

7.2.3   Strategies

Task performance is a complex process, therefore, involving the strategic interplay of a range of learner competences and task-related factors. In responding to the demands of a task the language user or learner activates those general and communicative strategies which are most efficient for accomplishing the particular task. The user or learner naturally adapts, adjusts and filters task inputs, goals, conditions and constraints to fit his or her own resources, purposes and (in a language learning context) particular learning style.

In carrying out a communication task, an individual selects, balances, activates and co-ordinates the appropriate components of those competences necessary for task planning, execution, monitoring/evaluation, and (where necessary) repair, with a view to the effective achievement of his or her intended communicative purpose. Strategies (general and communicative) provide a vital link between the different competences that the learner has (innate or acquired) and successful task completion (see sections 4.4 and 4.5).

7.3   Task difficulty

Individuals may differ considerably in their approach to the same task. Consequently the difficulty of any particular task for an individual, and the strategies which he or she adopts to cope with the demands of the task, are the result of a number of interrelated factors arising from his or her competences (general and communicative) and individual characteristics, and the specific conditions and constraints under which the task is carried out. For these reasons the ease or difficulty of tasks cannot be predicted with certainty, least of all for individual learners, and in language learning contexts consideration needs to be given to ways of building flexibility and differentiation into task design and implementation.

In spite of the problems associated with establishing task difficulty, the effective use of classroom learning experiences requires a principled and coherent approach to task selection and sequencing. This means taking into account the specific competences of the learner and factors that affect task difficulty, and manipulating task parameters in order to modify the task according to the needs and capabilities of the learner.

In considering levels of task difficulty, therefore, it is necessary to take into account:

- user/learner's competences and characteristics, including the learner's own purposes and learning style;
- task conditions and constraints which may affect the language user/learner's performance in carrying out specific tasks, and which, in learning contexts, may be adjusted to accommodate learner competences and characteristics.

7.3.1 Learner competences and learner characteristics

The learner's different competences are closely related to individual characteristics of a cognitive, affective and linguistic nature which need to be taken into account in establishing the potential difficulty of a given task for a particular learner.

7.3.1.1 Cognitive factors

Task familiarity: cognitive load may be lessened and successful task completion facilitated according to the extent of the learner's familiarity with:

- the type of task and operations involved;
- the theme(s);
- type of text (genre);
- interactional schemata (scripts and frames) involved as the availability to the learner of unconscious or 'routinised' schemata can free the learner to deal with other aspects of performance, or assists in anticipating text content and organisation;
- necessary background knowledge (assumed by the speaker or writer);
- relevant sociocultural knowledge, e.g. knowledge of social norms and variations, social conventions and rules, language forms appropriate to the context, references connected with national or cultural identity, and distinctive differences between the learner's culture and the target culture (see section 5.1.1.2) and intercultural awareness (see 5.1.1.3).

Skills: task completion depends on the learner's ability to exercise, *inter alia*:

- the organisational and interpersonal skills necessary to carry out the different steps of the task;

- the learning skills and strategies that facilitate task completion, including coping when linguistic resources are inadequate, discovering for oneself, planning and monitoring task implementation;
- intercultural skills (see section 5.1.2.2), including the ability to cope with what is implicit in the discourse of native speakers.

Ability to cope with processing demands: a task is likely to make greater or lesser demands depending on the learner's capacity to:

- handle the number of steps or 'cognitive operations' involved, and their concrete or abstract nature;
- attend to the processing demands of the task (amount of 'on-line thinking') and to relating different steps of the task to one another (or to combining different but related tasks).

7.3.1.2 Affective factors

Self-esteem: a positive self-image and lack of inhibition is likely to contribute to successful task completion where the learner has the necessary self-confidence to persist in carrying out the task; for example, assuming control of interaction when necessary (e.g. intervening to obtain clarification, to check understanding, willingness to take risks, or, when faced with comprehension difficulties, continuing to read or listen and making inferences etc.); the degree of inhibition may be influenced by the particular situation or task.

Involvement and motivation: successful task performance is more likely where the learner is fully involved; a high level of intrinsic motivation to carry out the task – due to interest in the task or because of its perceived relevance, for example to real life needs or to the completion of another linked task (task interdependence) – will promote greater learner involvement; extrinsic motivation *may* also play a role, for example where there are external pressures to complete the task successfully (e.g. to earn praise or in order not to lose face, or for competitive reasons).

State: performance is influenced by the learner's physical and emotional state (an alert and relaxed learner is more likely to learn and to succeed than a tired and anxious one).

Attitude: the difficulty of a task which introduces new sociocultural knowledge and experiences will be affected by, for example: the learner's interest in and openness to otherness; willingness to relativise his or her own cultural viewpoint and value system; willingness to assume the role of 'cultural intermediary' between his or her own and the foreign culture and to resolve intercultural misunderstanding and conflict.

7.3.1.3 Linguistic factors

The stage of development of the learner's linguistic resources is a primary factor to be considered in establishing the suitability of a particular task or in manipulating task parameters: level of knowledge and control of grammar, vocabulary and phonology or orthography required to carry out the task, i.e. language resources such as range, grammatical and lexical accuracy, and aspects of language use such as fluency, flexibility, coherence, appropriacy, precision.

A task may be linguistically demanding but cognitively simple, or vice versa, and consequently one factor may be offset against the other in task selection for pedagogic purposes (although an appropriate response to a cognitively demanding task may be linguistically challenging in a real life context). In carrying out a task learners have to handle both content and form. Where they do not need to devote undue attention to formal aspects, then more resources are available to attend to cognitive aspects, and vice versa. The availability of routinised schematic knowledge frees the learner to deal with content and, in the case of interaction and spontaneous production activities, to concentrate on more accurate use of less well established forms. The learner's ability to compensate for 'gaps' in his or her linguistic competence is an important factor in successful task completion for all activities (see communication strategies, section 4.4).

7.3.2   Task conditions and constraints

A range of factors may be manipulated with regard to conditions and constraints in classroom tasks involving:

- interaction and production;
- reception.

7.3.2.1   Interaction and production

Conditions and constraints affecting the difficulty of interaction and production tasks:

- Support
- Time
- Goal
- Predictability
- Physical conditions
- Participants

- *Support:*

The provision of adequate information concerning contextual features and the availability of language assistance can help reduce task difficulty.

- amount of *contextualisation* provided: task accomplishment may be facilitated by the provision of sufficient and relevant information about participants, roles, content, goals, setting (including visuals) and relevant, clear and adequate instructions or guidelines for carrying out the task;
- extent to which *language assistance* is provided: in interaction activities, task rehearsal or carrying out a parallel task in a preparatory phase, and the provision of language support (key words, etc.) helps to create expectations and to activate prior knowledge or experience and acquired schemata; non-immediate production activ-

ities will obviously be facilitated by the availability of resources such as reference works, relevant models, and assistance from others.

* *Time:*

The less time available for task preparation and performance, the more demanding the task is likely to be. Temporal aspects to be considered include:

* time available for *preparation*, i.e. the extent to which planning or rehearsal is possible: in spontaneous communication intentional planning is not possible and consequently a highly developed and subconscious use of strategies is required for successful task completion; in other instances the learner may be under less severe time pressure and can exercise relevant strategies at a more conscious level, for example where communication schemata are fairly predictable or determined in advance as in routine transactions, or where there is adequate time for planning, executing, evaluating, and editing text as is normally the case with interaction tasks which do not require an immediate response (corresponding by letter) or non-immediate spoken or written production tasks;
* time available for *execution*: the greater the degree of urgency inherent in the communicative event, or the shorter the time allowed for learners to complete the task, the greater the pressure in carrying out the task in spontaneous communication; however, non-spontaneous interaction or production tasks may also create time pressure, for example, to meet a deadline for completing a text, which in turn reduces the time available for planning, execution, evaluation and repair;
* *duration of turns*: longer turns in spontaneous interaction (e.g. recounting an anecdote) are normally more demanding than short turns;
* *duration of the task*: where cognitive factors and performance conditions are constant, a lengthy spontaneous interaction, a (complex) task with many steps, or the planning and execution of a lengthy spoken or written text is likely to be more demanding than a corresponding task of a shorter duration.

* *Goal:*

The greater the amount of negotiation required to achieve the task goal(s) the more demanding the task is likely to be. In addition, the extent to which expectations with regard to task outcomes are shared by the teacher and learners will facilitate the acceptance of diversified but acceptable task accomplishment.

* *convergence or divergence* of task goal(s): in an interaction task a convergent goal normally involves more 'communicative stress' than a divergent goal, i.e. the former requires participants to arrive at a single, agreed outcome (such as reaching a consensus on a course of action to be followed) which may involve considerable negotiation as specific information which is essential for successful task completion is exchanged, whereas the latter has no single, specific intended outcome (e.g. a simple exchange of views);
* *learner and teacher attitudes* to goal(s): teacher and learner awareness of the possibility and acceptability of different outcomes (as opposed to learners' (perhaps subconscious) striving for a single 'correct' outcome) may influence task execution.

- *Predictability:*

Regular changes in task parameters during task execution are likely to increase demands on interlocutors.

- in an interaction task, the introduction of an unexpected element (event, circumstances, information, participant) obliges the learner to activate relevant strategies to cope with the dynamics of the new and more complex situation; in a production task the development of a 'dynamic' text (e.g. a story involving regular changes of characters, scenes and with time shifts) is likely to be more demanding than producing a 'static' text (e.g. describing a lost or stolen object).

- *Physical conditions:*

Noise can add to the processing demands in interaction:

- *interference:* background noise or a poor telephone line, for example, may require participants to draw on prior experience, schematic knowledge, inferencing skills, etc. to compensate for 'gaps' in the message.

- *Participants:*

In addition to the above parameters, a variety of participant-related factors, although they cannot normally be manipulated, need to be taken into account when considering conditions influencing the ease of difficulty of real life tasks involving interaction.

- *co-operativeness of interlocutor(s):* a sympathetic interlocutor will facilitate successful communication by ceding a degree of control over the interaction to the user/learner, e.g. in negotiating and accepting modification of goals, and in facilitating comprehension, for example by responding positively to requests to speak more slowly, to repeat, to clarify;
- *features of speech of interlocutors*, e.g. rate, accent, clarity, coherence;
- *visibility of interlocutors* (accessibility of paralinguistic features in face to face communication facilitates communication);
- *general and communicative competences of interlocutors*, including behaviour (degree of familiarity with norms in a particular speech community), and knowledge of the subject matter.

7.3.2.2 Reception

Conditions and constraints affecting the difficulty of comprehension tasks:

- Task support
- Text characteristics
- Type of response required

- *Task support*

The introduction of various forms of support can reduce the possible difficulty of texts, for example, a preparatory phase can provide orientation and activate prior knowledge, clear task instructions help to avoid possible confusion, and work arrangements involving small group settings offer possibilities for learner co-operation and mutual assistance.

- *preparatory phase*: creating expectations, providing necessary background knowledge, activating schematic knowledge, and filtering specific linguistic difficulties during a pre-listening/viewing or pre-reading phase reduce the processing load and consequently task demands; contextual assistance may be provided also by studying questions accompanying a text (and therefore ideally placed before a written text), and from clues such as visuals, layout, headings, etc.;
- *task instructions*: uncomplicated, relevant and sufficient task instructions (neither too much nor too little information) lessen the possibility of confusion about task procedures and goals;
- *small group setting*: for certain learners, and particularly but not exclusively for slower learners, a small group work arrangement involving co-operative listening/reading is more likely to result in successful task completion than individual work, as learners can share the processing load and obtain assistance and feedback on their understanding from one another.

- **Text characteristics**

In evaluating a text for use with a particular learner or group of learners, factors such as linguistic complexity, text type, discourse structure, physical presentation, length of the text and its relevance for the learner(s), need to be considered.

- *linguistic complexity*: particularly complex syntax consumes attentional resources that might otherwise be available for dealing with content; for example, long sentences with a number of subordinate clauses, non-continuous constituents, multiple negation, scope ambiguity, use of anaphorics and deictics without clear antecedents or reference. Syntactic over-simplification of authentic texts, however, may actually have the effect of increasing the level of difficulty (because of the elimination of redundancies, clues to meaning etc.);
- *text type*: familiarity with the genre and domain (and with assumed background and sociocultural knowledge) helps the learner in anticipating and comprehending text structure and content; the concrete or abstract nature of the text is also likely to play a role; for example, concrete description, instructions or narratives (particularly with adequate visual supports), for example, are likely to be less demanding than abstract argumentation or explanation;
- *discourse structure*: textual coherence and clear organisation (for example, temporal sequencing, main points clearly signalled and presented before illustration of the points), the explicit rather than implicit nature of information presented, the absence of conflicting or surprising information, all contribute to reducing information processing complexity;
- *physical presentation*: written and spoken texts obviously make differing demands because of the need to process information in spoken text in real time. In addition, noise, distortion and interference (e.g. weak radio/television reception, or untidy/smudged handwriting) increase the difficulty of comprehension; in the case

of spoken (audio) text the greater the number of speakers and the less distinct their voices, the more difficult it is to identify and understand individual speakers; other factors which increase difficulty in listening/viewing include overlapping speech, phonetic reduction, unfamiliar accents, speed of delivery, monotony, low volume, etc.;

- *length of text*: in general a short text is less demanding than a long text on a similar topic as a longer text requires more processing and there is an additional memory load, risk of fatigue and distraction (especially in the case of younger learners). However, a long text which is not too dense and contains considerable redundancy may be easier than a short dense text presenting the same information;

- *relevance to the learner*: a high level of motivation to understand due to personal interest in the content will help to sustain the learner's efforts to understand (although it will not necessarily assist comprehension directly); while the occurrence of low frequency vocabulary may be expected to increase the difficulty of a text in general, a text containing quite specific vocabulary on a familiar and relevant topic is likely to be less demanding for a specialist in the field than a text containing wide-ranging vocabulary of a more general nature, and it may be approached with greater confidence.

Encouraging learners to express their personal knowledge, ideas and opinions within a comprehension task may increase motivation and confidence, and activate linguistic competence related to the text. Embedding a comprehension task within another task may also help to make it inherently purposeful and increase learner involvement.

- *Type of response required*

While a text may be relatively difficult the type of response required by the task which is set may be manipulated in order to accommodate the learner's competences and characteristics. Task design may also depend on whether the aim is to develop comprehension skills or to check understanding. Accordingly, the type of response demanded may vary considerably, as numerous typologies of comprehension tasks illustrate.

A comprehension task may require global or selective comprehension, or understanding of important points of detail. Certain tasks may require the reader/listener to show understanding of the main information clearly stated in a text, while others may require the use of inferencing skills. A task may be summative (to be completed on the basis of the complete text), or may be structured so as to relate to manageable units (e.g. accompanying each section of a text) and thus making less demands on memory.

The response may be non-verbal (no overt response or a simple action such as ticking a picture) or a verbal response (spoken or written) may be required. The latter may, for instance, involve identifying and reproducing information from a text for a particular purpose or may, for example, require the learner to complete the text or to produce a new text through related interaction or production tasks.

The time allowed for the response may be varied so as to decrease or increase task difficulty. The more time a listener or reader has to replay or reread a text, the more he or she is likely to understand and the greater the opportunity to apply a range of strategies for coping with difficulties in understanding the text.

Users of the Framework may wish to consider and where appropriate state:

- *principles for the selection and weighting of 'real life' and 'pedagogic' tasks for their purposes, including the appropriateness of different types of tasks in particular learning contexts;*
- *the criteria for selecting tasks which are purposeful and meaningful for the learner, and provide a challenging but realistic and attainable goal, involving the learner as fully as possible, and allowing for differing learner interpretations and outcomes;*
- *the relationship between tasks that are primarily meaning-oriented and learning experiences specifically focused on form so that the learner's attention might be focused in a regular and useful manner on both aspects in a balanced approach to the development of accuracy and fluency;*
- *ways of taking into account the pivotal role of the learner's strategies in relating competences and performance in the successful accomplishment of challenging tasks under varying conditions and constraints (see section 4.4); ways of facilitating successful task accomplishment and learning (including activation of the learner's prior competences in a preparatory phase);*
- *criteria and options for selecting tasks, and where appropriate manipulating task parameters in order to modify the level of task difficulty so as to accommodate learners' differing and developing competences, and diversity in learner characteristics (ability, motivation, needs, interests);*
- *how the perceived level of difficulty of a task might be taken into account in the evaluation of successful task completion and in (self) assessment of the learner's communicative competence (Chapter 9).*

8 Linguistic diversification and the curriculum

8.1 Definition and initial approach

Plurilingual and pluricultural competence refers to the ability to use languages for the purposes of communication and to take part in intercultural interaction, where a person, viewed as a social agent has proficiency, of varying degrees, in several languages and experience of several cultures. This is not seen as the superposition or juxtaposition of distinct competences, but rather as the existence of a complex or even composite competence on which the user may draw.

The customary approach is to present learning a foreign language as an addition, in a compartmentalised way, of a competence to communicate in a foreign language to the competence to communicate in the mother tongue. The concept of plurilingual and pluricultural competence tends to:

- move away from the supposed balanced dichotomy established by the customary L1/L2 pairing by stressing plurilingualism where bilingualism is just one particular case;
- consider that a given individual does not have a collection of distinct and separate competences to communicate depending on the languages he/she knows, but rather a plurilingual and pluricultural competence encompassing the full range of the languages available to him/her;
- stress the pluricultural dimensions of this multiple competence but without necessarily suggesting links between the development of abilities concerned with relating to other cultures and the development of linguistic communicative proficiency.

A general observation can nevertheless be made, linking different distinct language learning components and paths. It is generally the case that language teaching in schools has to a large extent tended to stress objectives concerned with either the individual's *general competence* (especially at primary school level) or *communicative language competence* (particularly for those aged between 11 and 16), while courses for adults (students or people already working) formulate objectives in terms of specific *language activities* or functional ability in a particular *domain*. This emphasis, in the case of the former on the construction and development of competences, and in the latter case on optimal preparation for activities concerned with functioning in a specific context, corresponds no doubt to the distinct roles of general initial education on the one hand, and specialised and continuing education on the other. In this context, rather than treating these as opposites, the common framework of reference can help to relate these different practices with respect to one another and show that they should in fact be complementary.

8.2 Options for curricular design

8.2.1 *Diversification within an overall concept*

Discussion about curricula in relation to the Framework may be guided by three main principles.

The first is that discussion on curricula should be in line with the overall objective of promoting plurilingualism and linguistic diversity. This means that the teaching and learning of any one language should also be examined in conjunction with the provision for other languages in the education system and the paths which learners might choose to follow in the long term in their efforts to develop a variety of language skills.

The second principle is that this diversification is only possible, particularly in schools, if the cost efficiency of the system is considered, so as to avoid unnecessary repetition and to promote the economies of scale and the transfer of skills which linguistic diversity facilitates. If, for example, the education system allows pupils to begin learning two foreign languages at a pre-determined stage in their studies, and provides for optional learning of a third language, the objectives or kinds of progression in each of the chosen languages need not necessarily be the same (e.g. the starting point need not always be preparation for functional interaction satisfying the same communicative needs nor would one necessarily continue to emphasise learning strategies).

The third principle is, therefore, that considerations and measures relating to curricula should not just be limited to a curriculum for each language taken in isolation, nor even an integrated curriculum for several languages. They should also be approached in terms of their role in a general language education, in which linguistic knowledge (*savoir*) and skills (*savoir-faire*), along with the ability to learn (*savoir-apprendre*), play not only a specific role in a given language but also a transversal or transferable role across languages.

8.2.2 *From the partial to the transversal*

Between 'related' languages in particular – though not just between these – knowledge and skills may be transferred by a kind of osmosis. And, with reference to curricula, it should be stressed that:

• all knowledge of a language is partial, however much of a 'mother tongue' or 'native language' it seems to be. It is always incomplete, never as developed or perfect in an ordinary individual as it would be for the utopian, 'ideal native speaker'. In addition, a given individual never has equal mastery of the different component parts of the language in question (for example of oral and written skills, or of comprehension and interpretation compared to production skills);
• any partial knowledge is also more than it might seem. For instance, in order to achieve the 'limited' goal of increasing understanding of specialised texts in a given foreign language on very familiar subjects it is necessary to acquire knowledge and

skills which can also be used for many other purposes. Such 'spin-off' value is however a matter for the learner rather than the responsibility of the curriculum planner;

- those who have learnt one language also know a great deal about many other languages without necessarily realising that they do. The learning of further languages generally facilitates the activation of this knowledge and increases awareness of it, which is a factor to be taken into account rather than proceeding as if it did not exist.

Although leaving a very broad freedom of choice in drawing up curricula and progression, these different principles and observations also aim to encourage efforts to adopt a transparent and coherent approach when identifying options and making decisions. It is in this process that a framework of reference will be of particular value.

8.3 Towards curriculum scenarios

8.3.1 Curriculum and variation of objectives

From the above, it can be seen that each of the major components and sub-components of the proposed model may, if selected as a main learning objective, result in various choices in relation to content approaches and means to facilitate successful learning. For example, whether it is a matter of 'skills' (general competences of the individual learner/language user) or the 'sociolinguistic component' (within communicative language competence) or strategies, or comprehension (under the heading of language activities), in each case it is a question of components (and for quite distinct elements of the taxonomy proposed in the Framework) upon which a curriculum might or might not place emphasis and which might be considered in different instances as an objective, a means or a prerequisite. And for each of these components the question of the internal structure adopted (for example, which sub-components to select in the sociolinguistic component? how to sub-categorise strategies?) and the criteria for any system of progression over time (e.g. linear ranking of different types of comprehension activities?) could at least be identified and considered, if not treated in detail. This is the direction in which the other sections of this document invite the reader to approach the questions and consider the options appropriate to his or her own particular situation.

This 'exploded' view is all the more appropriate in the light of the generally accepted notion that the selection and ordering of objectives on which to base language learning may vary enormously depending on the context, the target group and the level in question. Furthermore, it should be stressed that objectives for the same type of public in the same context and at the same level could also vary regardless of the weight of tradition and the constraints imposed by the education system.

The discussion surrounding modern language teaching in primary schools illustrates this in that there is a great deal of variety and controversy – at national or even regional level within a country – concerning the definition of the initial, inevitably 'partial' aims to be set for this type of teaching. Should pupils: learn some basic rudiments of the foreign language system (linguistic component)?; develop linguistic awareness (more general linguistic knowledge (*savoir*), skills (*savoir-faire*) and *savoir-être*?; become more objective with regard to their native language and culture or be made to feel more at home in it?; be given confidence from the realisation and confirmation that they are capable of learning another language?; learn how to learn?; acquire a minimum of oral comprehension skills?; play with a foreign language and become familiar with it (in particular some of its phonetic and rhythmic characteristics) through counting-rhymes and songs? It goes without saying that it is possible to keep several irons in the fire and that many objectives could be combined or accommodated with others. However, it should be emphasised that in drawing up a curriculum the selection and balancing of objectives, content, ordering and means of assessment are closely linked to the analysis which has been made for each of the specified components.

These considerations imply that:

- throughout the language learning period – and this is equally applicable to schools – there may be continuity with regard to objectives or they may be modified and their order of priority adjusted;
- in a language curriculum accommodating several languages, the objectives and syllabuses of the different languages may either be similar or different;
- quite radically different approaches are possible and each can have its own transparency and coherence with regard to options chosen, and each can be explained with reference to the Framework;
- reflection on the curriculum may therefore involve the consideration of possible scenarios for the development of plurilingual and pluricultural competences and the role of the school in this process.

8.3.2 Some examples of differentiated curriculum scenarios

In the following brief illustration of what might be envisaged by scenario options or variations, two types of organisation and curriculum decisions for a particular school system are outlined, to include, as suggested above, two modern languages other than the language of instruction (conventionally, but mistakenly, referred to below as the native language, since everybody knows that the teaching language, even in Europe, is often not the native language of the pupils): one language starting in primary school (foreign language 1, hereafter FL1) and the other in lower secondary school (foreign language 2, hereafter FL2), with a third (FL3) being introduced as an optional subject at upper secondary level.

In these examples of scenarios a distinction is made between primary, lower secondary and upper secondary which does not correspond to all national education systems. However, these illustrative programmes can easily be transposed and adapted, even in contexts where the range of languages on offer is narrower or where the first institutional learning of a foreign language comes later than primary level. He who can do more can do less. The alternatives offered here include forms of learning for three foreign languages (two out of several on offer forming part of the compulsory programme and the third, which can also be chosen, being offered as an optional extra or in lieu of other optional subjects) because this seems to be the most realistic in the majority of cases and represents a useful basis to illustrate this point. The central argument is that for a given context various scenarios can be conceived and there can be local diversification, provided that in each case due attention is paid to the overall coherence and structure of any particular option.

a) **First scenario:**

Primary school:

The first foreign language (FL1) begins in primary school with the main aim of developing 'language awareness', a general consciousness of linguistic phenomena (relationship with the native language or other languages present in the classroom environment). The focus here is on partial objectives concerned above all with an individual's general competences – (discovery or recognition by the school of the plurality of languages and cultures, preparation for moving away from ethnocentrism, relativisation but also confirmation of the learner's own linguistic and cultural identity; attention paid to body language and gestures, sound aspects, music and rhythm, experience of the physical and aesthetic dimensions of certain elements of another language) – and their relationship with communicative competence, but without there being a structured and explicit attempt to develop this specific competence.

Lower secondary school:

- FL1 continues with the emphasis from now on placed on a gradual development of communicative competence (in its linguistic, sociolinguistic and pragmatic dimensions) but taking full account of achievements at primary level in the area of language awareness.
- The second foreign language (FL2, not taught at primary school) would not start from scratch either; it too would take account of what had been covered at primary school on the basis of and in relation to FL1, whilst at the same time pursuing slightly different objectives from those now pursued in FL1 (for instance, by giving priority to comprehension activities over production activities).

Upper secondary level:

Continuing the example in this scenario, consideration should now be given to:

- reducing the formal teaching of FL1 and using the language instead on a regular or occasional basis for teaching another subject (a form of domain-related learning and 'bilingual education');
- maintaining the emphasis with regard to FL2 on comprehension, concentrating in particular on different text types and the organisation of discourse, and relating this work to what is being done or has already been done in the mother tongue, whilst also using skills learnt in FL1;
- inviting pupils who choose to study the optional third foreign language (FL3) initially to take part in discussions and activities relating to types of learning and learning strategies that they have already experienced; they are then encouraged to work more autonomously, using a resource centre and contributing to the drawing up of a group or individual work programme designed to achieve the objectives set by the group or the institution.

b) **Second scenario:**

Primary school:

The first foreign language (FL1) starts at primary school with the emphasis on basic oral communication and a clearly predetermined linguistic content (with the aim of establishing the beginnings of a basic linguistic component, primarily phonetic and syntactic aspects, while promoting elementary oral interaction in class).

Lower secondary school:

For FL1, FL2 (when this second foreign language is introduced) and the native language, time is spent going over the learning methods and techniques encountered in primary school for FL1 and, separately, for the native language: the aim at this stage would be to promote sensitivity to and increase awareness of the learner's approach to languages and learning activities.

- For FL1 a 'regular' programme designed to develop the different skills continues until the end of secondary school but, at various intervals, this is supplemented with revision and discussion sessions relating to the resources and methods used for teaching and learning so as to accommodate an increasing differentiation between the profiles of different pupils and their expectations and interests.
- For FL2 at this stage particular emphasis could be placed on the sociocultural and sociolinguistic elements as perceived through increasing familiarity with the media (popular press, radio and television) and possibly linked with the native language course and benefiting from what has been covered in FL1. In this curriculum model, FL2, which continues until the end of secondary school, is the main forum for cultural and intercultural discussion fuelled through contact with the other languages in the curriculum and taking media-related texts as its main focus. It could also incorporate the experience of an international exchange with the focus on intercultural relations. Consideration should also be given to using other subjects (e.g. history or geography) to help initiate a well thought-out approach to pluriculturalism.

Upper secondary level:

- FL1 and FL2 each continue in the same direction but at a more complex and demanding level. Learners who opt for a third foreign language (FL3) do so primarily for 'vocational' purposes and relate their language learning to a more professionally-oriented or other academic branch of their studies (for example orientation towards the language of commerce, economics or technology).

It should be stressed that in this second scenario, as in the first, the final plurilingual and pluricultural profile of the learners may be 'uneven' to the extent that:

- the level of proficiency in the languages making up plurilingual competence varies;
- the cultural aspects are unequally developed for the different languages;
- it is not necessarily the case that for the languages in which linguistic aspects received most attention the cultural aspect is also the most developed;
- 'partial' competences, as described above, are integrated.

To these brief indications it may be added that in all cases time should be allowed at some point or other, in the case of all languages, for considering the approaches and learning paths to which learners, in their respective development, are exposed or for which they opt. This implies building into curriculum design at school scope for explicitness, the progressive development of 'learning awareness' and the introduction of general language education which helps learners establish metacognitive control over their own competences and strategies. Learners situate these in relation to other possible competences and strategies and with regard to the language activities in which they are applied in order to accomplish tasks within specific domains.

In other words, one of the aims of curriculum design, whatever the particular curriculum, is to make learners aware of categories and their dynamic interrelationship as proposed in the model adopted for the reference framework.

8.4   Assessment and school, out-of-school and post-school learning

If the curriculum is defined, as suggested by its primary meaning, in terms of the path travelled by a learner through a sequence of educational experiences, whether under the control of an institution or not, then a curriculum does not end with leaving school, but continues in some way or other thereafter in a process of life-long learning.

In this perspective, therefore, the curriculum of the school as institution has the aim of developing in the learner a plurilingual and pluricultural competence which at the end of school studies may take the form of differentiated profiles depending on individuals and the paths they have followed. It is clear that the form of this competence is not immutable and the subsequent personal and professional experiences of each social agent, the direction of his or her life, will cause it to evolve and change its balance through further development, reduction and reshaping. It is here that adult education and continuing training, among other things, play a role. Three complementary aspects may be considered in relation to this.

8.4.1   *The place of the school curriculum*

To accept the notion that the educational curriculum is not limited to school and does not end with it is also to accept that plurilingual and pluricultural competence may begin before school and continue to develop out of school in ways which proceed parallel with its development in school. This may happen through family experience and learning, history and contacts between generations, travel, expatriation, emigration, and more generally belonging to a multilingual and multicultural environment or moving from one environment to another, but also through reading and through the media.

While this is stating the obvious, it is also clear that the school is a long way from always taking this into account. It is therefore useful to think of the school curriculum as part of a much broader curriculum, but a part which also has the function of giving learners:

- an initial differentiated plurilingual and pluricultural repertoire (with some possible ways being suggested in the two scenarios outlined above);
- a better awareness of, knowledge of and confidence in their competences and the capacities and resources available to them, inside and outside the school, so that they may extend and refine these competences and use them effectively in particular domains.

8.4.2   Portfolio and profiling

It follows, therefore, that the recognition and assessment of knowledge and skills should be such as to take account of the circumstances and experiences through which these competences and skills are developed. The development of a *European Language Portfolio (ELP)* enabling an individual to record and present different aspects of his or her language biography represents a step in this direction. It is designed to include not only any officially awarded recognition obtained in the course of learning a particular language but also a record of more informal experiences involving contacts with languages and other cultures.

However, in order to stress the relationship between the school curriculum and the out-of-school curriculum, when language learning is assessed on the completion of secondary education, it would be valuable to try to provide formal recognition for plurilingual and pluricultural competence as such, perhaps by specifying an exit profile which can accommodate varying combinations rather than using as a basis a single predetermined level in a given language, or languages, as the case may be.

'Official' recognition of partial competences may be a step in this direction (and it would be helpful if the major international qualifications were to show the way by adopting such an approach, for example by acknowledging separately the four skills covered by comprehension/expression and written/spoken, and not necessarily all of them grouped together). But it would be helpful if the ability to cope with several languages or cultures could also be taken into account and recognised. Translating (or summarising) a second foreign language into a first foreign language, participating in an oral discussion involving several languages, interpreting a cultural phenomenon in relation to another culture, are examples of mediation (as defined in this document) which have their place to play in assessing and rewarding the ability to manage a plurilingual and pluricultural repertoire.

8.4.3   A multidimensional and modular approach

This chapter aims to draw attention generally to the shift in focus or at least the increasing complexity of curriculum design, and the implications for assessment and certification. It is clearly important to define stages in relation to content and progression. This may be done in terms of one primary component (linguistic or notional/functional, for example) or in terms of promoting progress in all dimensions for a particular language. It is equally important to distinguish clearly the components of a *multidimensional curriculum* (taking account in particular of the different dimensions of the reference framework) and to differentiate methods of evaluation, working towards *modular* learning and certification arrangements. This would permit, synchronically (i.e. at a given moment in the learning path) or diachronically (i.e. through differentiated stages along this path), the development and recognition of plurilingual and pluricultural competences with 'variable geometry' (i.e. the components and structure of which vary from one individual to another and change over time for a given individual).

At certain times in the learner's school career, following the school curriculum and the scenarios outlined briefly above, short cross-curricular modules involving the various languages might be introduced. Such 'translanguage' modules could encompass the various learning approaches and resources, ways of using the out-of-school environment, and dealing with misunderstandings in intercultural relations. They would give greater overall coherence and transparency to the underlying curricular choices and would improve the general structure without upsetting the programmes devised for other subjects.

Furthermore, a modular approach to qualifications would enable a specific assessment to be made, in an *ad hoc* module, of the plurilingual and pluricultural management abilities referred to above.

Multidimensionality and modularity thus appear as key concepts in developing a sound basis for linguistic diversification in the curriculum and in assessment. The reference framework is structured in a manner that allows it, through the categories it offers, to indicate the directions for such a modular or multidimensional organisation. However, the way forward is clearly to implement projects and experimental work in the school environment and in a variety of contexts.

Users of the Framework may wish to consider and where appropriate state:

- *whether the learners concerned already have some experience of linguistic and cultural plurality, and the nature of this experience;*
- *whether learners are already able, even if only at a very basic level, to function in several linguistic and/or cultural communities, and how this competence is distributed and differentiated according to the contexts of language use and activities;*
- *what experience of linguistic and cultural diversity learners may have at the time of their learning (for example parallel to and outside their attendance at a learning institution);*
- *how this experience might be built on in the learning process;*
- *what types of objectives appear best suited to learners (see section 1.2) at a particular point in the development of a plurilingual and pluricultural competence, taking account of their characteristics, expectations, interests, plans and needs as well as their previous learning path and their existing resources;*
- *how to encourage, for the learners concerned, the decompartmentalisation and establishment of an effective relationship between the different components of plurilingual and pluricultural competence in the process of being developed; in particular, how to focus attention on and draw on the learners' existing transferable and transversal knowledge and skills;*
- *which partial competences (of what kind and for what purposes) might enrich, complexify and differentiate learners' existing competences;*
- *how to fit learning concerned with a particular language or culture coherently into an overall curriculum in which the experience of several languages and several cultures is developed:*
- *what options or what forms of differentiation in curriculum scenarios exist for managing the development of a diversified competence for particular learners; what economies of scale can be envisaged and achieved, if appropriate;*
- *what forms of organisation of learning (a modular approach, for example) are likely to favour management of the learning path in the case of the learners in question;*
- *what approach to evaluation or assessment will make it possible to take account of and accord proper recognition to the partial competences and the diversified plurilingual and pluricultural competence of learners.*

---

9 Assessment

9.1 Introduction

Assessment is used in this chapter in the sense of the assessment of the proficiency of the language user. All language tests are a form of assessment, but there are also many forms of assessment (e.g. checklists used in continuous assessment; informal teacher observation) which would not be described as tests. Evaluation is a term which is again broader than assessment. All assessment is a form of evaluation, but in a language programme a number of things are evaluated other than learner proficiency. These may include the effectiveness of particular methods or materials, the kind and quality of discourse actually produced in the programme, learner/teacher satisfaction, teaching effectiveness, etc. This chapter is concerned with assessment, and not with broader issues of programme evaluation.

There are three concepts that are traditionally seen as fundamental to any discussion of assessment: validity, reliability and feasibility. It is useful in relation to the discussion in this chapter to have an overview of what is meant by these terms, how they relate to one another, and how they are relevant to the Framework.

Validity is the concept with which the Framework is concerned. A test or assessment procedure can be said to have validity to the degree that it can be demonstrated that what is actually assessed (the construct) is what, in the context concerned, *should* be assessed, and that the information gained is an accurate representation of the proficiency of the candidates(s) concerned.

Reliability, on the other hand, is a technical term. It is basically the extent to which the same rank order of candidates is replicated in two separate (real or simulated) administrations of the same assessment.

What is in fact more important than reliability is the *accuracy of decisions* made in relation to a standard. If the assessment reports results as pass/fail or Levels A2+/B1/B1+, how accurate are these decisions? The accuracy of the decisions will depend on the validity of the particular standard (e.g. Level B1) for the context. It will also depend on the validity of the criteria used to reach the decision and the validity of the procedures with which those criteria were developed.

If two different organisations or regions use criteria related to the same standards in order to inform their assessment decisions for the same skill, if the standards themselves are valid and appropriate for the two contexts concerned, and if the standards are interpreted consistently in the design of the assessment tasks and the interpretation of the performances, the results in the two systems will correlate. Traditionally the correlation between two tests thought to assess the same construct is known as '*concurrent validity*'.

This concept is obviously related to reliability, since unreliable tests will not correlate. However, what is more central is the extent of communality between the two tests regarding *what is assessed*, and *how performance is interpreted*.

It is with these two questions that the Common European Framework is concerned. The next section outlines three main ways in which the Framework can be used:

1.	For the specification of the content of tests and examinations:	*what is assessed*
2.	For stating the criteria to determine the attainment of a learning objective:	*how performance is interpreted*
3.	For describing the levels of proficiency in existing tests and examinations thus enabling comparisons to be made across different systems of qualifications:	*how comparisons can be made*

These issues relate to different kinds of assessment in different ways. There are many different kinds and traditions of assessment. It is a mistake to assume that one approach (e.g. a public examination) is necessarily superior in its educational effects to another approach (e.g. teacher assessment). It is indeed a major advantage of a set of common standards – such as the Common Reference Levels of the Framework – that they make it possible to relate different forms of assessment to one another.

The third section of the chapter lays out choices between different types of assessment. The choices are presented in the form of contrasting pairs. In each case the terms used are defined and the relative advantages and disadvantages are discussed in relation to the purpose of the assessment in its educational context. The implications of exercising one or another of the alternative options are also stated. The relevance of the Framework to the type of assessment concerned is then pointed out.

An assessment procedure also needs to be practical, to be *feasible*. Feasibility is particularly an issue with performance testing. Assessors operate under time pressure. They are only seeing a limited sample of performance and there are definite limits to the type and number of categories they can handle as criteria. The Framework seeks to provide a point of reference, not a practical assessment tool. The Framework must be comprehensive, but all its users must be selective. Selectivity may well involve the use of a simpler operational scheme, which collapses categories separated in the Framework. For instance, the categories used in the illustrative scales of descriptors juxtaposed to the text in Chapters 4 and 5 are frequently considerably simpler than the categories and exponents discussed in the text itself. The final section of this chapter discusses this issue, with examples.

9.2 The Framework as a resource for assessment

9.2.1 The specification of the content of tests and examinations

The description of 'Language Use and the Language User', in Chapter 4 and in particular section 4.4 on 'Communicative Language Activities', can be consulted when drawing up a task specification for a communicative assessment. It is increasingly recognised that valid assessment requires the sampling of a range of relevant types of discourse. For example, in relation to the testing of speaking, a recently developed test illustrates this point. First, there is a simulated *Conversation* which functions as a warm up; then there is an *Informal Discussion* of topical issues in which the candidate declares an interest. This is followed by a *Transaction* phase, which takes the form either of a face-to-face or simulated telephone information seeking activity. This is followed by a *Production* phase, based upon a written *Report* in which the candidate gives a *Description* of his/her academic field and plans. Finally there is a *Goal-orientated Co-operation*, a consensus task between candidates.

To summarise, the Framework categories for communicative activities employed are:

	Interaction (Spontaneous, short turns)	**Production** (Prepared, long turns)
Spoken:	*Conversation* *Informal discussion* *Goal-orientated co-operation*	*Description* of his/her academic field
Written:		*Report/Description* of his/her academic field

In constructing the detail of the task specifications the user may wish to consult section 4.1, on 'the context of language use' (domains, conditions and constraints, mental context), section 4.6 on 'Texts', and Chapter 7 on 'Tasks and their Role in Language Teaching', specifically section 7.3 on 'Task difficulty'.

Section 5.2 on 'Communicative language competences' will inform the construction of the test items, or phases of a spoken test, in order to elicit evidence of the relevant linguistic, sociolinguistic and pragmatic competences. The set of content specifications at Threshold Level produced by the Council of Europe for over 20 European languages (see Bibliography items listed on p. 200) and at Waystage and Vantage Level for English, plus their equivalents when developed for other languages and levels, can be seen as ancillary to the main Framework document. They offer examples of a further layer of detail to inform test construction for Levels A1, A2, B1 and B2.

9.2.2 The criteria for the attainment of a learning objective

The scales provide a source for the development of rating scales for the assessment of the attainment of a particular learning objective and the descriptors may assist in the formulation of criteria. The objective may be a broad level of general language proficiency, expressed as a Common Reference Level (e.g. B1). It may on the other hand be a specific constellation of activities, skills and competences as discussed in section 6.1.4 on 'Partial Competences and Variation in Objectives in relation to the Framework'. Such a modular objective might be profiled on a grid of categories by levels, such as that presented in Table 2.

In discussing the use of descriptors it is essential to make a distinction between:

1. Descriptors of communicative activities, which are located in Chapter 4.
2. Descriptors of aspects of proficiency related to particular competences, which are located in Chapter 5.

The former are very suitable for teacher- or self-assessment with regard to real-world tasks. Such teacher- or self-assessments are made on the basis of a detailed picture of the learner's language ability built up during the course concerned. They are attractive because they can help to focus both learners and teachers on an action-oriented approach.

However, it is *not* usually advisable to include descriptors of communicative activities in the criteria for an assessor to rate performance in a particular speaking or writing test if one is interested in reporting results in terms of a level of proficiency attained. This is because to report on proficiency, the assessment should not be primarily concerned with any one particular performance, but should rather seek to judge the generalisable competences evidenced by that performance. There may of course be sound educational reasons for focusing on success at completing a given activity, especially with younger Basic Users (Levels A1; A2). Such results will be less generalisable, but generalisability of results is not usually the focus of attention in the earlier stages of language learning.

This reinforces the fact that assessments can have many different functions. What is appropriate for one assessment purpose may be inappropriate for another.

9.2.2.1 Descriptors of communicative activities

Descriptors of communicative activities (Chapter 4) can be used in three separate ways in relation to the attainment of objectives.

1. **Construction**: As discussed above in section 9.2.1 scales for communicative activities help in the definition of a specification for the design of assessment tasks.

2. **Reporting**: Scales for communicative activities can also be very useful for reporting results. Users of the products of the educational system, such as employers, are often interested in the overall outcomes rather than in a detailed profile of competence.

3. **Self- or teacher-assessment**: Finally, descriptors for communicative activities can be used for self- and teacher-assessment in various ways, of which the following are some examples:

   • *Checklist:* For continuous assessment or for summative assessment at the end of a course. The descriptors at a particular level can be listed. Alternatively, the content of descriptors can be 'exploded'. For example the descriptor *Can ask for and provide personal information* might be exploded into the implicit constituent parts *I can introduce myself; I can say where I live; I can say my address in French; I can say how old I am*, etc. and *I can ask someone what their name is; I can ask someone where they live; I can ask someone how old they are,* etc.

   • *Grid:* For continuous or summative assessment, rating a profile onto a grid of selected categories (e.g. *Conversation; Discussion; Exchanging Information*) defined at different levels (B1+, B2, B2+).

The use of descriptors in this way has become more common in the last 10 years. Experience has shown that the consistency with which teachers and learners can interpret descriptors is enhanced if the descriptors describe not only WHAT the learner can do, but also HOW WELL they do it.

9.2.2.2   Descriptors of aspects of proficiency related to particular competences

Descriptors of aspects of proficiency can be used in two main ways in relation to the attainment of objectives.

1. *Self- or teacher-assessment:* Provided the descriptors are *positive, independent statements* they can be included in checklists for self- and teacher-assessment. However, it is a weakness of the majority of existing scales that the descriptors are often negatively worded at lower levels and norm-referenced around the middle of the scale. They also often make purely verbal distinctions between levels by replacing one or two words in adjacent descriptions which then have little meaning outside the co-text of the scale. Appendix A discusses ways of developing descriptors that avoid these problems.

2. *Performance assessment:* A more obvious use for scales of descriptors on aspects of competence from Chapter 5 is to offer starting points for the development of assessment criteria. By guiding personal, non-systematic impressions into considered judgements, such descriptors can help develop a shared frame of reference among the group of assessors concerned.

There are basically three ways in which descriptors can be presented for use as assessment criteria:

•   Firstly, descriptors can be presented as a *scale* – often combining descriptors for different categories into one holistic paragraph per level. This is a very common approach.

•   Secondly, they can be presented as a *checklist*, usually with one checklist per relevant level, often with descriptors grouped under headings, i.e. under categories. Checklists are less usual for live assessment.

•   Thirdly, they can be presented as a *grid* of selected categories, in effect as a set of parallel scales for separate categories. This approach makes it possible to give a diagnostic profile. However, there are limits to the number of categories that assessors can cope with.

There are two distinctly different ways in which one can provide a grid of sub-scales:

Proficiency Scale: by providing a profile grid defining the relevant levels for certain categories, for example from Levels A2 to B2. Assessment is then made directly onto those levels, possibly using further refinements like a second digit or pluses to give greater differentiation if desired. Thus even though the performance test was aimed at Level B1, and even if none of the learners had reached Level B2, it would still be possible for stronger learners to be credited with B1+, B1++ or B1.8.

Examination Rating Scale: by selecting or defining a descriptor for each relevant category which describes the desired pass standard or norm for a particular module or examination for that category. That descriptor is then named 'Pass' or '3' and the scale is norm-referenced around that standard (a very weak performance = '1', an excellent performance = '5'). The formulation of '1' & '5' might be other descriptors drawn or adapted from the adjacent levels on the scale from the appropriate section of Chapter 5, or the descriptor may be formulated in relation to the wording of the descriptor defined as '3'.

9.2.3 Describing the levels of proficiency in tests and examinations to aid comparison

The scales for the Common References Levels are intended to facilitate the description of the level of proficiency attained in existing qualifications – and so aid comparison between systems. The measurement literature recognises five classic ways of linking separate assessments: (1) equating; (2) calibrating; (3) statistical moderation; (4) benchmarking, and (5) social moderation.

The first three methods are traditional: (1) producing alternative versions of the same test (equating), (2) linking the results from different tests to a common scale (calibrating), and (3) correcting for the difficulty of test papers or the severity of examiners (statistical moderation).

The last two methods involve building up a common understanding through discussion (social moderation) and the comparison of work samples in relation to standardised definitions and examples (benchmarking). Supporting this process of building a common understanding is one of the aims of the Framework. This is the reason why the scales of descriptors to be used for this purpose have been standardised with a rigorous development methodology. In education this approach is increasingly described as standards-oriented assessment. It is generally acknowledged that the development of a standards-oriented approach takes time, as partners acquire a feel for the meaning of the standards through the process of exemplification and exchange of opinions.

It can be argued that this approach is potentially the strongest method of linking because it involves the development and validation of a common view of the construct. The fundamental reason why it is difficult to link language assessments, despite the statistical wizardry of traditional techniques, is that the assessments generally test radically different things even when they are intending to cover the same domains. This is partly due to (a) under-conceptualisation and under-operationalisation of the construct, and partly to due to (b) related interference from the method of testing.

The Framework offers a principled attempt to provide a solution to the first and underlying problem in relation to modern language learning in a European context. Chapters 4 to 7 elaborate a descriptive scheme, which tries to conceptualise language use, competences and the processes of teaching and learning in a practical way which will help partners to operationalise the communicative language ability we wish to promote.

The scales of descriptors make up a conceptual grid which can be used to:

a) relate national and institutional frameworks to each other, through the medium of the Common Framework;
b) map the objectives of particular examinations and course modules using the categories and levels of the scales.

Appendix A provides readers with an overview of methods to develop scales of descriptors, and relate them to the Framework scale.

The User Guide for Examiners produced by ALTE (Document CC-Lang (96) 10 rev) provides detailed advice on operationalising constructs in tests, and avoiding unnecessary distortion though test method effects.

9.3 Types of assessment

A number of important distinctions can be made in relation to assessment. The following list is by no means exhaustive. There is no significance to whether one term in the distinction is placed on the left or on the right.

Table 7. *Types of assessment*

1	Achievement assessment	Proficiency assessment
2	Norm-referencing (NR)	Criterion-referencing (CR)
3	Mastery learning CR	Continuum CR
4	Continuous assessment	Fixed assessment points
5	Formative assessment	Summative assessment
6	Direct assessment	Indirect assessment
7	Performance assessment	Knowledge assessment
8	Subjective assessment	Objective assessment
9	Checklist rating	Performance rating
10	Impression	Guided judgement
11	Holistic assessment	Analytic assessment
12	Series assessment	Category assessment
13	Assessment by others	Self-assessment

9.3.1 Achievement assessment/proficiency assessment

Achievement assessment is the assessment of the achievement of specific objectives – assessment of what has been taught. It therefore relates to the week's/term's work, the course book, the syllabus. Achievement assessment is oriented to the course. It represents an internal perspective.

Proficiency assessment on the other hand is assessment of what someone can do/knows in relation to the application of the subject in the real world. It represents an external perspective.

Teachers have a natural tendency to be more interested in achievement assessment in order to get feedback for teaching. Employers, educational administrators and adult learners tend to be more interested in proficiency assessment: assessment of outcomes, what the person can now do. The advantage of an achievement approach is that it is close to the learner's experience. The advantage of a proficiency approach is that it helps everyone to see where they stand; results are transparent.

In communicative testing in a needs-oriented teaching and learning context one can argue that the distinction between achievement (oriented to the content of the course) and proficiency (oriented to the continuum of real world ability) should ideally be small. To the extent that an achievement assessment tests practical language use in relevant situations and aims to offer a balanced picture of emerging competence, it has a proficiency angle. To the extent that a proficiency assessment consists of language and communicative tasks based on a transparent relevant syllabus, giving the learner the opportunity to show what they have achieved, that test has an achievement element.

The scales of illustrative descriptors relate to proficiency assessment: the continuum of real world ability. The importance of achievement testing as a reinforcement to learning is discussed in Chapter 6.

9.3.2 Norm-referencing (NR)/criterion-referencing (CR)

Norm-referencing is the placement of learners in rank order, their assessment and ranking in relation to their peers.

Criterion-referencing is a reaction against norm-referencing in which the learner is assessed purely in terms of his/her ability in the subject, irrespective of the ability of his/her peers.

Norm-referencing can be undertaken in relation to the class (you are 18th) or the demographic cohort (you are 21,567th; you are in the top 14%) or the group of learners taking a test. In the latter case, raw test scores may be adjusted to give a 'fair' result by plotting the distribution curve of the test results onto the curve from previous years in order to maintain a standard and ensure that the same percentage of learners are given 'A' grades every year, irrespective of the difficulty of the test or the ability of the pupils. A common use of norm-referenced assessment is in placement tests to form classes.

Criterion-referencing implies the mapping of the continuum of proficiency (vertical) and range of relevant domains (horizontal) so that individual results on a test can be situated in relation to the total criterion space. This involves (a) the definition of the relevant domain(s) covered by the particular test/module, and (b) the identification of 'cut-off points': the score(s) on the test deemed necessary to meet the proficiency standard set.

The scales of illustrative descriptors are made up of criterion statements for categories in the descriptive scheme. The Common Reference Levels present a set of common standards.

9.3.3 Mastery CR/continuum CR

The *mastery criterion-referencing* approach is one in which a single 'minimum competence standard' or 'cut-off point' is set to divide learners into 'masters' and 'non-masters', with no degrees of quality in the achievement of the objective being recognised.

The *continuum criterion-referencing* approach is an approach in which an individual ability is referenced to a defined continuum of all relevant degrees of ability in the area in question.

There are in fact many approaches to CR, but most of them can be identified as primarily a 'mastery learning' or 'continuum' interpretation. Much confusion is caused by the misidentification of criterion-referencing exclusively with the mastery approach. The mastery approach is an achievement approach related to the content of the course/module. It puts less emphasis on situating that module (and so achievement in it) on the continuum of proficiency.

The alternative to the mastery approach is to reference results from each test to the relevant continuum of proficiency, usually with a series of grades. In this approach, that continuum is the 'criterion', the external reality which ensures that the test results mean something. Referencing to this external criterion can be undertaken with a scalar analysis (e.g. Rasch model) to relate results from all the tests to each other and so report results directly onto a common scale.

The Framework can be exploited with mastery or continuum approach. The scale of levels used in a continuum approach can be matched to the Common Reference Levels; the objective to be mastered in a mastery approach can be mapped onto the conceptual grid of categories and levels offered by the Framework.

9.3.4 Continuous assessment/fixed point assessment

Continuous assessment is assessment by the teacher and possibly by the learner of class performances, pieces of work and projects throughout the course. The final grade thus reflects the whole course/year/semester.

Fixed point assessment is when grades are awarded and decisions made on the basis of an examination or other assessment which takes place on a particular day, usually the end of the course or before the beginning of a course. What has happened beforehand is irrelevant; it is what the person can do now that is decisive.

Assessment is often seen as something outside the course which takes place at fixed points in order to make decisions. Continuous assessment implies assessment which is integrated into the course and which contributes in some cumulative way to the assessment at the end of the course. Apart from marking homework and occasional or regular short achievement tests to reinforce learning, continuous assessment may take the form of checklists/grids completed by teachers and/or learners, assessment in a series of focused tasks, formal assessment of coursework, and/or the establishment of a portfolio of samples of work, possibly in differing stages of drafting, and/or at different stages in the course.

Both approaches have advantages and disadvantages. Fixed point assessment assures that people can still do things that might have been on the syllabus two years ago. But it leads to examination traumas and favours certain types of learners. Continuous assessment allows more account to be taken of creativity and different strengths, but is very much dependent on the teacher's capacity to be objective. It can, if taken to an extreme, turn life into one long never-ending test for the learner and a bureaucratic nightmare for the teacher.

Checklists of criterion statements describing ability with regard to communicative activities (Chapter 4) can be useful for continuous assessment. Rating scales developed in relation to the descriptors for aspects of competence (Chapter 5) can be used to award grades in fixed point assessment.

9.3.5 *Formative assessment/summative assessment*

Formative assessment is an ongoing process of gathering information on the extent of learning, on strengths and weaknesses, which the teacher can feed back into their course planning and the actual feedback they give learners. Formative assessment is often used in a very broad sense so as to include non-quantifiable information from questionnaires and consultations.

Summative assessment sums up attainment at the end of the course with a grade. It is not necessarily proficiency assessment. Indeed a lot of summative assessment is norm-referenced, fixed-point, achievement assessment.

The strength of formative assessment is that it aims to improve learning. The weakness of formative assessment is inherent in the metaphor of feedback. Feedback only works if the recipient is in a position (a) *to notice*, i.e. is attentive, motivated and familiar with the form in which the information is coming, (b) *to receive*, i.e. is not swamped with information, has a way of recording, organising and personalising it; (c) *to interpret*, i.e. has sufficient pre-knowledge and awareness to understand the point at issue, and not to take counterproductive action and (d) *to integrate* the information, i.e. has the time, orientation and relevant resources to reflect on, integrate and so remember the new information. This implies self-direction, which implies training towards self-direction, monitoring one's own learning, and developing ways of acting on feedback.

Such learner training or awareness raising has been called *évaluation formatrice*. A variety of techniques may be used for this awareness training. A basic principle is to compare impression (e.g. what you say you can do on a checklist) with the reality, (e.g. actually listening to material of the type mentioned in the checklist and seeing if you do understand it). DIALANG relates self-assessment to test performance in this way. Another important technique is discussing samples of work – both neutral examples and samples from learners and encouraging them to develop a personalised metalanguage on aspects of quality. They can then use this metalanguage to monitor their work for strengths and weaknesses and to formulate a self-directed learning contract.

Most formative or diagnostic assessment operates at a very detailed level of the particular language points or skills recently taught or soon to be covered. For diagnostic assessment the lists of exponents given in section 5.2 are still too generalised to be of practical use; one would need to refer to the particular specification which was relevant (Waystage, Threshold, etc.). Grids consisting of descriptors defining different aspects of competence at different levels (Chapter 4) can, however, be useful to give formative feedback from a speaking assessment.

The Common Reference Levels would appear to be most relevant to summative assessment. However, as the DIALANG Project demonstrates, feedback from even a summative assessment can be diagnostic and so formative.

9.3.6 *Direct assessment/indirect assessment*

Direct assessment is assessing what the candidate is actually doing. For example, a small group are discussing something, the assessor observes, compares with a criteria grid, matches the performances to the most appropriate categories on the grid, and gives an assessment.

Indirect assessment, on the other hand, uses a test, usually on paper, which often assesses enabling skills.

Direct assessment is effectively limited to speaking, writing and listening in interaction, since you can never see receptive activity directly. Reading can, for example, only be assessed indirectly by requiring learners to demonstrate evidence of understanding by ticking boxes, finishing sentences, answering questions, etc. Linguistic range and control can be assessed either directly through judging the match to criteria or indirectly by interpreting and generalising from the responses to test questions. A classic direct test is an interview; a classic indirect test is a cloze.

Descriptors defining different aspects of competence at different levels in Chapter 5 can be used to develop assessment criteria for direct tests. The parameters in Chapter 4 can inform the selection of themes, texts and test tasks for direct tests of the productive skills and indirect tests of listening and reading. The parameters of Chapter 5 can in addition inform the identification of key linguistic competences to include in an indirect test of language knowledge, and of key pragmatic, sociolinguistic and linguistic competences to focus on in the formulation of test questions for item-based tests of the four skills.

9.3.7 *Performance assessment/knowledge assessment*

Performance assessment requires the learner to provide a sample of language in speech or writing in a direct test.

Knowledge assessment requires the learner to answer questions which can be of a range of different item types in order to provide evidence of the extent of their linguistic knowledge and control.

Unfortunately one can never test competences directly. All one ever has to go on is a range of performances, from which one seeks to generalise about proficiency. Proficiency can be seen as competence put to use. In this sense, therefore, all tests assess only performance, though one may seek to draw inferences as to the underlying competences from this evidence.

However, an interview requires more of a 'performance' than filling gaps in sentences, and gap-filling in turn requires more 'performance' than multiple choice. In this sense the word 'performance' is being used to mean the production of language. But the word 'performance' is used in a more restricted sense in the expression 'performance tests'. Here the word is taken to mean a relevant performance in a (relatively) authentic and often work or study-related situation. In a slightly looser use of this term 'performance assessment', oral assessment procedures could be said to be performance tests in that they generalise about proficiency from performances in a range of discourse styles considered to be relevant to the learning context and needs of the learners. Some tests balance the performance assessment with an assessment of knowledge of the language as a system; others do not.

This distinction is very similar to the one between direct and indirect tests. The Framework can be exploited in a similar way. The Council of Europe specifications for different levels (Waystage, Threshold Level, Vantage Level) offer in addition appropriate detail on target language knowledge in the languages for which they are available.

9.3.8   *Subjective assessment/objective assessment*

Subjective assessment is a judgement by an assessor. What is normally meant by this is the judgement of the quality of a performance.

Objective assessment is assessment in which subjectivity is removed. What is normally meant by this is an indirect test in which the items have only one right answer, e.g. multiple choice.

However the issue of subjectivity/objectivity is considerably more complex.

An indirect test is often described as an 'objective test' when the marker consults a definitive key to decide whether to accept or reject an answer and then counts correct responses to give the result. Some test types take this process a stage further by only having one possible answer to each question (e.g. multiple choice, and c-tests, which were developed from cloze for this reason), and machine marking is often adopted to eliminate marker error. In fact the objectivity of tests described as 'objective' in this way is somewhat over-stated since someone decided to restrict the assessment to techniques offering more control over the test situation (itself a subjective decision others may disagree with). Someone then wrote the test specification, and someone else may have written the item as an attempt to operationalise a particular point in the specification. Finally, someone selected the item from all the other possible items for this test. Since all those decisions involve an element of subjectivity, such tests are perhaps better described as objectively scored tests.

In direct performance assessment grades are generally awarded on the basis of a judgement. That means that the decision as to how well the learner performs is made subjectively, taking relevant factors into account and referring to any guidelines or criteria and experience. The advantage of a subjective approach is that language and communication are very complex, do not lend themselves to atomisation and are greater than the sum of their parts. It is very often difficult to establish what exactly a test item is testing. Therefore to target test items on specific aspects of competence or performance is a lot less straightforward than it sounds.

Yet, in order to be fair, all assessment should be as objective as possible. The effects of the personal value judgements involved in subjective decisions about the selection of content and the quality of performance should be reduced as far as possible, particularly where summative assessment is concerned. This is because test results are very often used by third parties to make decisions about the future of the persons who have been assessed.

Subjectivity in assessment can be reduced, and validity and reliability thus increased by taking steps like the following:

- developing a **specification for the content** of the assessment, for example based upon a framework of reference common to the context involved
- using **pooled judgements** to select content and/or to rate performances
- adopting **standard procedures** governing how the assessments should be carried out
- providing **definitive marking keys** for indirect tests and basing judgements in direct tests on **specific defined criteria**
- requiring **multiple judgements** and/or **weighting of different factors**
- undertaking appropriate **training** in relation to **assessment guidelines**

- checking the quality of the assessment (validity, reliability) by *analysing assessment data*

As discussed at the beginning of this chapter, the first step towards reducing the subjectivity of judgements made at all stages in the assessment process is to build a common understanding of the construct involved, a common frame of reference. The Framework seeks to offer such a basis for the *specification for the content* and a source for the development of *specific defined criteria* for direct tests.

9.3.9   Rating on a scale/rating on a checklist

Rating on a scale: judging that a person is at a particular level or band on a scale made up of a number of such levels or bands.

Rating on a checklist: judging a person in relation to a list of points deemed to be relevant for a particular level or module.

In 'rating on a scale' the emphasis is on placing the person rated on a series of bands. The emphasis is vertical: how far up the scale does he/she come? The meaning of the different bands/levels should be made clear by scale descriptors. There may be several scales for different categories, and these may be presented on the same page as a grid or on different pages. There may be a definition for each band/level or for alternate ones, or for the top, bottom and middle.

The alternative is a checklist, on which the emphasis is on showing that relevant ground has been covered, i.e. the emphasis is horizontal: how much of the content of the module has he/she successfully accomplished? The checklist may be presented as a list of points like a questionnaire. It may on the other hand be presented as a wheel, or in some other shape. The response may be Yes/No. The response may be more differentiated, with a series of steps (e.g. 0–4) preferably with steps identified with labels, with definitions explaining how the labels should be interpreted.

Because the illustrative descriptors constitute independent, criterion statements which have been calibrated to the levels concerned, they can be used as a source to produce *both* a checklist for a particular level, as in some versions of the Language Portfolio, *and* rating scales or grids covering all relevant levels, as presented in Chapter 3, for self-assessment in Table 2 and for examiner assessment in Table 3.

9.3.10   Impression/guided judgement

Impression: fully subjective judgement made on the basis of experience of the learner's performance in class, without reference to specific criteria in relation to a specific assessment.

Guided judgement: judgement in which individual assessor subjectivity is reduced by complementing impression with conscious assessment in relation to specific criteria.

An 'impression' is here used to mean when a teacher or learner rates purely on the basis of their experience of performance in class, homework, etc. Many forms of subjective rating, especially those used in continuous assessment, involve rating an impression on the basis of reflection or memory possibly focused by conscious observation of the person concerned over a period of time. Very many school systems operate on this basis.

The term 'guided judgement' is here used to describe the situation in which that impression is guided into a considered judgement through an assessment approach. Such an approach implies (a) an assessment activity with some form of procedure, and/or (b) a set of defined criteria which distinguish between the different scores or grades, and (c) some form of standardisation training. The advantage of the guided approach to judging is that if a common framework of reference for the group of assessors concerned is established in this way, the consistency of judgements can be radically increased. This is especially the case if 'benchmarks' are provided in the form of samples of performance and fixed links to other systems. The importance of such guidance is underlined by the fact that research in a number of disciplines has shown repeatedly that with untrained judgements the differences in the severity of the assessors can account for nearly as much of the differences in the assessment of learners as does their actual ability, leaving results almost purely to chance.

The scales of descriptors for the common reference levels can be exploited to provide a set of defined criteria as described in (b) above, or to map the standards represented by existing criteria in terms of the common levels. In the future, benchmark samples of performance at different common reference levels may be provided to assist in standardisation training.

9.3.11   Holistic/analytic

Holistic assessment is making a global synthetic judgement. Different aspects are weighted intuitively by the assessor.

Analytic assessment is looking at different aspects separately.

There are two ways in which this distinction can be made: (a) in terms of what is looked for; (b) in terms of how a band, grade or score is arrived at. Systems sometimes combine an analytic approach at one level with a holistic approach at another.

a)   What to assess: some approaches assess a global category like 'speaking' or 'interaction', assigning one score or grade. Others, more analytic, require the assessor to assign separate results to a number of independent aspects of performance. Yet other approaches require the assessor to note a global impression, analyse by different categories and then come to a considered holistic judgement. The advantage of the separate categories of an analytic approach is that they encourage the assessor to observe closely. They provide a metalanguage for negotiation between assessors, and for feedback to learners. The disadvantage is that a wealth of evidence suggests that assessors cannot easily keep the categories separate from a holistic judgement. They also get cognitive overload when presented with more than four or five categories.

b)   Calculating the result: some approaches holistically match observed performance to descriptors on a rating scale, whether the scale is holistic (one global scale) or analytic (3–6 categories in a grid). Such approaches involve no arithmetic. Results are reported either as a single number or as a 'telephone number' across categories. Other more analytical approaches require giving a certain mark for a number of different points and then adding them up to give a score, which may then convert into a grade. It is characteristic of this approach that the categories are weighted, i.e. the categories do not each account for an equal number of points.

Tables 2 and 3 in Chapter 3 provide self-assessment and examiner assessment examples respectively of *analytic* scales of criteria (i.e. grids) used with a *holistic* rating strategy (i.e. match what you can deduce from the performance to the definitions, and make a judgement).

9.3.12 Series assessment/category assessment

Category assessment involves a single assessment task (which may well have different phases to generate different discourse as discussed in section 9.2.1.) in which performance is judged in relation to the categories in an assessment grid: the analytic approach outlined in 9.3.11.

Series assessment involves a series of isolated assessment tasks (often roleplays with other learners or the teacher), which are rated with a simple holistic grade on a labelled scale of e.g. 0–3 or 1–4.

A series assessment is one way of coping with the tendency in category assessments for results on one category to affect those on another. At lower levels the emphasis tends to be on task achievement, the aim is to fill out a checklist of what the learner can do on the basis of teacher/learner assessment of actual performances rather than simple impression. At higher levels, tasks may be designed to show particular aspects of proficiency in the performance. Results are reported as a profile.

The scales for different categories of language competence juxtaposed with the text in Chapter 5 offer a source for the development of the criteria for a category assessment. Since assessors can only cope with a small number of categories, compromises have to be made in the process. The elaboration of relevant types of communicative activities in section 4.4. and the list of different types of functional competence outlined in section 5.2.3.2 may inform the identification of suitable tasks for a series assessment.

9.3.13 Assessment by others/self-assessment

Assessment by others: judgements by the teacher or examiner.
Self-assessment: judgements about your own proficiency.
Learners can be involved in many of the assessment techniques outlined above. Research suggests that provided 'high stakes' (e.g. whether or not you will be accepted for a course) are not involved, self-assessment can be an effective complement to tests and teacher assessment. Accuracy in self-assessment is increased (a) when assessment is in relation to clear descriptors defining standards of proficiency and/or (b) when assessment is related to a specific experience. This experience may itself even be a test activity. It is also probably made more accurate when learners receive some training. Such structured self-assessment can achieve correlations to teachers' assessments and tests equal to the correlation (level of concurrent validation) commonly reported between teachers themselves, between tests and between teacher assessment and tests.

The main potential for self-assessment, however, is in its use as a tool for motivation and awareness raising: helping learners to appreciate their strengths, recognise their weaknesses and orient their learning more effectively.

Users of the Framework may wish to consider and where appropriate state:

- *which of the types of assessment listed above are:*
  - *more relevant to the needs of the learner in their system*
  - *more appropriate and feasible in the pedagogic culture of their system*
  - *more rewarding in terms of teacher development through 'washback' effect*
- *the way in which the assessment of achievement (school-oriented; learning-oriented) and the assessment of proficiency (real world-oriented; outcome-oriented) are balanced and complemented in their system, and the extent to which communicative performance is assessed as well as linguistic knowledge.*
- *the extent to which the results of learning are assessed in relation to defined standards and criteria (criterion-referencing) and the extent to which grades and evaluations are assigned on the basis of the class a learner is in (norm-referencing).*
- *the extent to which teachers are:*
  - *informed about standards (e.g. common descriptors, samples of performance)*
  - *encouraged to become aware of a range of assessment techniques*
  - *trained in techniques and interpretation*
- *the extent to which it is desirable and feasible to develop an integrated approach to continuous assessment of coursework and fixed point assessment in relation to related standards and criteria definitions*
- *the extent to which it is desirable and feasible to involve learners in self-assessment in relation to defined descriptors of tasks and aspects of proficiency at different levels, and operationalisation of those descriptors in – for example – series assessment*
- *the relevance of the specifications and scales provided in the Framework to their context, and the way in which they might be complemented or elaborated.*

Self-assessment and examiner versions of rating grids are presented in Table 2 and in Table 3 in Chapter 3. The most striking distinction between the two – apart from the purely surface formulation as *I can do . . .* or *Can do . . .* is that whereas Table 2 focuses on communicative activities, Table 3 focuses on generic aspects of competence apparent in any spoken performance. However, a slightly simplified self-assessment version of Table 3 can easily be imagined. Experience suggests that at least adult learners are capable of making such qualitative judgements about their competence.

9.4 Feasible assessment and a metasystem

The scales interspersed in Chapters 4 and 5 present an example of a set of categories related to but simplified from the more comprehensive descriptive scheme presented in the text of Chapters 4 and 5. It is not the intention that anyone should, in a practical assessment approach, use all the scales at all the levels. Assessors find it difficult to cope with a large number of categories and in addition, the full range of levels presented may not be appropriate in the context concerned. Rather, the set of scales is intended as a reference tool.

Whatever approach is being adopted, any practical assessment system needs to reduce the number of possible categories to a feasible number. Received wisdom is that more than 4 or 5 categories starts to cause cognitive overload and that 7 categories is psychologically an upper limit. Thus choices have to be made. In relation to oral assessment, if interaction strategies are considered a qualitative aspect of communication relevant in oral assessment, then the illustrative scales contain 12 qualitative categories relevant to oral assessment:

Turntaking strategies
Co-operating strategies
Asking for clarification
Fluency
Flexibility
Coherence
Thematic development
Precision
Sociolinguistic competence
General range
Vocabulary range
Grammatical accuracy
Vocabulary control
Phonological control

It is obvious that, whilst descriptors on many of these features could possibly be included in a general checklist, 12 categories are far too many for an assessment of any performance. In any practical approach, therefore, such a list of categories would be approached selectively. Features need to be combined, renamed and reduced into a smaller set of assessment criteria appropriate to the needs of the learners concerned, to the requirements of the assessment task concerned and to the style of the pedagogic culture concerned. The resultant criteria might be equally weighted, or alternatively certain factors considered more crucial to the task at hand might be more heavily weighted.

The following four examples show ways in which this can be done. The first three examples are brief notes on the way categories are used as test criteria in existing assessment approaches. The fourth example shows how descriptors in scales in the Framework were merged and reformulated in order to provide an assessment grid for a particular purpose on a particular occasion.

Example 1:
Cambridge Certificate in Advanced English (CAE), Paper 5: Criteria for Assessment (1991)

Test criteria	Illustrative scales	Other categories
Fluency	Fluency	
Accuracy and range	General range Vocabulary range Grammatical accuracy Vocabulary control	
Pronunciation	Phonological control	
Task achievement	Coherence Sociolinguistic appropriacy	Task success Need for interlocutor support
Interactive communication	Turntaking strategies Co-operative strategies Thematic development	Extent and ease of maintaining contribution

Note on other categories: In the illustrative scales, statements about task success are found in relation to the kind of activity concerned under *Communicative Activities*. *Extent and ease of contribution* is included under *Fluency* in those scales. An attempt to write and calibrate descriptors on *Need for Interlocutor Support* to include in the illustrative set of scales was unsuccessful.

Example 2:
International Certificate Conference (ICC): Certificate in English for Business Purposes, Test 2: Business Conversation (1987)

Test criteria	Illustrative scales	Other categories
Scale 1 (not named)	Sociolinguistic appropriacy Grammatical accuracy Vocabulary control	Task success
Scale 2 (Use of discourse features to initiate and maintain flow of conversation)	Turntaking strategies Co-operative strategies Sociolinguistic appropriacy	

Example 3:
Eurocentres – Small Group Interaction Assessment (RADIO) (1987)

Test criteria	Illustrative scales	Other categories
Range	General range Vocabulary range	
Accuracy	Grammatical accuracy Vocabulary control Socio-linguistic appropriacy	
Delivery	Fluency Phonological control	
Interaction	Turntaking strategies Co-operating strategies	

Example 4:
Swiss National Research Council: Assessment of Video Performances

Context: The illustrative descriptors were scaled in a research project in Switzerland as explained in Appendix A. At the conclusion of the research project, teachers who had participated were invited to a conference to present the results and to launch experimentation in Switzerland with the European Language Portfolio. At the conference, two of the subjects of discussion were (a) the need to relate continuous assessment and self-assessment checklists to an overall framework, and (b) the ways in which the descriptors scaled in the project could be exploited in different ways in assessment. As part of this process of discussion, videos of some of the learners in the survey were rated onto the assessment grid presented as Table 3 in Chapter 3. It presents a selection from the illustrative descriptors in a merged, edited form.

Test criteria	Illustrative scales	Other categories
Range	General range Vocabulary range	
Accuracy	Grammatical accuracy Vocabulary control	
Fluency	Fluency	
Interaction	Global interaction Turntaking Co-operating	
Coherence	Coherence	

Different systems with different learners in different contexts simplify, select and combine features in different ways for different kinds of assessment. Indeed rather than being too long, the list of 12 categories is probably unable to accommodate *all* the variants people choose, and would need to be expanded to be fully comprehensive.

Users of the Framework may wish to consider and where appropriate state:

- *the way in which theoretical categories are simplified into operational approaches in their system;*
- *the extent to which the main factors used as assessment criteria in their system can be situated in the set of categories introduced in Chapter 5 for which sample scales are provided in the Appendix, given further local elaboration to take account of specific domains of use.*

General Bibliography

N.B. Starred publications and documents have been produced in English and French.

The following reference works contain entries relevant to many sections of the Framework:

Bussmann, Hadumond (1996) *Routledge dictionary of language and linguistics*. London, Routledge.

Byram, M. (in press) *The Routledge encyclopedia of language teaching and learning*. London, Routledge.

Clapham, C. and Corson, D. (eds.) (1998) *Encyclopedia of language and education*. Dordrecht, Kluwer.

Crystal, D. (ed.) (1987) *The Cambridge encyclopedia of language*. Cambridge, CUP.

Foster, P. and Skehan, P. (1994) *The Influence of Planning on Performance in Task-based Learning.* Paper presented at the British Association of Applied Linguistics

Galisson, R. & Coste, D. (eds.) (1976) *Dictionnaire de didactique des languages*. Paris, Hachette.

Johnson, K. (1997) *Encyclopedic dictionary of applied linguistics*. Oxford, Blackwells.

Richards, J.C., Platt, J. & Platt, H. (1993) *Longman dictionary of language teaching and applied linguistics*. London, Longman.

Skehan, P. (1995) 'A framework for the implementation of task-based instruction', Applied Linguistics, 16/4, 542–566.

Spolsky, B. (ed.) (1999) *Concise encyclopedia of educational linguistics*. Amsterdam, Elsevier.

The following works are of relevance mainly to the chapter under which they are listed:

Chapter 1

*Council of Europe (1992) *Transparency and coherence in language learning in Europe: objectives, evaluation, certification. (Report edited by B. North of a Symposium held in Rüschlikon 1991).* Strasbourg, Council of Europe.

*(1997) *European language portfolio: proposals for development*. Strasbourg, Council of Europe.

*(1982) 'Recommendation no.R(82)18 of the Committee of Ministers to member States concerning modern languages'. Appendix A to Girard & Trim 1988.

*(1997) *Language learning for European citizenship: final report of the Project*. Strasbourg, Council of Europe.

*(1998) 'Recommendation no.R(98)6 of the Committee of Ministers to member States concerning modern languages'. Strasbourg, Council of Europe.

*Girard, D. and Trim, J.L.M. (eds.) (1998) *Project no.12 'Learning and teaching modern languages for communication': Final Report of the Project Group (activities 1982–87)*. Strasbourg, Council of Europe.

Gorosch, M., Pottier, B. and Riddy, D.C. (1967) *Modern languages and the world today. Modern languages in Europe, 3*. Strasbourg, AIDELA in co-operation with the Council of Europe.

Malmberg, P. (1989) *Towards a better language teaching: a presentation of the Council of Europe's language projects*. Uppsala, University of Uppsala In-service Training Department.

Chapter 2

a) The following 'Threshold Level'-type publications have so far appeared:

Baldegger, M., Müller, M. & Schneider, G. in Zusammenarbeit mit Näf, A. (1980) *Kontaktschwelle Deutsch als Fremdsprache*. Berlin, Langenscheidt.

Belart, M. & Rancé, L. (1991) *Nivell Llindar per a escolars (8–14 anys)*. Gener, Generalitat de Catalunya.

Castaleiro, J.M., Meira, A. & Pascoal, J. (1988) *Nivel limiar (para o ensino/aprendizagem do Portugues como lingua segunda/lingua estrangeira)*. Strasbourg, Council of Europe.

Coste, D., J. Courtillon, V. Ferenczi, M. Martins-Baltar et E. Papo (1976) *Un niveau-seuil*. Paris, Hatier.

Dannerfjord, T. (1983) *Et taerskelniveau for dansk – Appendix – Annexe – Appendiks*. Strasbourg, Council of Europe.

Efstathiadis, S. (ed.) (1998) *Katofli gia ta nea Ellenika*. Strasbourg, Council of Europe.

Ehala, M., Liiv. S., Saarso, K., Vare, S. & Õispuu, J. (1997) *Eesti keele suhtluslävi*. Strasbourg, Council of Europe.

Ek, J.A. van (1977) *The Threshold Level for modern language learning in schools*. London, Longman.

Ek, J.A. van & Trim, J.L.M. (1991) *Threshold Level 1990*. Cambridge, CUP.

　(1991) *Waystage 1990*. Cambridge, CUP.

　(1997) *Vantage Level*. Strasbourg, Council of Europe (to be republished by CUP c. November 2000).

Galli de' Paratesi, N. (1981) *Livello soglia per l'insegnamento dell'italiano come lingua straniera*. Strasbourg, Council of Europe.

Grinberga, I., Martinsone, G., Piese, V., Veisberg, A. & Zuicena, I. (1997) *Latvie šu valodas prasmes limenis*. Strasbourg, Council of Europe.

Jessen, J. (1983) *Et taerskelniveau for dansk*. Strasbourg, Council of Europe.

Jones, G.E., Hughes, M., & Jones, D. (1996) *Y lefel drothwy: ar gyfer y gymraeg*. Strasbourg, Council of Europe.

Kallas, E. (1990) *Yatabi lebaaniyyi: un livello sogla per l'insegnamento/apprendimento dell' arabo libanese nell' universitá italiana*. Venezia, Cafoscarina.

King, A. (ed.) (1988) *Atalase Maila*. Strasbourg, Council of Europe.

Mas, M., Melcion, J., Rosanas, R. & Vergé, M.H. (1992) *Nivell llindar per a la llengua catalana*. Barcelona, Generalitat de Catalunya.

Mifsud, M. & Borg, A.J. (1997) *Fuq l-ghatba tal-Malti*. Strasbourg, Council of Europe.

Narbutas E., Pribu_auskaite, J., Ramoniene, M., Skapiene, S. & Vilkiene, L. (1997) *Slenkstis*. Strasbourg, Council of Europe.

Porcher, L. (ed.) (1980) *Systèmes d'apprentissage des langues vivantes par les adultes (option travailleurs migrants): Un niveau-seuil intermediaire*. Strasbourg, Council of Europe.

Porcher, L., M. Huart et Mariet, F. (1982) *Adaptation de 'Un niveau-seuil' pour des contextes scholaires. Guide d'emploi*. Paris, Hatier.

Pushkin Russian Language Institute and Moscow Linguistic University (1966) *Porogoviy uroveny russkiy yazik*. Strasbourg, Council of Europe.

Salgado, X.A.F., Romero, H.M. & Moruxa, M.P. (1993) *Nivel soleira lingua galega*. Strasbourg, Council of Europe.

Sandström, B. (ed.) (1981) *Tröskelnivå: förslag till innehåll och metod i den grundläggande utbildnigen i svenska för vuxna invandrare*. Stockholm, Skolöverstyrelsen.

Slagter, P.J. (1979) *Un nivel umbral*. Strasbourg, Council of Europe.

Svanes, B., Hagen, J.E., Manne, G. & Svindland, A.S. (1987) *Et terskelnivå for norsk*. Strasbourg, Council of Europe.

Wynants, A. (1985) *Drempelniveau: nederlands als vreemde taal*. Strasbourg, Council of Europe.

b) Other publications of relevance:

Hest, E. van & Oud-de Glas, M. (1990) *A survey of techniques used in the diagnosis and analysis of foreign language needs in industry*. Brussels, Lingua.

Lüdi, G. and Py, B. (1986) *Etre bilingue*. Bern, Lang.

Lynch, P. Stevens, A. & Sands, E.P. (1993) *The language audit*. Milton Keynes, Open University.

Porcher, L. et al. (1982) *Identification des besoins langagiers de travailleurs migrants en France*. Strasbourg, Council of Europe.

Richterich, R. (1985) *Objectifs d'apprentissage et besoins langagiers*. Col. F. Paris, Hachette.

(ed.) (1983) *Case studies in identifying language needs*. Oxford, Pergamon.

Richterich, R. and J.-L. Chancerel (1980) *Identifying the needs of adults learning a foreign language*. Oxford, Pergamon.

(1981) *L'identification des besoins des adultes apprenant une langue étrangère*. Paris, Hatier.

Trim, J.L.M. (1980) *Developing a Unit/Credit scheme of adult language learning*. Oxford, Pergamon.

Trim, J.L.M. Richterich, R., van Ek, J.A. & Wilkins, D.A. (1980) *Systems development in adult language learning*. Oxford, Pergamon.

*Trim, J.L.M., Holec, H. Coste, D. and Porcher, L. (eds.) (1984) *Towards a more comprehensive framework for the definition of language learning objectives. Vol I Analytical summaries of the preliminary studies. Vol II Preliminary studies* (contributions in English and French). Strasbourg, Council of Europe.

Widdowson, H.G. (1989) 'Knowledge of Language and Ability for Use'. *Applied Linguistics* 10/2, 128–137.

Wilkins, D.A. (1972) *Linguistics in language teaching*. London, Edward Arnold.

Chapter 3

*van Ek, J.A. (1985–86) *Objectives for foreign language learning: vol.I Scope. vol.II Levels*. Strasbourg, Council of Europe.

North, B. (2000) *The Development of a Common Reference Scale of Language Proficiency*. New York, Peter Lang.

(1994) *Perspectives on language proficiency and aspects of competence: a reference paper discussing issues in defining categories and levels*. Strasbourg, Council of Europe.

North B. and Schneider, G. (1998): 'Scaling Descriptors for Language Proficiency Scales'. *Language Testing* 15/2: 217–262.

Schneider, G. and North, B. (2000) *Fremdsprachen können – was heisst das? Skalen zur Becshreibung, Beurteilung und Selbsteinschätzung der fremdsprachlichen Kommunkationsfähigkeit*. Chur/Zürich, Verlag Rüegger AG.

Chapter 4

Bygate, M. (1987) *Speaking*. Oxford, OUP.

Canale, M. & Swain, M. (1981) 'A theoretical framework for communicative competence'. In Palmer, A.S., Groot, P.G. & Trosper, S.A. (eds.) *The construct validation of tests of communicative competence*. Washington, DC., TESOL.

Carter, R. & Lang, M.N. (1991) *Teaching literature*. London, Longman.

Davies, Alan (1989): 'Communicative Competence as Language Use'. *Applied Linguistics* 10/2, 157–170.

Denes, P.B. and Pinson, E.N. (1993) *The Speech chain: the physics and biology of spoken language*. 2nd. edn. New York, Freeman.

Faerch, C. & Kasper, G. (eds.) (1983) *Strategies in interlanguage communication*. London, Longman.

Firth, J.R. (1964) *The tongues of men and Speech*. London, OUP.

Fitzpatrick, A. (1994) *Competence for vocationally oriented language learning: descriptive parameters, organisation and assessment*. Doc. CC-LANG (94)6. Strasbourg, Council of Europe.

Fry, D.B. (1977) *Homo loquens*. Cambridge CUP.

Hagège, C. (1985) *L'homme des paroles*. Paris, Fayard.

*Holec, H., Little, D. & Richterich, R. (1996) *Strategies in language learning and use*. Strasbourg, Council of Europe.

Kerbrat-Orecchioli, C. (1990, 1994) *Les interactions verbales (3 vols.)*. Paris, Colins.

Laver, J. & Hutcheson, S. (1972) *Communication in face-to-face interaction*. Harmondsworth, Penguin.

Levelt, W.J.M. (1993) *Speaking: from intention to articulation*. Cambridge, Mass, MIT.

Lindsay, P.H. & Norman, D.A. (1977) *Human information processing*. New York, Academic Press.

Martins-Baltar, M., Boutgain, D. Coste, D. Ferenczi, V. et M.-A. Mochet (1979) *L'écrit et les écrits: problèmes d'analyse et considérations didactiques*. Paris, Hatier.

Swales, J.M. (1990) *Genre analysis: English in academic and research settings*. Cambridge, CUP.

Chapter 5

Allport, G. (1979) *The Nature of Prejudice*. Reading MA, Addison-Wesley.

Austin, J.L. (1962) *How to do things with words*. Oxford, OUP.

Cruttenden, A. (1986) *Intonation*. Cambridge, CUP.

Crystal, D. (1969) *Prosodic systems and intonation in English*. Cambridge, CUP.

Furnham, A. and Bochner, S. (1986) *Culture Shock: psychological reactions in unfamiliar environments*. London, Methuen.

Gardner, R.C. (1985) *Social psychology and second language learning: the role of attitude and motivation*. London, Edward Arnold.

Grice, H.P. (1975) 'Logic and conversation'. In Cole, P. and Morgan, J.L. (eds.) *Speech acts*. New York, Academic Press, 41–58.

Gumperz, J.J. (1971) *Language in social groups*. Stamford, Stamford University Press.

Gumperz, J.J. & Hymes, D. (1972) *Directions in sociolinguistics: the ethnography of communication*. New York, Holt, Rinehart & Wiston.

Hatch, E. & Brown, C. (1995) *Vocabulary, semantics and language education*. Cambridge, CUP.

Hawkins, E.W. (1987) *Awareness of language: an introduction. revised edn*. Cambridge, CUP.

Hymes, D. (1974) *Foundations in sociolinguistics: an ethnographic approach*. Philadelphia, University of Pennsylvania Press.

Hymes, D.H. (1972) On communicative competence. In Pride and Holmes (1972).

Hymes, D.H. (1984) *Vers la compétence de communication*. Paris, Hatier.

Kingdon, R. (1958) *The groundwork of English intonation*. London, Longman.

Knapp-Potthoff, A. and Liedke, M. (eds.) (1977) *Aspekte interkultureller Kommunikationsfähigkeit*. Munich: iudicium verlag.

Labov, W. (1972) *Sociolinguistic patterns*. Philadelphia, University of Pennsylvania Press.

Lehrer, A. (1974) *Semantic fields and lexical structure*. London & Amsterdam.

Levinson, S.C. (1983) *Pragmatics*. Cambridge, CUP.

Lyons, J. (1977) *Semantics.vols. I and II*. Cambridge, CUP.

Mandelbaum, D.G. (1949) *Selected writings of Edward Sapir*. Berkeley, University of California Press.

Matthews, P.H. (1974) *Morphology: an introduction to the theory of word-structure*. Cambridge, CUP. (1981) *Syntax*. Cambridge, CUP.

Neuner, G. (1988) *A socio-cultural framework for communicative teaching and learning of foreign languages at the school level*. Doc. CC-GP12(87)24. Strasbourg, Council of Europe.

O'Connor, J.D. & Arnold, G.F. (1973) *The intonation of colloquial English*. 2nd edn. London, Longman.

O'Connor, J.D. (1973) *Phonetics*. Harmondsworth, Penguin.

Pride, J.B. & Holmes, J. (eds.) (1972) *Sociolinguistics*. Harmondsworth, Penguin.

Rehbein, J. (1977) *Komplexes Handeln: Elemente zur Handlungstheorie der Sprache*. Stuttgart, Metzler.

Robinson, G.L.N. (1985) *Crosscultural Understanding*. Oxford: Pergamon.

Robinson, W.P. (1972) *Language and social behaviour*. Harmondsworth, Penguin.

Roulet, E. (1972) *Théories grammaticales, descriptions et enseignement des langues*. Paris, Nathan.

Sapir, E. (1921) *Language*. New York, Harcourt Brace.

Searle, J. (1969) *Speech acts: an essay in the philosophy of language*. Cambridge, CUP.

Searle, J.R. (1976) 'The classification of illocutionary acts'. *Language in society*, vol.51, no.1, 1–24.

Trudgill, P. (1983) *Sociolinguistics* 2nd edn. Harmondsworth, Penguin.

Ullmann, S. (1962) *Semantics: an introduction to the science of meaning*. Oxford, Blackwell.

Wells, J.C. & Colson, G. (1971) *Practical phonetics*. Bath, Pitman.

Widdowson, H.G. (1992) *Practical stylistics: an approach to poetry*. Oxford, OUP.

Wray, A. (1999) 'Formulaic language in learners and native speakers'. *Language teaching 32,4*. Cambridge, CUP.

Wunderlich, D. (ed.) (1972) *Linguistische Pragmatik*. Frankfurt, Athanäum.

Zarate, G. (1986) *Enseigner une culture étrangère*. Paris, Hachette.

(1993) *Représentations de l'étranger et didactique des langues*. Paris, Hachette.

Chapter 6

Berthoud, A.-C. (ed.) (1996) 'Acquisition des compétences discursives dans un contexte plurilingue'. *Bulletin Suisse de linguistique appliquée*. VALS/ASLA 64.

Berthoud, A.-C. and Py, B. (1993) *Des linguistes et des enseignants. Maîtrise et acquisition des langues secondes*. Bern, Lang.

Besse, H. and Porquier, R. (1984) *Grammaire et didactique des langues*. Collection L.A.L. Paris, Hatier.

Blom, B.S. (1956) *Taxonomy of educational objectives*. London, Longman.

Bloom, B.S. (1976) *Human characteristics and school learning*. New York, McGraw.

Broeder, P. (ed.) (1988) *Processes in the developing lexicon. Vol. III of Final Report of the European Science Foundation Project 'Second language acquisition by adult immigrants'*. Strasbourg, Tilburg and Göteborg, ESF.

Brumfit, C. (1984) *Communicative Methodology in Language Teaching. The roles of fluency and accuracy*. Cambridge. CUP.

(1987) 'Concepts and Categories in Language Teaching Methodology'. *AILA Review* 4, 25–31.

Brumfit, C. & Johnson, K (eds.) (1979) *The communicative approach to language teaching*. Oxford, OUP.

Byram, M. (1997) *Teaching and assessing intercultural communicative competence*. Clevedon, Multilingual Matters.

Byram, M. (1989) *Cultural Studies and Foreign Language Education*. Clevedon, Multilingual Matters.

Byram, M. (1997), *Teaching and Assessing Intercultural Communicative Competence*. Clevedon, Multilingual Matters.

Byram, M., Zarate, G. & Neuner, G. (1997) *Sociocultural competences in foreign language teaching and learning*. Strasbourg, Council of Europe.

Callamand, M. (1981) *Méthodologie de la prononciation*. Paris, CLE International.

Canale, M. & Swain, M. (1980) 'Theoretical bases of communicative approaches to second language teaching and testing'. *Applied linguistics* vol. 1, no.1.

Conférence suisse des directeurs cantonaux de l'instruction publique (ed.) (1998) *Enseignement des langues étrangères – Recherche dans le domaine des langues et pratique de l'enseignement des langues étrangères. Dossier 52*. Berne, CDIP.

Cormon, F. (1992) *L'enseignement des langues*. Paris, Chronique sociale.

Coste, D. (1997) 'Eduquer pour une Europe des langues et des cultures'. *Etudes de linguistique appliquée 98*.

*Coste, D., Moore, D. & Zarate, G. (1997) *Plurilingual and pluricultural competence*. Strasbourg, Council of Europe.

Cunningsworth, A. (1984) *Evaluating and selecting EFL materials*. London, Heinemann.

*Girard, D. (ed.) (1988) *Selection and distribution of contents in language syllabuses*. Strasbourg, Council of Europe.

Dalgallian, G., Lieutaud, S. & Weiss, F. (1981) *Pour un nouvel enseignement des langues*. Paris, CLE.

Dickinson, L. (1987) *Self-instruction in language learning*. Cambridge, CUP.

Gaotrac, L. (1987) *Théorie d'apprentissage et acquisition d'une langue étrangère*. Collection L.A.L. Paris, Hatier.

Gardner, R.C. & MacIntyre, P.D. (1992–3) 'A student's contribution to second language learning': Part I 'cognitive variables' & Part II 'affective variables'. *Language teaching. Vol. 25 no. 4 & vol. 26 no 1*.

Girard, D. (1995) *Enseigner les langues: méthodes et pratiques*. Paris, Bordas.

Grauberg, W. (1997) *The elements of foreign language teaching*. Clevedon, Multilingual Matters.

Hameline, D., (1979) *Les objectifs pédagogiques en formation initiale et en formation continué*. Paris, E.S.F.

Hawkins, E.W. (1987) *Modern languages in the curriculum, revised edn*. Cambridge, CUP.

Hill, J. (1986) *Literature in language teaching*. London, Macmillan.

Holec, H. (1982) *Autonomie et apprentissage des langues étrangères*. Paris, Hatier.

(1981) *Autonomy and foreign language learning*. Oxford, Pergamon.

*(ed.) (1988) *Autonomy and self-directed learning: present fields of application* (with contributions in English and French). Strasbourg, Council of Europe.

Komensky, J.A. (Comenius) (1658) *Orbis sensualium pictus*. Nuremberg.

Kramsch, C. (1993) *Context and Culture in Language Teaching*. Oxford, OUP.

Krashen, S.D. (1982) *Principles and practice of second language acquisition*. Oxford, Pergamon.

Krashen, S.D. & Terrell, T.D. (1983) *The natural approach: language acquisition in the classroom*. Oxford, Pergamon.

Little, D., Devitt, S. & Singleton, D. (1988) *Authentic texts in foreign language teaching: theory and practice*. Dublin, Authentik.

MacKay, W.F. (1965) *Language teaching analysis*. London, Longman.

McDonough, S.H. (1981) *Psychology in foreign language teaching*. London, Allen & Unwin.

Melde, W. (1987) *Zur Integration von Landeskunde und Kommunikation im Fremdsprachenunterricht* Tübingen, Gunter Narr Verlag.

Pêcheur, J. and Viguer, G. (eds.) (1995) *Méthodes et méthodologies*. Col. Recherches et applications. Paris, Le français dans le monde.

Piepho, H.E. (1974) *Kommunikative Kompetenz als übergeordnetes Lernziel*. München, Frankonius.

*Porcher, L. (1980) *Reflections on language needs in the school*. Strasbourg, Council of Europe.

(ed.) (1992) *Les auto-apprentissages*. Col. Recherches et applications. Paris, Le français dans le monde.

Py, B. (ed.) (1994) 'l'acquisition d'une langue seconde. Quelques développements récents'. *Bulletin suisse de linguistique appliquée*. VALS/ASLA.

Rampillon, U. and Zimmermann, G. (eds.) (1997) *Strategien und Techniken beim Erwerb fremder Sprachen*. Ismaning, Hueber.

Savignon, S.J. (1983) *Communicative Competence: Theory and Classroom Practice*. Reading (Mass.), Addison-Wesley.

*Sheils, J. (1988) *Communication in the modern language classroom*. Strasbourg, Council of Europe (also available in German, Russian and Lithuanian).

Schmidt, R. W. (1990) 'The Role of Consciousness in Second Language Learning'. *Applied Linguistics* 11/2, 129–158.

Skehan, P. (1987) *Individual differences in second language learning*. London, Arnold.

Spolsky, B. (1989) *Conditions for second language learning*. Oxford, OUP.

Stern, H.H. (1983) *Fundamental concepts of language teaching*. Oxford, OUP.

Stern, H.H. and A. Weinrib (1977) 'Foreign languages for younger children: trends and assessment'. *Language Teaching and Linguistics: Abstracts 10*, 5–25.

The British Council (1978) *The teaching of comprehension*. London, British Council.

Trim, J.L.M. (1991) 'Criteria for the evaluation of classroom-based materials for the learning and teaching of languages for communication'. In Grebing, R. *Grenzenlöses Sprachenlernen. Festschrift für Reinhold Freudenstein*. Berlin, Cornelsen.

Williams, E. (1984) *Reading in the language classroom*. London, Macmillan.

Chapter 7

Jones, K. (1982) *Simulations in language teaching*. Cambridge, CUP.

Nunan, D. (1989) *Designing tasks for the communicative classroom*. Cambridge, CUP.

Yule, G. (1997) *Referential communication tasks*. Mahwah, N.J., Lawrence Erlbaum.

Chapter 8

Breen, M.P. (1987) 'Contemporary paradigms in syllabus design', Parts I and II. *Language Teaching*, vol. 20 nos. 2 & 3, p.81–92 & 157–174.

Burstall, C., Jamieson, M. Cohen, S. and Margreaves, M. (1974) *Primary French in the balance*. Slough, NFER.

Clark, J.L. (1987) *Curriculum Renewal in School Foreign Language Learning*. Oxford, OUP.

*Coste, D. (ed.) (1983) *Contributions à une rénovation de l'apprentissage et de l'enseignement des languages. Quelques expériences en cours en Europe*. Paris, Hatier.

Coste, D. and Lehman, D. (1995) 'Langues et curriculum. Contenus, programmes et parcours'. *Etudes de linguistique appliquée, 98*.

Damen, L. (1987) *Culture Learning: the Fifth Dimension in the Language Classroom*. Reading, Mass: Addison Wesley.

Fitzpatrick, A. (1994) *Competence for vocationally oriented language learning: descriptive parameters, organisation and assessment*. Doc. CC-LANG 994) 6. Strasbourg, Council of Europe.

Johnson, K. (1982) *Communicative syllabus design and methodology*. Oxford, Pergamon.

Labrie, C. (1983) *La construction de la Communauté européenne*. Paris, Champion.

Munby, J. (1972) *Communicative syllabus design*. Cambridge, CUP.

Nunan, D. (1988) *The learner-centred curriculum: a study in second language teaching*. Cambridge, CUP.

Roulet, E. (1980) *Langue maternelle et langue seconde. Vers une pédagogie intégrée*. Col. L.A.'L' Paris, Hatier.

Schneider, G., North, B., Flügel, Ch. and Koch, L. (1999) *Europäisches Sprachenportfolio – Portfolio européen des langues – Portfolio europeo delle lingue – European Language Portfolio, Schweizer Version*. Bern EDK. Also available online: http//www.unifr.ch/ids/portfolio.

Schweizerische Konferenz der kantonalen Erzeihungsdirektoren EDK (1995) *Mehrsprachiges Land – mehrsprachige Schulen. 7. Schweizerisches Forum Langue 2. Dossier 33*. Bern, EDK.

Vigner, G. (ed.) (1996) 'Promotion, réforme des langues et systèmes éducatifs'. *Etudes de linguistique appliquée, 103*.

*Wilkins, D. (1987) *The educational value of foreign language learning*. Doc. CC-GP(87)10. Strasbourg, Council of Europe.

Wilkins, D.A. (1976) *Notional syllabuses*. Oxford, OUP.

Chapter 9

Alderson, J.C., Clapham, C. and Wall, D. (1995) *Language Test Construction and Evaluation*. Cambridge, CUP.

Alderson, J.C. (2000) *Assessing Reading*. Cambridge Language Assessment Series (eds. J.C. Alderson and L.F. Bachman). Cambridge, CUP.

Bachman, L.F. (1990) *Fundamental considerations in language testing*. Oxford, OUP.

Brindley, G. (1989) *Assessing Achievement in the Learner-Centred Curriculum*. NCELTR Research Series (National Centre for English Language Teaching and Research). Sydney: Macquarie University.

Coste, D. and Moore, D. (eds.) (1992) 'Autour de l'évaluation de l'oral'. *Bulletin CILA 55*.

Douglas, D. (2000) Assessing Languages for Specific Purposes. Cambridge Language Assessment Series (eds. J.C. Alderson and L.F. Bachman). Cambridge, CUP.

Lado, R. (1961) *Language testing: the construction and use of foreign tests*. London, Longman.

Lussier, D. (1992) *Evaluer les apprentissages dans une approche communicative*. Col. F. Paris, Hachette.

Monnerie-Goarin, A. and Lescure, R. (eds.) 'Evaluation et certifications en langue étrangère'. *Recherches et applications. Numéro spécial. Le français dans le monde, août-septembre 1993*.

Oskarsson, M. (1980) *Approaches to self-assessment in foreign language learning*. Oxford, Pergamon.

(1984) *Self-assessment of foreign language skills: a survey of research and development work*. Strasbourg, Council of Europe.

General Bibliography

Reid, J. (2000) *Assessing Vocabulary*. (Cambridge Language Assessment Series, eds. J.C. Alderson and L.F. Bachman). Cambridge, CUP.
Tagliante, C. (ed.) (1991) *L'évaluation*. Paris, CLE International.
University of Cambridge Local Examinations Syndicate (1998) *The multilingual glossary of language testing terms (Studies in language testing 6)*. Cambridge, CUP.

Appendix A: developing proficiency descriptors

This appendix discusses technical aspects of describing levels of language attainment. Criteria for descriptor formulation are discussed. Methodologies for scale development are then listed, and an annotated bibliography is provided.

Descriptor formulation

Experience of scaling in language testing, the theory of scaling in the wider field of applied psychology, and preferences of teachers when involved in consultation processes (e.g. UK graded objectives schemes, Swiss project) suggest the following set of guidelines for developing descriptors:

- *Positiveness:* It is a common characteristic of assessor-orientated proficiency scales and of examination rating scales for the formulation of entries at lower levels to be negatively worded. It is more difficult to formulate proficiency at low levels in terms of what the learner can do rather than in terms of what they can't do. But if levels of proficiency are to serve as objectives rather than just as an instrument for screening candidates, then positive formulation is desirable. It is sometimes possible to formulate the same point either positively or negatively, e.g. in relation to range of language (see Table A1).

  An added complication in avoiding negative formulation is that there are some features of communicative language proficiency which are not additive. The less there is the better. The most obvious example is what is sometimes called Independence, the extent to which the learner is dependent on (a) speech adjustment on the part of the interlocutor (b) the chance to ask for clarification and (c) the chance to get help with formulating what he/she wants to say. Often these points can be dealt with in provisos attached to positively worded descriptors, for example:

    Can generally understand clear, standard speech on familiar matters directed at him/her, provided he/she can ask for repetition or reformulation from time to time.
    Can understand what is said clearly, slowly and directly to him/her in simple everyday conversation; can be made to understand, if the speaker can take the trouble.
  or:
    Can interact with reasonable ease in structured situations and short conversations, provided the other person helps if necessary.

Table A1. *Assessment: positive and negative criteria*

Positive	Negative
• has a repertoire of basic language and strategies which enables him or her to deal with predictable everyday situations. (Eurocentres Level 3: certificate) • basic repertoire of language and strategies sufficient for most everyday needs, but generally requiring compromise of the message and searching for words. (Eurocentres Level 3: assessor grid)	• has a narrow language repertoire, demanding constant rephrasing and searching for words. (ESU Level 3) • limited language proficiency causes frequent breakdowns and misunderstandings in non-routine situations. (Finnish Level 2) • communication breaks down as language constraints interfere with message. (ESU Level 3)
• vocabulary centres on areas such as basic objects, places, and most common kinship terms. (ACTFL Novice)	• has only a limited vocabulary. (Dutch Level 1) • limited range of words and expressions hinders communication of thoughts and ideas. (Gothenburg U)
• produces and recognises a set of words and short phrases learnt by heart. (Trim 1978 Level 1)	• can produce only formulaic utterances lists and enumerations. (ACTFL Novice)
• can produce brief everyday expressions in order to satisfy simple needs of a concrete type (in the area of salutation, information, etc.). (Elviri; Milan Level 1 1986)	• has only the most basic language repertoire, with little or no evidence of a functional command of the language. (ESU Level 1)

• *Definiteness:* Descriptors should describe concrete tasks and/or concrete degrees of skill in performing tasks. There are two points here. Firstly, the descriptor should avoid vagueness, like, for example 'Can use a range of appropriate strategies'. What is meant by strategy? Appropriate to what? How should we interpret 'range'? The problem with vague descriptors is that they can read quite nicely, but an apparent ease of acceptance can mask the fact that everyone is interpreting them differently. Secondly, since the 1940s, it has been a principle that distinctions between steps on a scale should not be dependent on replacing a qualifier like 'some' or 'a few' with 'many' or 'most' or by replacing 'fairly broad' with 'very broad' or 'moderate' with 'good' at the next level up. Distinctions should be real, not word-processed and this may mean gaps where meaningful, concrete distinctions cannot be made.

• *Clarity:* Descriptors should be transparent, not jargon-ridden. Apart from the barrier to understanding, it is sometimes the case that when jargon is stripped away, an apparently impressive descriptor can turn out to be saying very little. Secondly, they should be written in simple syntax with an explicit, logical structure.

• *Brevity:* One school of thought is associated with holistic scales, particularly those used in America and Australia. These try to produce a lengthy paragraph which comprehensibly covers what are felt to be the major features. Such scales achieve 'definiteness' by a very comprehensive listing which is intended to transmit a detailed portrait of what raters can recognise as a typical learner at the level concerned, and are as a result very rich sources of description. There are two disadvantages to such an approach however. Firstly, no individual is actually 'typical'. Detailed features co-occur in different ways. Secondly, a descriptor which is longer than a two clause sentence cannot realistically be referred to during the assessment process. Teachers consistently seem to prefer short descriptors. In the project which produced the illustrative descriptors, teachers tended to reject or split descriptors longer than about 25 words (approximately two lines of normal type).

• *Independence:* There are two further advantages of short descriptors. Firstly they are more likely to describe a behaviour about which one can say 'Yes, this person can do this'. Consequently shorter, concrete descriptors can be used as independent criteria statements in checklists or questionnaires for teacher continuous assessment and/or self-assessment. This kind of independent integrity is a signal that the descriptor could serve as an objective rather than having meaning only relative to the formulation of other descriptors on the scale. This opens up a range of opportunities for exploitation in different forms of assessment (see Chapter 9).

Users of the Framework may wish to consider and where appropriate state:

• *Which of the criteria listed are most relevant, and what other criteria are used explicitly or implicitly in their context;*
• *To what extent it is desirable and feasible that formations in their system meet criteria such as those listed.*

Scale development methodologies

The existence of a series of levels presupposes that certain things can be placed at one level rather than another and that descriptions of a particular degree of skill belong to one level rather than another. This implies a form of scaling, consistently applied. There are a number of possible ways in which descriptions of language proficiency can be assigned to different levels. The available methods can be categorised in three groups: intuitive methods, qualitative methods and quantitative methods. Most existing scales of language proficiency and other sets of levels have been developed through one of the three intuitive methods in the first group. The best approaches combine all three approaches in a complementary and cumulative process. Qualitative methods require the intuitive preparation and selection of material and intuitive interpretation of results. Quantitative methods should quantify qualitatively pre-tested material, and will require intuitive interpretation of results. Therefore in developing the Common Reference Levels, a combination of intuitive, qualitative and quantitative approaches was used.

If qualitative and quantitative methods are used then there are two possible starting points: descriptors or performance samples.

Starting with descriptors: One starting point is to consider what you wish to describe, and then write, collect or edit draft descriptors for the categories concerned as input to the qualitative phase. Methods 4 and 9, the first and last in the qualitative group below, are examples of this approach. It is particularly suitable for developing descriptors for curriculum-related categories such as communicative language activities, but can also be used to develop descriptors for aspects of competence. The advantage of starting with categories and descriptors is that a theoretically balanced coverage can be defined.

Starting with performance samples. The alternative, which can only be used to develop descriptors to rate performances, is to start with representative samples of performances. Here one can ask representative raters what they see when they work with the samples (qualitative). Methods 5–8 are variants on this idea. Alternatively, one can just ask the raters to assess the samples and then use an appropriate statistical technique to identify what key features are actually driving the raters' decisions (quantitative). Methods 10 and 11 are examples of this approach. The advantage of analysing performance samples is that one can arrive at very concrete descriptions based on data.

The last method, No 12, is the only one to actually *scale* the descriptors in a mathematical sense. This was the method used to develop the Common Reference Levels and illustrative descriptors, after Method 2 (intuitive) and Methods 8 and 9 (qualitative). However, the same statistical technique can be also used after the development of the scale, in order to validate the use of the scale in practice, and identify needs for revision.

Intuitive methods:

These methods do not require any structured data collection, just the principled interpretation of experience.

No 1. *Expert:* Someone is asked to write the scale, which they may do by consulting existing scales, curriculum documents and other relevant source material, possibly after undertaking a needs analysis of the target group in question. They may then pilot and revise the scale, possibly using informants.

No 2. *Committee:* As expert, but a small development team is involved, with a larger group as consultants. Drafts would be commented on by consultants. The consultants may operate intuitively on the basis of their experience and/or on the basis of comparison to learners or samples of performance. Weaknesses of curriculum scales for secondary school modern language learning produced by committee in the UK and Australia are discussed by Gipps (1994) and Scarino (1996; 1997).

No 3. *Experiential:* As committee, but the process lasts a considerable time within an institution and/or specific assessment context and a 'house consensus' develops. A core of people come to share an understanding of the levels and the criteria. Systematic piloting and feedback may follow in order to refine the wording. Groups of raters may discuss performances in relation to the definitions, and the definitions in relation to sample performances. This is the traditional way proficiency scales have been developed (Wilds 1975; Ingram 1985; Liskin-Gasparro 1984; Lowe 1985, 1986).

Qualitative methods:

These methods all involve small workshops with groups of informants and a qualitative rather than statistical interpretation of the information obtained.

No 4.   *Key concepts: formulation:* Once a draft scale exists, a simple technique is to chop up the scale and ask informants typical of the people who will use the scale to (a) put the definitions in what they think is the right order, (b) explain why they think that, and then once the difference between their order and the intended order has been revealed, to (c) identify what key points were helping them, or confusing them. A refinement is to sometimes remove a level, giving a secondary task to identify where the gap between two levels indicates that a level is missing between them. The Eurocentres certification scales were developed in this way.

No 5.   *Key concepts: performances:* Descriptors are matched to typical performances at those band levels to ensure a coherence between what was described and what occurred. Some of the Cambridge examination guides take teachers through this process, comparing wordings on scales to grades awarded to particular scripts. The IELTS (International English Language Testing System) descriptors were developed by asking groups of experienced raters to identify 'key sample scripts' for each level, and then agree the 'key features' of each script. Features felt to be characteristic of different levels are then identified in discussion and incorporated in the descriptors (Alderson 1991; Shohamy *et al.* 1992).

No 6.   *Primary trait:* Performances (usually written) are sorted by individual informants into rank order. A common rank order is then negotiated. The principle on which the scripts have actually been sorted is then identified and described at each level – taking care to highlight features salient at a particular level. What has been described is the trait (feature, construct) which determines the rank order (Mullis 1980). A common variant is to sort into a certain number of piles, rather than into rank order. There is also an interesting multi-dimensional variant on the classic approach. In this version, one first determines through the identification of key features (No 5 above) what the most significant traits are. Then one sorts the samples into order for each trait separately. Thus at the end one has an analytic, multiple trait scale rather than a holistic, primary trait one.

No 7.   *Binary decisions:* Another variant of the primary trait method is to first sort representative samples into piles by levels. Then in a discussion focusing on the boundaries between levels, one identifies key features (as in No 5 above).

However, the feature concerned is then formulated as a short criterion question with a Yes/No answer. A tree of binary choices is thus built up. This offers the assessor an algorithm of decisions to follow (Upshur and Turner 1995).

No 8. *Comparative judgements:* Groups discuss pairs of performances stating which is better – and why. In this way the categories in the metalanguage used by the raters is identified, as are the salient features working at each level. These features can then be formulated into descriptors (Pollitt and Murray 1996).

No 9. *Sorting tasks:* Once draft descriptors exist, informants can be asked to sort them into piles according to categories they are supposed to describe and/or according to levels. Informants can also be asked to comment on, edit/amend and/or reject descriptors, and to identify which are particularly clear, useful, relevant, etc. The descriptor pool on which the set of illustrative scales was based was developed and edited in this way (Smith and Kendall 1963; North 1996/2000).

Quantitative methods:

These methods involve a considerable amount of statistical analysis and careful interpretation of the results.

No 10. *Discriminant analysis:* First, a set of performance samples which have already been rated (preferably by a team) are subjected to a detailed discourse analysis. This qualitative analysis identifies and counts the incidence of different qualitative features. Then, multiple regression is used to determine which of the identified features are significant in apparently determining the rating which the assessors gave. Those key features are then incorporated in formulating descriptors for each level (Fulcher 1996).

No 11. *Multidimensional scaling:* Despite the name, this is a descriptive technique to identify key features and the relationship between them. Performances are rated with an analytic scale of several categories. The output from the analysis technique demonstrates which categories were actually decisive in determining level, and provides a diagram mapping the proximity or distance of the different categories to each other. This is thus a research technique to identify and validate salient criteria (Chaloub-Deville 1995).

No 12. *Item response theory (IRT) or 'latent trait' analysis:* IRT offers a family of measurement or scaling models. The most straightforward and robust one is the *Rasch* model named after George Rasch, the Danish mathematician. IRT is a development from probability theory and is used mainly to determine the difficulty of individual test items in an item bank. If you are advanced, your chances of answering an elementary question are very high; if you are elementary your chances of answering an advanced item are very low. This simple fact is developed into a scaling methodology with the Rasch model, which can be used to calibrate items to the same scale. A development of the approach allows it to be used to scale descriptors of communicative proficiency as well as test items.

In a Rasch analysis, different tests or questionnaires can be formed into an overlapping chain through the employment of 'anchor items', which are common to adjacent forms. In the diagram below, the anchor items are shaded grey. In this way, forms can be targeted to particular groups of learners, yet linked into a common scale. Care must, however, be taken in this process, since the model distorts results for the high scores and low scores on each form.

```
                                         Test C
                      Test B
       Test A
```

The advantage of a Rasch analysis is that it can provide sample-free, scale-free measurement, that is to say scaling that is independent of the samples or the tests/questionnaires used in the analysis. Scale values are provided which remain constant for future groups provided those future subjects can be considered new groups within the same statistical population. Systematic shifts in values over time (e.g. due to curriculum change or to assessor training) can be quantified and adjusted for. Systematic variation between types of learners or assessors can be quantified and adjusted for (Wright and Masters 1982; Lincare 1989).

There are a number of ways in which Rasch analysis can be employed to scale descriptors:

(a) Data from the qualitative techniques Nos 6, 7 or 8 can be put onto an arithmetic scale with Rasch.
(b) Tests can be carefully developed to operationalise proficiency descriptors in particular test items. Those test items can then be scaled with Rasch and their scale values taken to indicate the relative difficulty of the descriptors (Brown et al. 1992; Carroll 1993; Masters 1994; Kirsch 1995; Kirsch and Mosenthal 1995).
(c) Descriptors can be used as questionnaire items for teacher assessment of their learners (Can he/she do X?). In this way the descriptors can be calibrated directly onto an arithmetic scale in the same way that test items are scaled in item banks.
(d) The scales of descriptors included in Chapters 3, 4 and 5 were developed in this way. All three projects described in Appendices B, C and D have used Rasch methodology to scale descriptors, and to equate the resulting scales of descriptors to each other.

In addition to its usefulness in the development of a scale, Rasch can also be used to analyse the way in which the bands on an assessment scale are actually used. This may help to highlight loose wording, underuse of a band, or overuse of a band, and inform revision (Davidson 1992; Milanovic et al. 1996; Stansfield and Kenyon 1996; Tyndall and Kenyon 1996).

> *Users of the Framework may wish to consider and where appropriate state:*
>
> - *the extent to which grades awarded in their system are given shared meaning through common definitions;*
> - *which of the methods outlined above, or which other methods, are used to develop such definitions.*

Select annotated bibliography: language proficiency scaling

Alderson, J.C. 1991: Bands and scores. In: Alderson, J.C. and North, B. (eds.): *Language testing in the 1990s*, London: British Council/ Macmillan, Developments in ELT, 71–86.

Discusses problems caused by confusion of purpose and orientation, and development of IELTS speaking scales.

Brindley, G. 1991: Defining language ability: the criteria for criteria. In Anivan, S. (ed.) *Current developments in language testing*, Singapore, Regional Language Centre.

Principled critique of the claim of proficiency scales to represent criterion-referenced assessment.

Brindley, G. 1998: Outcomes-based assessment and reporting in language learning programmes, a review of the issues. *Language Testing* 15 (1), 45–85.

Criticises the focus on outcomes in terms of what learners can do, rather than focusing on aspects of emerging competence.

Brown, Annie, Elder, Cathie, Lumley, Tom, McNamara, Tim and McQueen, J. 1992: *Mapping abilities and skill levels using Rasch techniques*. Paper presented at the 14th Language Testing Research Colloquium, Vancouver. Reprinted in *Melbourne Papers in Applied Linguistics* 1/1, 37–69.

Classic use of Rasch scaling of test items to produce a proficiency scale from the reading tasks tested in the different items.

Carroll, J.B. 1993: Test theory and behavioural scaling of test performance. In Frederiksen, N., Mislevy, R.J. and Bejar, I.I. (eds.) *Test theory for a new generation of tests*. Hillsdale N.J. Lawrence Erlbaum Associates: 297–323.

Seminal article recommending the use of Rasch to scale test items and so produce a proficiency scale.

Chaloub-Deville M. 1995: Deriving oral assessment scales across different tests and rater groups. *Language Testing* 12 (1), 16–33.

Study revealing what criteria native speakers of Arabic relate to when judging learners. Virtually the only application of multi-dimensional scaling to language testing.

Davidson, F. 1992: Statistical support for training in ESL composition rating. In Hamp-Lyons (ed.): *Assessing second language writing in academic contexts*. Norwood N.J. Ablex: 155–166.

Very clear account of how to validate a rating scale in a cyclical process with Rasch analysis. Argues for a 'semantic' approach to scaling rather than the 'concrete' approach taken in, e.g., the illustrative descriptors.

Fulcher 1996: Does thick description lead to smart tests? A data-based approach to rating scale construction. *Language Testing* 13 (2), 208–38.

Systematic approach to descriptor and scale development starting by proper analysis of what is actually happening in the performance. Very time-consuming method.

Gipps, C. 1994: *Beyond testing.* London, Falmer Press.

Promotion of teacher 'standards-oriented assessment' in relation to common reference points built up by networking. Discussion of problems caused by vague descriptors in the English National Curriculum. Cross-curricula.

Kirsch, I.S. 1995: Literacy performance on three scales: definitions and results. In *Literacy, economy and society: Results of the first international literacy survey.* Paris, Organisation for Economic Cooperation and development (OECD): 27–53.

Simple non-technical report on a sophisticated use of Rasch to produce a scale of levels from test data. Method developed to predict and explain the difficulty of new test items from the tasks and competences involved – i.e. in relation to a framework.

Kirsch, I.S. and Mosenthal, P.B. 1995: Interpreting the IEA reading literacy scales. In Binkley, M., Rust, K. and Wingleee, M. (eds.) Methodological issues in comparative educational studies: The case of the IEA reading literacy study. Washington D.C.: US Department of Education, National Center for Education Statistics: 135–192.

More detailed and technical version of the above tracing the development of the method through three related projects.

Linacre, J. M. 1989: *Multi-faceted Measurement.* Chicago: MESA Press.

Seminal breakthrough in statistics allowing the severity of examiners to be taken into account in reporting a result from an assessment. Applied in the project to develop the illustrative descriptors to check the relationship of levels to school years.

Liskin-Gasparro, J. E. 1984: The ACTFL proficiency guidelines: Gateway to testing and curriculum. In: *Foreign Language Annals* 17/5, 475–489.

Outline of the purposes and development of the American ACTFL scale from its parent Foreign Service Institute (FSI) scale.

Lowe, P. 1985: The ILR proficiency scale as a synthesising research principle: the view from the mountain. In: James, C.J. (ed.): *Foreign Language Proficiency in the Classroom and Beyond.* Lincolnwood (Ill.): National Textbook Company.

Detailed description of the development of the US Interagency Language Roundtable (ILR) scale from the FSI parent. Functions of the scale.

Lowe, P. 1986: Proficiency: panacea, framework, process? A Reply to Kramsch, Schulz, and particularly, to Bachman and Savignon. In: *Modern Language Journal* 70/4, 391–397.

Defence of a system that worked well – in a specific context – against academic criticism prompted by the spread of the scale and its interviewing methodology to education (with ACTFL).

Masters, G. 1994: Profiles and assessment. *Curriculum Perspectives* 14,1: 48–52.

Brief report on the way Rasch has been used to scale test results and teacher assessments to create a curriculum profiling system in Australia.

Milanovic, M., Saville, N., Pollitt, A. and Cook, A. 1996: Developing rating scales for CASE: Theoretical concerns and analyses. In Cumming, A. and Berwick, R. *Validation in language testing.* Clevedon, Avon, Multimedia Matters: 15–38.

Classic account of the use of Rasch to refine a rating scale used with a speaking test – reducing the number of levels on the scale to the number assessors could use effectively.

Mullis, I.V.S. 1981: *Using the primary trait system for evaluating writing*. Manuscript No. 10-W-51. Princeton N.J.: Educational Testing Service.

Classic account of the primary trait methodology in mother tongue writing to develop an assessment scale.

North, B. 1993: *The development of descriptors on scales of proficiency: perspectives, problems, and a possible methodology*. NFLC Occasional Paper, National Foreign Language Center, Washington D.C., April 1993.

Critique of the content and development methodology of traditional proficiency scales. Proposal for a project to develop the illustrative descriptors with teachers and scale them with Rasch from teacher assessments.

North, B. 1994: *Scales of language proficiency: a survey of some existing systems*, Strasbourg, Council of Europe CC-LANG (94) 24.

Comprehensive survey of curriculum scales and rating scales later analysed and used as the starting point for the project to develop illustrative descriptors.

North, B. 1996/2000: *The development of a common framework scale of language proficiency*. PhD thesis, Thames Valley University. Reprinted 2000, New York, Peter Lang.

Discussion of proficiency scales, how models of competence and language use relate to scales. Detailed account of development steps in the project which produced the illustrative descriptors – problems encountered, solutions found.

North, B. forthcoming: *Scales for rating language performance in language tests: descriptive models, formulation styles* and presentation formats. TOEFL Research Paper. Princeton NJ; Educational Testing Service.

Detailed analysis and historical survey of the types of rating scales used with speaking and writing tests: advantages, disadvantages, pitfalls, etc.

North, B. and Schneider, G. 1998: Scaling descriptors for language proficiency scales. *Language Testing* 15/2: 217–262.

Overview of the project which produced the illustrative descriptors. Discusses results and stability of scale. Examples of instruments and products in an appendix.

Pollitt, A. and Murray, N.L. 1996: What raters really pay attention to. In Milanovic, M. and Saville, N. (eds.) 1996: *Performance testing, cognition and assessment*. Studies in Language Testing 3. Selected papers from the 15th Language Testing Research Colloquium, Cambridge and Arnhem, 2–4 August 1993. Cambridge: University of Cambridge Local Examinations Syndicate: 74–91.

Interesting methodological article linking repertory grid analysis to a simple scaling technique to identify what raters focus on at different levels of proficiency.

Scarino, A. 1996: Issues in planning, describing and monitoring long-term progress in language learning. In Proceedings of the AFMLTA 10th National Languages Conference: 67–75.

Criticises the use of vague wording and lack of information about how well learners perform in typical UK and Australian curriculum profile statements for teacher assessment.

Scarino, A. 1997: Analysing the language of frameworks of outcomes for foreign language learning. In Proceedings of the AFMLTA 11th National Languages Conference: 241–258.

As above.

Schneider, G and North, B. 1999: *'In anderen Sprachen kann ich' . . . Skalen zur Beschreibung, Beurteilung und Selbsteinschätzung der fremdsprachlichen Kommunikationsfähigkeit.* Bern/Aarau: NFP 33/SKBF (Umsetzungsbericht).

Short report on the project which produced the illustrative scales. Also introduces Swiss version of the Portfolio (40 page A5).

Schneider, G and North, B. 2000: 'Dans d'autres langues, je suis capable de ...' Echelles pour la description, l'évaluation et l'auto-évaluation des competences en langues étrangères. Berne/Aarau PNR33/CSRE (rapport de valorisation)

As above.

Schneider, G and North, B. 2000: *Fremdsprachen können – was heisst das? Skalen zur Beschreibung, Beurteilung und Selbsteinschätzung der fremdsprachlichen Kommunikationsfähigkeit.* Chur/Zürich, Verlag Rüegger AG.

Full report on the project which produced the illustrative scales. Straightforward chapter on scaling in English. Also introduces Swiss version of the Portfolio.

Skehan, P. 1984: Issues in the testing of English for specific purposes. In: *Language Testing* 1/2, 202–220.

Criticises the norm-referencing and relative wording of the ELTS scales.

Shohamy, E., Gordon, C.M. and Kraemer, R. 1992: The effect of raters' background and training on the reliability of direct writing tests. *Modern Language Journal* 76: 27–33.

Simple account of basic, qualitative method of developing an analytic writing scale. Led to astonishing inter-rater reliability between untrained non-professionals.

Smith, P. C. and Kendall, J.M. 1963: Retranslation of expectations: an approach to the construction of unambiguous anchors for rating scales. In: *Journal of Applied Psychology*, 47/2.

The first approach to scaling descriptors rather than just writing scales. Seminal. Very difficult to read.

Stansfield C.W. and Kenyon D.M. 1996: Comparing the scaling of speaking tasks by language teachers and the ACTFL guidelines. In Cumming, A. and Berwick, R. *Validation in language testing.* Clevedon, Avon, Multimedia Matters: 124–153.

Use of Rasch scaling to confirm the rank order of tasks which appear in the ACTFL guidelines. Interesting methodological study which inspired the approach taken in the project to develop the illustrative descriptors.

Takala, S. and F. Kaftandjieva (forthcoming). Council of Europe scales of language proficiency: A validation study. In J.C. Alderson (ed.) *Case studies of the use of the Common European Framework.* Council of Europe.

Report on the use of a further development of the Rasch model to scale language self-assessments in relation to adaptations of the illustrative descriptors. Context: DIALANG project: trials in relation to Finnish.

Tyndall, B. and Kenyon, D. 1996: Validation of a new holistic rating scale using Rasch multifaceted analysis. In Cumming, A. and Berwick, R. *Validation in language testing.* Clevedon, Avon, Multimedia Matters: 9–57.

Simple account of the validation of a scale for ESL placement interviews at university entrance. Classic use of multi-faceted Rasch to identify training needs.

Upshur, J. and Turner, C. 1995: Constructing rating scales for second language tests. *English Language Teaching Journal* 49 (1), 3–12.

Wilds, C.P. 1975: The oral interview test. In: Spolsky, B. and Jones, R. (Eds): *Testing language proficiency*. Washington D.C.: Center for Applied Linguistics, 29–44.

Sophisticated further development of the primary trait technique to produce charts of binary decisions. Very relevant to school sector.

The original coming out of the original language proficiency rating scale. Worth a careful read to spot nuances lost in most interview approaches since then.

Appendix B: The illustrative scales of descriptors

This appendix contains a description of the Swiss project which developed the illustrative descriptors for the CEF. Categories scaled are also listed, with references to the pages where they can be found in the main document. The descriptors in this project were scaled and used to create the CEF levels with Method No 12c (Rasch modelling) outlined at the end of Appendix A.

The Swiss research project

Origin and Context

The scales of descriptors included in Chapters 3, 4 and 5 have been drawn up on the basis of the results of a Swiss National Science Research Council project which took place between 1993 and 1996. This project was undertaken as a follow-up to the 1991 Rüschlikon Symposium. The aim was to develop transparent statements of proficiency of different aspects of the CEF descriptive scheme, which might also contribute to the development of a European Language Portfolio.

A 1994 survey concentrated on Interaction and Production and was confined to English as a Foreign Language and to teacher assessment. A 1995 survey was a partial replication of the 1994 study, with the addition of Reception, but French and German proficiency were surveyed as well as English. Self-assessment and some examination information (Cambridge; Goethe; DELF/DALF) were also added to the teacher assessment.

Altogether almost 300 teachers and some 2,800 learners representing approximately 500 classes were involved in the two surveys. Learners from lower secondary, upper secondary, vocational and adult education, were represented in the following proportions:

	Lower secondary	Upper secondary	Vocational	Adult
1994	35%	19%	15%	31%
1995	24%	31%	17%	28%

Teachers from the German- French- Italian- and Romansch-speaking language regions of Switzerland were involved, though the numbers involved from the Italian- and

Romansch-speaking regions was very limited. In each year about a quarter of the teachers were teaching their mother tongue. Teachers completed questionnaires in the target language. Thus in 1994 the descriptors were used just in English, whilst in 1995 they were completed in English, French and German.

Methodology

Briefly, the methodology of the project was as follows:

Intuitive phase:
1. Detailed analysis of those scales of language proficiency in the public domain or obtainable through Council of Europe contacts in 1993; a list is given at the end of this summary.

2. Deconstruction of those scales into descriptive categories related those outlined in Chapters 4 and 5 to create an initial pool of classified, edited descriptors.

Qualitative phase:
3. Category analysis of recordings of teachers discussing and comparing the language proficiency demonstrated in video performances in order to check that the metalanguage used by practitioners was adequately represented.

4. 32 workshops with teachers (a) sorting descriptors into categories they purported to describe; (b) making qualitative judgements about clarity, accuracy and relevance of the description; (c) sorting descriptors into bands of proficiency.

Quantitative phase:
5. Teacher assessment of representative learners at the end of a school year using an overlapping series of questionnaires made up of the descriptors found by teachers in the workshops to be the clearest, most focused and most relevant. In the first year a series of 7 questionnaires each made up of 50 descriptors was used to cover the range of proficiency from learners with 80 hours English to advanced speakers.

6. In the second year a different series of five questionnaires was used. The two surveys were linked by the fact that descriptors for spoken interaction were reused in the second year. Learners were assessed for each descriptor on a 0–4 scale describing the relation to performance conditions under which they could be expected to perform as described in the descriptor. The way the descriptors were interpreted by teachers was analysed using the Rasch rating scale model. This analysis had two aims:

    (a) to mathematically scale a 'difficulty value' for each descriptor.
    (b) to identify statistically significant variation in the interpretation of the

descriptors in relation to different educational sectors, language regions and target languages in order to identify descriptors with a very high stability of values across different contexts to use in constructing holistic scales summarising the Common Reference Levels.

7. Performance assessment by all participating teachers of videos of some of the learners in the survey. The aim of this assessment was to quantify differences in severity of participating teachers in order to take such variation in severity into account in identifying the range of achievement in educational sectors in Switzerland.

Interpretation phase:
8. Identification of 'cut-points' on the scale of descriptors to produce the set of Common Reference Levels introduced in Chapter 3. Summary of those levels in a holistic scale (Table 1), a self-assessment grid describing language activities (Table 2) and a performance assessment grid describing different aspects of communicative language competence (Table 3).

9. Presentation of illustrative scales in Chapters 4 and 5 for those categories that proved scaleable.

10. Adaptation of the descriptors to self-assessment format in order to produce a Swiss trial version of the European Language Portfolio. This includes: (a) a self-assessment grid for Listening, Speaking, Spoken Interaction, Spoken Production, Writing (Table 2); (b) a self-assessment checklist for each of the Common Reference Levels.

11. A final conference in which research results were presented, experience with the Portfolio was discussed and teachers were introduced to the Common Reference Levels.

Results

Scaling descriptors for different skills and for different kinds of competences (linguistic, pragmatic, sociocultural) is complicated by the question of whether or not assessments of these different features will combine in a single measurement dimension. This is not a problem caused by or exclusively associated with Rasch modelling, it applies to all statistical analysis. Rasch, however, is less forgiving if a problem emerges. Test data, teacher assessment data and self-assessment data may behave differently in this regard. With assessment by teachers in this project, certain categories were less successful and had to be removed from the analysis in order to safeguard the accuracy of the results. Categories lost from the original descriptor pool included the following:

Appendix B: The illustrative scales of descriptors

a) Sociocultural competence

Those descriptors explicitly describing sociocultural and sociolinguistic competence. It is not clear how much this problem was caused (a) by this being a separate construct from language proficiency; (b) by rather vague descriptors identified as problematic in the workshops, or (c) by inconsistent responses by teachers lacking the necessary knowledge of their students. This problem extended to descriptors of ability to read and appreciate fiction and literature.

b) Work-related

Those descriptors asking teachers to guess about activities (generally work-related) beyond those they could observe directly in class, for example telephoning; attending formal meetings; giving formal presentations; writing reports & essays; formal correspondence. This was despite the fact that the adult and vocational sectors were well represented.

c) Negative concept

Those descriptors relating to need for simplification; need to get repetition or clarification, which are implicitly negative concepts. Such aspects worked better as provisos in positively worded statements, for example:

> *Can generally understand clear, standard speech on familiar matters directed at him/her, provided he/she can ask for repetition or reformulation from time to time.*

Reading proved to be on a separate measurement dimension to spoken interaction and production for these teachers. However, the data collection design made it possible to scale reading separately and then to equate the reading scale to the main scale after the event. Writing was not a major focus of the study, and the descriptors for written production included in Chapter 4 were mainly developed from those for spoken production. The relatively high stability of the scale values for descriptors for reading and writing taken from the CEF being reported by both DIALANG and ALTE (see Appendices C and D respectively), however, suggests that the approaches taken to reading and to writing were reasonably effective.

   The complications with the categories discussed above are all related to the scaling issue of uni- as opposed to multi-dimensionality. Multi-dimensionality shows itself in a second way in relation to the population of learners whose proficiency is being described. There were a number of cases in which the difficulty of a descriptor was dependent on the educational sector concerned. For example, adult beginners are considered by their teachers to find 'real life' tasks significantly easier than 14 year olds. This seems intuitively sensible. Such variation is known as 'Differential Item Function (DIF)'. In as far as this was feasible, descriptors showing DIF were avoided when constructing the summaries of the Common Reference Levels introduced in Tables 1 and 2 in Chapter 3. There were very few significant effects by target language, and none by mother tongue, other than a suggestion that native speaker teachers may have a stricter interpretation of the word 'understand' at advanced levels, particularly with regard to literature.

Exploitation

The illustrative descriptors in Chapters 4 and 5 have been either (a) situated at the level at which that actual descriptor was empirically calibrated in the study; (b) written by recombining elements of descriptors so calibrated to that level (for a few categories like *Public Announcements* which were not included in the original survey), or (c) selected on the basis of the results of the qualitative phase (workshops), or (d) written during the interpretative phase to plug a gap on the empirically calibrated sub-scale. This last point applies almost entirely to *Mastery*, for which very few descriptors had been included in the study.

Follow up

A project for the university of Basle in 1999–2000 adapted CEF descriptors for a self-assessment instrument designed for university entrance. Descriptors were also added for sociolinguistic competence and for note taking in a university context. The new descriptors were scaled to the CEF levels with the same methodology used in the original project, and are included in this edition of the CEF. The correlation of the scale values of the CEF descriptors between their original scale values and their values in this study was 0.899.

References

North, B. 1996/2000: *The development of a common framework scale of language proficiency*. PhD thesis, Thames Valley University. Reprinted 2000, New York, Peter Lang.

   forthcoming: Developing descriptor scales of language proficiency for the CEF Common Reference Levels. In J.C. Alderson (ed.) *Case studies of the use of the Common European Framework*. Council of Europe.

   forthcoming: A CEF-based self-assessment tool for university entrance. In J.C. Alderson (ed.) *Case studies of the use of the Common European Framework*. Council of Europe.

North, B. and Schneider, G. 1998: Scaling descriptors for language proficiency scales. *Language Testing* 15/2: 217–262.

Schneider and North 1999: '*In anderen Sprachen kann ich*' . . . *Skalen zur Beschreibung, Beurteilung und Selbsteinschätzung der fremdsprachlichen Kommunikationmsfähigkeit*. Berne, Project Report, National Research Programme 33, Swiss National Science Research Council.

The descriptors in the Framework

In addition to the tables used in Chapter 3 to summarise the Common Reference Levels, illustrative descriptors are interspersed in the text of Chapters 4 and 5 as follows:

Document B1   Illustrative scales in Chapter 4: Communicative activities

R E C E P T I O N	**Spoken**	• Overall listening comprehension
		    • Understanding Interaction between native speakers
		    • Listening as a member of a live audience
		    • Listening to announcements and instructions
		    • Listening to radio & audio recordings

	Audio/Visual	• Watching TV & film

	Written	• Overall reading comprehension
		    • Reading correspondence
		    • Reading for orientation
		    • Reading for information and argument
		    • Reading instructions

I N T E R A C T I O N	**Spoken**	• Overall spoken interaction
		    • Comprehension in interaction
		    • Understanding a native speaker interlocutor
		    • Conversation
		    • Informal discussion
		    • Formal discussion (Meetings)
		    • Goal-oriented co-operation
		    • Obtaining goods and services
		    • Information exchange
		    • Interviewing & being interviewed

	Written	• Overall written interaction
		    • Correspondence
		    • Notes, messages & forms

P R O D U C T I O N	**Spoken**	• Overall spoken production
		    • Sustained monologue: describing experience
		    • Sustained monologue: putting a case (e.g. debate)
		    • Public announcements
		    • Addressing audiences

	Written	• Overall written production
		    • Creative writing
		    • Writing reports and essays

Document B2   Illustrative scales in Chapter 4: Communication strategies

RECEPTION	• Identifying cues and inferring
INTERACTION	• Taking the floor (turntaking) • Co-operating • Asking for clarification
PRODUCTION	• Planning • Compensating • Monitoring and repair

Document B3   Illustrative scales in Chapter 4: Working with text

TEXT
• Note taking in seminars and lectures • Processing text

Document B4   Illustrative scales in Chapter 5: Communicative language competence

LINGUISTIC		
	Range:	• General range • Vocabulary range
	Control:	• Grammatical accuracy • Vocabulary control • Phonological control • Orthographic control
SOCIOLINGUISTIC		
		• Sociolinguistic
PRAGMATIC		
		• Flexibility • Taking the floor (turntaking) – repeated • Thematic development • Coherence • Propositional precision • Spoken fluency

Document B5   Coherence in descriptor calibration

The position at which particular content appears on the scale demonstrates a high degree of coherence. As an example, one can take topics. No descriptors were included for topics, but topics were referred to in descriptors for various categories. The three most relevant categories were *Describing & narrating*, *Information exchange* and *Range*.

   The charts below compare the way topics are treated in those three areas. Although the content of the three charts is not identical, comparison demonstrates a considerable degree of coherence, which is reflected throughout the set of calibrated descriptors. Analysis of this kind has been the basis for producing descriptors for categories not included in the original survey (*e.g. Public announcements*) by recombining descriptor elements.

DESCRIBING & NARRATING:						
A1	**A2**		**B1**		**B2**	**C1**	**C2**

A1	**A2**		**B1**		**B2**	**C1**	**C2**
• where they live	• people, appearance • background, job • places & living conditions	• objects, pets, possessions • events & activities • likes/dislikes • plans/ arrangements • habits/routines • personal experience	• plot of book/film • experiences • reactions to both • dreams, hopes, ambitions • tell a story	• basic details of unpre-dictable occurrences e.g. accident		• clear detailed descrip-tion of complex subjects	

INFORMATION EXCHANGE:						

A1	**A2**		**B1**		**B2**	**C1**	**C2**
• them-selves & others • home • time	• simple, routine, direct • limited, work & free time	• simple directions & instructions • pastimes, habits, routines • past activities	• detailed directions	• accumu-lated factual info on familiar matters within field			

RANGE: SETTINGS:						

A1	**A2**		**B1**		**B2**	**C1**	**C2**
	• basic common needs • simple/ predictable survival • simple concrete needs: pers. details, daily routines, info requests	• routine everyday transactions • familiar situations & topics • everyday situations with predictable content	• most topics pertinent to everyday life: family hobbies interests, work travel, current events				

Document B4   Scales of language proficiency used as sources

Holistic scales of overall spoken proficiency
- Hofmann: Levels of Competence in Oral Communication 1974
- University of London School Examination Board: Certificate of Attainment – Graded Tests 1987
- Ontario ESL Oral Interaction Assessment Bands 1990
- Finnish Nine Level Scale of Language Proficiency 1993
- European Certificate of Attainment in Modern Languages 1993

Scales for different communicative activities
- Trim: Possible Scale for a Unit/Credit Scheme: Social Skills 1978
- North: European Language Portfolio Mock-up: Interaction Scales 1991

- Eurocentres/ELTDU Scale of Business English 1991
- Association of Language Testers in Europe, Bulletin 3, 1994

Scales for the four skills
- Foreign Service Institute Absolute Proficiency Ratings 1975
- Wilkins: Proposals for Level Definitions for a Unit/Credit Scheme: Speaking 1978
- Australian Second Language Proficiency Ratings 1982
- American Council on the Teaching of Foreign Languages Proficiency Guidelines 1986
- Elviri et al.: Oral Expression 1986 (in Van Ek 1986)
- Interagency Language Roundtable Language Skill Level Descriptors 1991
- English Speaking Union (ESU) Framework Project: 1989
- Australian Migrant Education Program Scale (Listening only)

Rating scales for oral assessment
- Dade County ESL Functional Levels 1978
- Hebrew Oral Proficiency Rating Grid 1981
- Carroll B.J. and Hall P.J. Interview Scale 1985
- Carroll B.J. Oral Interaction Assessment Scale 1980
- International English Testing System (IELTS): Band Descriptors for Speaking & Writing 1990
- Goteborgs Univeritet: Oral Assessment Criteria
- Fulcher: The Fluency Rating Scale 1993

Frameworks of syllabus content and assessment criteria for pedagogic stages of attainment
- University of Cambridge/Royal Society of Arts Certificates in Communicative Skills in English 1990
- Royal Society of Arts Modern Languages Examinations: French 1989
- English National Curriculum: Modern Languages 1991
- Netherlands New Examinations Programme 1992
- Eurocentres Scale of Language Proficiency 1993
- British Languages Lead Body: National Language Standards 1993

Appendix C: The DIALANG scales

This appendix contains a description of the DIALANG language assessment system which is an application for diagnostic purposes of the Common European Framework (CEF). The focus here is on the self-assessment statements used in the system and on the calibration study carried out on them as part of the development of the system. Two related descriptive scales, which are based on the CEF and used in reporting and explaining the diagnostic results to the learners, are also included. The descriptors in this project were scaled and equated to the CEF levels with Method No 12c (Rasch modelling) outlined at the end of Appendix A.

The DIALANG project

The DIALANG assessment system

DIALANG is an assessment system intended for language learners who want to obtain diagnostic information about their proficiency. The DIALANG project is carried out with the financial support of the European Commission, Directorate-General for Education and Culture (SOCRATES Programme, LINGUA Action D).

The system consists of self-assessment, language tests and feedback, which are all available in fourteen European languages: Danish, Dutch, English, Finnish, French, German, Greek, Icelandic, Irish, Italian, Norwegian, Portuguese, Spanish, and Swedish. DIALANG is delivered via the Internet free of charge.

DIALANG's Assessment Framework and the descriptive scales used for reporting the results to the users are directly based on the Common European Framework (CEF). The self-assessment statements used in DIALANG are also mostly taken from the CEF and adapted whenever necessary to fit the specific needs of the system.

Purpose of DIALANG

DIALANG is aimed at adults who want to know their level of language proficiency and who want to get feedback on the strengths and weaknesses of their proficiency. The system also provides the learners with advice about how to improve their language skills and, furthermore, it attempts to raise their awareness of language learning and proficiency. The system does not issue certificates.

The primary users of the system will be individual learners who study languages independently or on formal language courses. However, language teachers may also find many of the features of the system useful for their purposes.

Assessment procedure in DIALANG

The DIALANG assessment procedure has the following steps:

1. Choice of administration language (14 possible)
2. Registration
3. Choice of test language (14 possible)
4. Vocabulary Size Placement Test
5. Choice of skill (reading, listening, writing, vocabulary, structures)
6. Self-assessment (only in reading, listening, and writing)
7. System pre-estimates learner's ability
8. Test of appropriate difficulty is administered
9. Feedback

On entering the system, the learners first choose the language in which they wish to receive instructions and feedback. After registering, users are then presented with a placement test which also estimates the size of their vocabulary. After choosing the skill in which they then wish to be tested, users are presented with a number of self-assessment statements, before taking the test selected. These self-assessment statements cover the skill in question, and the learner has to decide whether or not s/he can do the activity described in each statement. Self-assessment is not available for the other two areas assessed by DIALANG, vocabulary and structures, because source statements do not exist in the CEF. After the test, as part of the feedback, the learners are told whether their self-assessed level of proficiency differs from the level of proficiency assigned to them by the system on the basis of their test performance. Users are also offered an opportunity to explore potential reasons for a mismatch between self-assessment and the test results in the Explanatory Feedback section.

Purpose of self-assessment in DIALANG

Self-assessment (SA) statements are used for two reasons in the DIALANG system. Firstly, self-assessment is considered an important activity in itself. It is believed to encourage autonomous learning, to give learners greater control over their learning and to enhance learner awareness of their learning process.

The second purpose of self-assessment in DIALANG is more 'technical': the system uses the Vocabulary Size Placement Test and self-assessment results to pre-estimate the learners' ability and then directs them to the test whose difficulty level best matches their ability.

The DIALANG self-assessment scales

Source

Most of the self-assessment statements used in DIALANG were taken from the English version of the Common European Framework (Draft 2, 1996). In this respect, DIALANG is a direct application of the Framework for assessment purposes.

Qualitative development

The DIALANG Working Group on Self-Assessment[1] reviewed all CEF statements in 1998 and chose those which appeared to be the most concrete, clear and simple; North's (1996/2000) empirical results on the statements were also consulted. More than a hundred statements were selected for reading, listening and writing. In addition, statements about speaking were chosen but as speaking is not part of the present DIALANG system, they were not included in the validation study described below and are thus not presented in this appendix.

The wording of the statements was changed from 'Can do' to 'I can' because they were to be used for self-assessment rather than teacher assessment purposes. Some of the statements were modified to simplify them further to suit the intended users; a few new statements were also developed where there was not enough material in the CEF to draw on (the new statements are in italics in the tables). All statements were audited by Dr Brian North, the originator of the statements in the CEF, and by a group of four language testing and teaching experts before the final wording of the statements was agreed.

Translation

Because DIALANG is a multilingual system, the self-assessment statements were then translated from English into the other thirteen languages. The translation followed an agreed procedure. Guidelines for translation and negotiation were agreed; comprehensibility to learners was a prime quality criterion. Initially, two to three experts per language translated the statements into their language independently and then met to discuss differences and to agree a consensus wording. The translations were forwarded to the Self-Assessment Group whose members had the linguistic proficiency to additionally cross-check the quality of the translations in nine languages. The translators were contacted and any questions related to wording were discussed and modifications agreed.

Calibration of the self-assessment statements

So far, the DIALANG project has carried out one calibration study on the self-assessment statements. (Calibration is a procedure in which the level of difficulty of

---

[1] The group consisted of Alex Teasdale (chair), Neus Figueras, Ari Huhta, Fellyanka Kaftandjieva, Mats Oscarson, and Sauli Takala.

items, statements, etc. is determined statistically and a scale is constructed of them.) The calibration was based on a sample of 304 subjects (complete test design) who also took a number of DIALANG tests in Finnish. The SA-statements were presented to them either in Swedish (for 250 subjects whose mother tongue was Swedish) or in English. In addition, most subjects could consult the Finnish language version of the statements.[2]

The data was analysed with the OPLM programme (Verhelst et al. 1985; Verhelst and Glass 1995).[3] The results of the analysis were very good: over 90% of the statements could be scaled (i.e. they 'fitted' the statistical model used). The three self-assessment scales which were constructed on the basis of the calibration of the statements were very homogeneous, as indicated by the high reliability indices (Cronbach's alpha): .91 for reading, .93 for listening and .94 for writing.[4]

Similar calibration studies will be carried out when the other 13 languages are piloted, following the approach developed by the Data Analysis Group. They will show to what extent the excellent results of the first study can be replicated and whether there is any tendency for some statements to be consistently better than the others, for self-assessment purposes.

Although the first calibration study is only one study, it is important to note that it tells about the quality of more than one language version of the SA statements in DIALANG. This is because most of the learners studied could choose any, even all, of the three versions (Swedish, English or Finnish) when completing the self-assessment part, although most of them probably relied on the Swedish one. Because of the careful translation procedure, we can safely assume that the SA statements are largely equivalent across the languages – an assumption which will obviously be tested as part of the other calibration studies.

Additional evidence for the quality of the DIALANG self-assessment scales – and for the CEF scales – was obtained by Dr Kaftandjieva by correlating the difficulty values of the statements in this study with the values for the same statements obtained by North (1996/2000) in a different context. The correlation was found to be very high (.83), or even .897, if one strangely behaving statement is excluded.

Document C1 presents the 107 self-assessment statements for reading, listening and writing which survived the calibration study based on Finnish data. The statements in each table are ordered in terms of difficulty from the easiest to the hardest. Statements which were not taken from the Framework are in *italics*.

Other DIALANG scales based on the Common European Framework

In addition to the self-assessment statements, DIALANG uses two sets of descriptive scales which are based on the CEF. The scales concern reading, writing and listening:

---

[2] The study was conducted in the Centre for Applied Language Studies at the University of Jyväskylä, which was the Coordinating Centre of the Project in 1996–1999, by the Working Group for Data Analysis consisting of Fellyanka Kaftandjieva (chair), Norman Verhelst, Sauli Takala, John de Jong, and Timo Törmäkangas. The Coordinating Centre in DIALANG Phase 2 is Freie Universität Berlin.

[3] OPLM is an extension of the Rasch model, which allows items to differ in their discrimination. The difference between it and the two-parameter model is that discrimination parameters are not estimated but inputted as known constants.

[4] The global data-model fit was also quite good (p=.26) when the statements were calibrated together. The statistical fit for skill-based calibration was also good (p=.10 for Reading, .84 for Writing and .78 for Listening).

- the more concise version accompanies the test score,
- the more extensive version is part of Advisory Feedback.

Concise scales

DIALANG uses the concise overall scales for reading, writing and listening to report scores on the DIALANG system. When learners get feedback on their performance, they are given a result on the CEF scale, A1 to C2, and the meaning of this score is described using these reporting scales. These were validated in the DIALANG context by asking 12 expert judges to assign each statement to one of six levels. These overall reporting scales were then used by the expert judges to assign each item in the DIALANG tests of Finnish to a CEF level. The scale is based on Table 2 of the CEF; the descriptions were slightly modified in the same way as SA statements. These scales are presented in Document C2.

Advisory feedback

The Advisory Feedback section of the assessment system uses scales which contain more extensive descriptions of proficiency in reading, writing and listening. The section provides the users with more detailed accounts of what learners can typically do with the language at each of the skill levels. The learners can also compare the description for a particular level with the descriptions for adjacent levels. These more detailed scales are also based on the scales on Table 2 in the CEF, but the descriptors were elaborated further with the help of other sections of the CEF and also other sources. These scales are presented in Document C3.

Readers interested in the results of the empirical studies reported here will find more detailed information about them in Takala and Kaftandjieva (forthcoming); for further information about the system in general and the feedback it provides, consult Huhta, Luoma, Oscarson, Sajavaara, Takala and Teasdale (forthcoming).

References

Huhta, A., S. Luoma, M. Oscarson, K. Sajavaara, S. Takala, and A. Teasdale (forthcoming). DIALANG – A Diagnostic Language Assessment System for Learners. In J.C. Alderson (ed.) Case Studies of the Use of the Common European Framework. Council of Europe.

North, B. (1996/2000). The Development of a Common Framework Scale of Language Proficiency Based on a Theory of Measurement. PhD thesis. Thames Valley University. Reprinted 2000: New York, Peter Lang.

Takala, S. and F. Kaftandjieva (forthcoming). Council of Europe Scales of Language Proficiency: A Validation Study. In J.C. Alderson (ed.) Case Studies of the Use of the Common European Framework. Council of Europe.

Verhelst, N., C. Glass and H. Verstralen (1985). One-Parameter Logistic Model: OPLM. Arnhem: CITO.

Verhelst, N. and C. Glass (1995). The One-Parameter Logistic Model. In G. Fisher and I. Molenaar (eds.) Rasch Models: Foundations, Recent Developments and Applications. New York: Springer-Verlag. 215–237.

Document C1   DIALANG self-assessment statements

CEF Level	*READING*
A1	I can understand the general idea of simple informational texts and short simple descriptions, especially if they contain pictures which help to explain the text.
A1	I can understand very short, simple texts, putting together familiar names, words and basic phrases, by for example rereading parts of the text.
A1	I can follow short, simple written instructions, especially if they contain pictures.
A1	I can recognise familiar names, words and very simple phrases on simple notices in the most common everyday situations.
A1	I can understand short, simple messages, e.g. on postcards.
A2	I can understand short, simple texts containing the most common words, including some shared international words.
A2	I can understand short, simple texts written in common everyday language.
A2	I can understand short simple texts related to my job.
A2	I can find specific information in simple everyday material such as advertisements, brochures, menus and timetables.
A2	I can identify specific information in simple written material such as letters, brochures and short newspaper articles describing events.
A2	I can understand short simple personal letters.
A2	I can understand standard routine letters and faxes on familiar topics.
A2	I can understand simple instructions on equipment encountered in everyday life – such as a public telephone.
A2	I can understand everyday signs and notices in public places, such as streets, restaurants, railway stations and in workplaces.
B1	I can understand straightforward texts on subjects related to my fields of interest.
B1	I can find and understand general information I need in everyday material, such as letters, brochures and short official documents.
B1	I can search one long or several short texts to locate specific information I need to help me complete a task.
B1	I can recognise significant points in straightforward newspaper articles on familiar subjects.
B1	I can identify the main conclusions in clearly written argumentative texts.
B1	I can recognise the general line of argument in a text but not necessarily in detail.
B1	I can understand the description of events, feelings and wishes in personal letters well enough to correspond with a friend or acquaintance.
B1	I can understand clearly written straightforward instructions for a piece of equipment.
B2	I can read correspondence relating to my fields of interest and easily understand the essential meaning.
B2	I can understand specialised articles outside my field, provided I can use a dictionary to confirm terminology.
B2	I can read many kinds of texts quite easily at different speeds and in different ways according to my purpose in reading and the type of text.
B2	I have a broad reading vocabulary, but I sometimes experience difficulty with less common words and phrases.
B2	I can quickly identify the content and relevance of news items, articles and reports on a wide range of professional topics, deciding whether closer study is worthwhile.
B2	I can understand articles and reports concerned with contemporary problems in which the writers adopt particular stances or viewpoints.
C1	I can understand any correspondence with an occasional use of dictionary.
C1	I can understand in detail long, complex instructions on a new machine or procedure even outside my own area of speciality if I can reread difficult sections.
C2	I can understand and interpret practically all forms of written language including abstract, structurally complex, or highly colloquial literary and non-literary writings.

CEF Level	WRITING
A1	I can write simple notes to friends.
A1	I can describe where I live.
A1	I can fill in forms with personal details.
A1	I can write simple isolated phrases and sentences.
A1	I can write a short simple postcard.
A1	I can write short letters and messages with the help of a dictionary.
A2	I can give short, basic descriptions of events and activities.
A2	I can write very simple personal letters expressing thanks and apology.
A2	I can write short, simple notes and messages relating to matters of everyday life.
A2	I can describe plans and arrangements.
A2	I can explain what I like or dislike about something.
A2	I can describe my family, living conditions, schooling, present or most recent job.
A2	I can describe past activities and personal experiences.
B1	I can write very brief reports, which pass on routine factual information and state reasons for actions.
B1	I can write personal letters describing experiences, feelings and events in detail.
B1	I can describe basic details of unpredictable occurrences, e.g., an accident.
B1	I can describe dreams, hopes and ambitions.
B1	I can take messages describing enquiries, problems, etc.
B1	I can describe the plot of a book or film and describe my reactions.
B1	I can briefly give reasons and explanations for opinions, plans and actions.
B2	I can evaluate different ideas and solutions to a problem.
B2	I can synthesise information and arguments from a number of sources.
B2	I can construct a chain of reasoned argument.
B2	I can speculate about causes, consequences and hypothetical situations.
C1	I can expand and support points of view at some length with subsidiary points, reasons and relevant examples.
C1	I can develop an argument systematically, giving appropriate emphasis to significant points, and presenting relevant supporting detail.
C1	I can give clear detailed descriptions of complex subjects.
(estim. C1)	*I can usually write without consulting a dictionary.*
(estim. C1)	*I can write so well that my language needs to be checked only if the text is an important one.*
C2	I can provide an appropriate and effective logical structure, which helps the reader to find significant points.
C2	I can produce clear, smoothly flowing, complex reports, articles or essays that present a case, or give critical appreciation of proposals or literary works.
(estim. C2)	*I can write so well that native speakers need not check my texts.*
(estim. C2)	*I can write so well that my texts cannot be improved significantly even by teachers of writing.*

CEF Level	*LISTENING*
A1	I can understand everyday expressions dealing with simple and concrete everyday needs, in clear, slow and repeated speech.
A1	I can follow speech which is very slow and carefully articulated, with long pauses for me to get the meaning.
A1	I can understand questions and instructions and follow short, simple directions.
A1	I can understand numbers, prices and times.
A2	I can understand enough to manage simple, routine exchanges without too much effort.
A2	I can generally identify the topic of discussion around me which is conducted slowly and clearly.
A2	I can generally understand clear, standard speech on familiar matters, although in a real life situation I might have to ask for repetition or reformulation.
A2	I can understand enough to be able to meet concrete needs in everyday life provided speech is clear and slow.
A2	I can understand phrases and expressions related to immediate needs.
A2	I can handle simple business in shops, post offices or banks.
A2	I can understand simple directions relating to how to get from X to Y, by foot or public transport.
A2	I can understand the essential information from short recorded passages dealing with predictable everyday matters which are spoken slowly and clearly.
A2	I can identify the main point of TV news items reporting events, accidents, etc, where the visual material supports the commentary.
A2	I can catch the main point in short, clear, simple messages and announcements.
B1	I can guess the meaning of occasional unknown words from the context and understand sentence meaning if the topic discussed is familiar.
B1	I can generally follow the main points of extended discussion around me, provided speech is clear and in standard language.
B1	I can follow clear speech in everyday conversation, though in a real life situation I will sometimes have to ask for repetition of particular words and phrases.
B1	I can understand straightforward factual information about common everyday or job-related topics, identifying both general messages and specific details, provided speech is clear and generally familiar accent is used.
B1	I can understand the main points of clear standard speech on familiar matters which occur regularly.
B1	I can follow a lecture or a talk within my own field, provided the subject matter is familiar and the presentation straightforward and clearly organised.
B1	I can understand simple technical information, such as operation instructions for everyday equipment.
B1	I can understand the information content of the majority of recorded or broadcast audio material about familiar subjects spoken relatively slowly and clearly.
B1	I can follow many films in which visuals and action carry much of the storyline, and in which the story is straightforward and the language clear.
B1	I can catch the main points in broadcasts on familiar topics and topics of personal interest when the language is relatively slow and clear.

CEF Level	LISTENING (continued)
B2	I can understand in detail what is said to me in the standard spoken language. I can do this even when there is some noise in the background.
B2	I can understand standard spoken language, live or broadcast, on both familiar and unfamiliar topics normally encountered in personal, academic or vocational life. Only extreme background noise, unclear structure and/or idiomatic usage causes some problems.
B2	I can understand the main ideas of complex speech on both concrete and abstract topics delivered in a standard language including technical discussions in my field of specialisation.
B2	I can follow extended speech and complex lines of argument provided the topic is reasonably familiar, and the direction of the talk is clearly stated by the speaker.
B2	I can follow the essentials of lectures, talks and reports and other forms of presentation which use complex ideas and language.
B2	I can understand announcements and messages on concrete and abstract topics spoken in standard language at normal speed.
B2	I can understand most radio documentaries and most other recorded or broadcast audio material delivered in standard language and can identify the speaker's mood, tone, etc.
B2	I can understand most TV news and current affairs programmes such as documentaries, live interviews, talk shows, plays and the majority of films in standard language.
B2	I can follow a lecture or talk within my own field, provided the presentation is clear.
C1	I can keep up with an animated conversation between native speakers.
C1	I can understand enough to follow extended speech on abstract and complex topics beyond my own field, though I may need to confirm occasional details, especially if the accent is unfamiliar.
C1	I can recognise a wide range of idiomatic expressions and colloquialisms and recognise changes in style.
C1	I can follow extended speech even when it is not clearly structured and when relationships between ideas are only implied and not stated explicitly.
C1	I can follow most lectures, discussions and debates with relative ease.
C1	I can extract specific information from poor quality public announcements.
C1	I can understand complex technical information, such as operating instructions, specifications for familiar products and services.
C1	I can understand a wide range of recorded audio material, including some non-standard language, and identify finer points of detail, including implicit attitudes and relationships between speakers.
C1	I can follow films which contain a considerable degree of slang and idiomatic usage.
C2	I can follow specialised lectures and presentations which use a high degree of colloquialism, regional usage or unfamiliar terminology.

Document C2   The overall (concise) scales for reporting DIALANG scores

CEF Level	*READING*
A1	Your test result suggests that you are at or below level **A1** in reading on the Council of Europe scale. At this level people can understand very simple sentences, for example on notices and posters or in catalogues.
A2	Your test result suggests that you are at level **A2** in reading on the Council of Europe scale. At this level people can understand very short, simple texts. They can find specific information they are looking for in simple everyday texts such as advertisements, leaflets, menus and timetables and they can understand short simple personal letters.
B1	Your test result suggests that you are at level **B1** in reading on the Council of Europe scale. At this level people can understand texts that contain everyday or job-related language. They can understand personal letters in which the writer describes events, feelings and wishes.
B2	Your test result suggests that you are at level **B2** in reading on the Council of Europe scale. At this level people can understand articles and reports about contemporary issues when the writer takes a particular position on a problem or expresses a particular viewpoint. They can understand most short stories and popular novels.
C1	Your test result suggests that you are at level **C1** in reading on the Council of Europe scale. At this level people can understand long and complex factual and literary texts as well as differences in style. They can understand "specialised" language in articles and technical instructions, even if these are not in their field.
C2	Your test result suggests that you are at or above level **C2** in reading on the Council of Europe scale. At this level people can read, without any problems, almost all forms of text, including texts which are abstract and contain difficult words and grammar. For example: manuals, articles on special subjects, and literary texts.

CEF Level	WRITING
A1	Your test result suggests that you are at level **A1** in writing on the Council of Europe scale. At this level, people can write a short simple postcard, for example sending holiday greetings. They can fill in forms with personal details, for example writing their name, nationality and address on a hotel registration form.
A2	Your test result suggests that you are at level **A2** in writing on the Council of Europe scale. At this level people can write short, simple notes and messages about everyday matters and everyday needs. They can write a very simple personal letter, for example thanking someone for something.
B1	Your test result suggests that you are at level **B1** in writing on the Council of Europe scale. At this level people can write simple texts on topics which are familiar or of personal interest. They can write personal letters describing experiences and impressions.
B2	Your test result suggests that you are at level **B2** in writing on the Council of Europe scale. At this level people can write clear detailed texts on a wide range of subjects related to their interests. They can write an essay or report, passing on information and presenting some arguments for or against a particular point of view. They can write letters highlighting the personal significance of events and experiences.
C1	Your test result suggests that you are at level **C1** in writing on the Council of Europe scale. At this level, people can write clear and well-structured text and express their points of view at some length. They can write about complex subjects in a letter, an essay or a report, underlining what they think are the most important points. They can write different kinds of texts in an assured and personal style which is appropriate to the reader in mind.
C2	Your test result suggests that you are at level **C2** in writing on the Council of Europe scale. At this level, people can write clearly and smoothly and in an appropriate style. They can write complex letters, reports or articles in such a way that helps the reader to notice and remember important points. They can write summaries and reviews of professional or literary texts.

CEF Level	LISTENING
A1	Your test result suggests that you are at or below level **A1** in listening on the Council of Europe scale. At this level, people can understand very simple phrases about themselves, people they know and things around them, when people speak slowly and clearly.
A2	Your test result suggests that you are at level **A2** in listening on the Council of Europe scale. At this level, people can understand expressions and the most common words about things which are important to them, e.g. very basic personal and family information, shopping, their jobs. They can get the main point in short, clear, simple messages and announcements.
B1	Your test result suggests that you are at level **B1** in listening on the Council of Europe scale. At this level, people can understand the main points of clear 'standard' speech on familiar matters connected with work, school, leisure etc. In TV and radio current-affairs programmes or programmes of personal or professional interest, they can understand the main points provided the speech is relatively slow and clear.
B2	Your test result suggests that you are at level **B2** in listening on the Council of Europe scale. At this level, people can understand longer stretches of speech and lectures and follow complex lines of argument provided the topic is reasonably familiar. They can understand most TV news and current affairs programmes.
C1	Your test result suggests that you are at level **C1** in listening on the Council of Europe scale. At this level, people can understand spoken language even when it is not clearly structured and when ideas and thoughts are not expressed in an explicit way. They can understand television programmes and films without too much effort.
C2	Your test result suggests that you are at level **C2** in listening on the Council of Europe scale. At this level, people can understand any kind of spoken language, both when they hear it live and in the media. They also understand a native speaker who speaks fast if they have some time to get used to the accent.

Document C3   Elaborated descriptive scales used in the advisory feedback section of DIALANG

READING			
	A1	**A2**	**B1**
What types of text I understand	Very short, simple texts, typically short, simple descriptions, especially if they contain pictures. Short, simple written instructions e.g. short simple postcards, simple notices.	Texts on familiar, concrete matters. Short, simple texts e.g. routine personal and business letters and faxes, most everyday signs and notices, Yellow Pages, advertisements.	Straightforward factual texts on subjects related to my field of interest. Everyday material, e.g. letters, brochures and short official documents. Straightforward newspaper articles on familiar subjects and descriptions of events. Clearly written argumentative texts. Personal letters expressing feelings and wishes. Clearly written, straightforward instructions for a piece of equipment.
What I understand	Familiar names, words, basic phrases.	Understand short, simple texts. Find specific information in simple everyday material.	Understand straightforward factual language. Understand clearly written general argumentation (but not necessarily all details). Understand straightforward instructions. Find general information I need in everyday material. Locate specific information by searching one long or several different texts.
Conditions and limitations	Single phrase at a time, re-reading part of text.	Restricted mainly to common everyday language and language related to my job.	Ability to identify main conclusions and follow argument restricted to straightforward texts.

B2	C1	C2
Correspondence relating to my field of interest. Longer texts, including specialised articles outside my field and highly specialised sources within my field. Articles and reports on contemporary problems with particular viewpoints.	Wide range of long, complex texts from social, professional or academic life. Complex instructions on a new unfamiliar machine or procedure outside my area.	Wide range of long and complex texts – practically all forms of written language. Abstract, structurally complex, or highly colloquial literary and non-literary writings.
Understanding aided by broad active reading vocabulary, difficulty with less common phrases and idioms and with terminology. Understand the essential meaning of correspondence in my field, and specialised articles outside my field (with dictionary). Obtain information, ideas and opinions from highly specialised sources within my field. Locate relevant details in long texts.	Identify fine points of detail including attitudes and opinions which are not explicitly stated. Understand in detail complex texts, including fine points of detail, attitudes and opinions (see conditions and limitations).	Understand subtleties of style and meaning which are both implicitly and explicitly stated.
Range and types of text only a minor limitation – can read different types of text at different speeds and in different ways according to purpose and type. Dictionary required for more specialised or unfamiliar texts.	Understanding of details of complex texts usually only if difficult sections are re-read. Occasional use of dictionary.	Few limitations – can understand and interpret practically all forms of written language. Very unusual or archaic vocabulary and phrases may be unknown but will rarely impair understanding.

WRITING	A1	A2	B1
What types of text I can write	Very short pieces of writing: isolated words and very short, basic sentences. For example, simple messages, notes, forms and postcards.	Usually short, simple pieces of writing. For example, simple personal letters, postcards, messages, notes, forms.	Can write a continuous, intelligible text in which elements are connected.
What I can write	Numbers and dates, own name, nationality, address, and other personal details required to fill in simple forms when travelling. Short, simple sentences linked with connectors such as 'and' or 'then'.	Texts typically describe immediate needs, personal events, familiar places, hobbies, work, etc. Texts typically consist of short, basic sentences. Can use the most frequent connectors (e.g. and, but, because) to link sentences in order to write a story or to describe something as a list of points.	Can convey simple information to friends, service people, etc. who feature in everyday life. Can get straightforward points across comprehensively. Can give news, express thoughts about abstract or cultural topics such as films, music, etc. Can describe experiences, feelings and events in some detail.
Conditions and limitations	Apart from the most common words and expressions, the writer needs to consult a dictionary.	Only on familiar and routine matters. Writing continuous coherent text is difficult.	Range of texts can be limited to more familiar and common ones, such as describing things and writing about sequences of actions; but argumentation and contrasting issues, for example, are difficult.

B2	C1	C2
Can write a variety of different texts.	Can write a variety of different texts. Can express oneself with clarity and precision, using language flexibly and effectively.	Can write a variety of different texts. Can convey finer shades of meaning precisely. Can write persuasively.
Can express news and views effectively, and relate to those of others. Can use a variety of linking words to mark clearly the relationships between ideas. Spelling and punctuation are reasonably accurate.	Can produce clear, smoothly flowing, well-structured writing, showing controlled use of organisational patterns, connectors and cohesive devices. Can qualify opinions and statements precisely in relation to degrees of, for example, certainty/uncertainty, belief/doubt, likelihood. Layout, paragraphing and punctuation are consistent and helpful. Spelling is accurate apart from occasional slips.	Can create coherent and cohesive text making full and appropriate use of a variety of organisational patterns and a wide range of cohesive devices. Writing is free of spelling errors.
Expressing subtle nuances in taking a stance or in telling about feelings and experiences is usually difficult.	Expressing subtle nuances in taking a stance or in telling about feelings and experiences can be difficult.	No need to consult a dictionary, except for occasional specialist terms in an unfamiliar area.

LISTENING			
	A1	**A2**	**B1**
What types of text I understand	Very simple phrases about myself, people I know and things around me. Questions, instructions and directions. Examples: everyday expressions, questions, instructions, short and simple directions.	Simple phrases and expressions about things important to me. Simple, everyday conversations and discussions. Everyday matters in the media. Examples: messages, routine exchanges, directions, TV and radio news items.	Speech on familiar matters and factual information. Everyday conversations and discussions. Programmes in the media and films. Examples: operation instructions, short lectures and talks.
What I understand	Names and simple words. General idea. Enough to respond: providing personal info, following directions.	Common everyday language. Simple, everyday conversations and discussions. The main point. Enough to follow.	The meaning of some unknown words, by guessing. General meaning and specific details.
Conditions and limitations	Clear, slow and carefully articulated speech. When addressed by a sympathetic speaker.	Clear and slow speech. Will require the help of sympathetic speakers and/or images. Will sometimes ask for repetition or reformulation.	Clear, standard speech. Will require the help of visuals and action. Will sometimes ask for repetition of a word or phrase.

B2	C1	C2
All kinds of speech on familiar matters. Lectures. Programmes in the media and films. Examples: technical discussions, reports, live interviews.	Spoken language in general. Lectures, discussions and debates. Public announcements. Complex technical information. Recorded audio material and films. Examples: native-speaker conversations.	Any spoken language, live or broadcast. Specialised lectures and presentations.
Main ideas and specific information. Complex ideas and language. Speaker's viewpoints and attitudes.	Enough to participate actively in conversations. Abstract and complex topics. Implicit attitudes and relationships between speakers.	Global and detailed understanding without any difficulties.
Standard language and some idiomatic usage, even in reasonably noisy backgrounds.	Need to confirm occasional details when the accent is unfamiliar.	None, provided there is time to get used to what is unfamiliar.

Appendix D: The ALTE 'Can Do' statements

This appendix contains a description of the ALTE 'Can Do' statements, which form part of a long-term research project being undertaken by the Association of Language Testers in Europe (ALTE). The purposes and nature of the 'Can Do' statements are described. An account is then given of the way the statements were developed, related to ALTE examinations, and anchored to the CEF. The descriptors in this project were scaled and equated to the CEF levels with method number 12c (Rasch modelling) outlined in Appendix A.

The ALTE Framework and the 'Can Do' project

The ALTE Framework

The ALTE 'Can Do' statements constitute a central part of a long-term research programme set by ALTE, the aim of which is to establish a framework of 'key levels' of language performance, within which exams can be objectively described.

Much work has already been done to place the exam systems of ALTE members within this framework, based on an analysis of exam content and task types, and candidate profiles. A comprehensive introduction to these exam systems is available in the *ALTE Handbook of European Language Examinations and Examination Systems* (see pages 27, 167).

The ALTE 'Can Dos' are user-orientated scales

The aim of the 'Can Do' project is to develop and validate a set of performance-related scales, describing what learners can actually do in the foreign language.

In terms of Alderson's (1991) distinction between *constructor, assessor* and *user* orientated scales, the ALTE 'Can Do' statements in their original conception are user-orientated. They assist communication between stakeholders in the testing process, and in particular the interpretation of test results by non-specialists. As such they provide:

a) a useful tool for those involved in teaching and testing language students. They can be used as a checklist of what language users can do and thus define the stage they are at;

244

b) a basis for developing diagnostic test tasks, activity-based curricula and teaching materials;
c) a means of carrying out an activity-based linguistic audit, of use to people concerned with language training and recruitment in companies;
d) a means of comparing the objectives of courses and materials in different languages but existing in the same context.

They will be of use to people in training and personnel management, as they provide easily understandable descriptions of performance, which can be used in specifying requirements to language trainers, formulating job descriptions, specifying language requirements for new posts.

The ALTE 'Can Do' statements are multilingual

An important aspect of the 'Can Do' statements is that they are multilingual, having been translated so far into 12 of the languages represented in ALTE. These languages are: Catalan, Danish, Dutch, English, Finnish, French, German, Italian, Norwegian, Portuguese, Spanish, Swedish. As language-neutral descriptions of levels of language proficiency they constitute a frame of reference to which different language exams at different levels can potentially be related. They offer the chance to demonstrate equivalences between the examination systems of ALTE members, in meaningful terms relating to the real-world language skills likely to be available to people achieving a pass in these exams.

Organisation of the 'Can Do' statements

The 'Can Do' scales consist currently of about 400 statements, organised into three general areas: *Social and Tourist, Work*, and *Study*. These are the three main areas of interest of most language learners. Each includes a number of more particular areas, e.g. the Social and Tourist area has sections on *Shopping, Eating out, Accommodation*, etc. Each of these includes up to three scales, for the skills of *Listening/speaking, Reading* and *Writing. Listening/speaking* combines the scales relating to interaction.

Each scale includes statements covering a range of levels. Some scales cover only a part of the proficiency range, as there are many situations in which only basic proficiency is required to achieve successful communication.

The development process

The original development process went through these stages:

a) describing users of ALTE language tests through questionnaires, reports from schools, etc.;
b) using this information to specify range of candidate needs and identify major concerns;

c)   using test specifications and internationally recognised levels such as Waystage and Threshold to draw up initial statements;
d)   moderating statements and assessing their relevance to test takers;
e)   trailing statements with teachers and students with a view to evaluating relevance and transparency;
f)   correcting, revising and simplifying the language of the statements in the light of the above.

Empirical validation of the ALTE 'Can Do' statements

The scales as developed above have been subjected to an extended process of empirical validation. The validation process is aimed at transforming the 'Can Do' statements from an essentially subjective set of level descriptions into a calibrated measuring instrument. This is a long-term, ongoing process, which will continue as more data become available across the range of languages represented by ALTE.

So far data collection has been based chiefly on self-report, the 'Can Do' scales being presented to respondents as a set of linked questionnaires. Nearly ten thousand respondents have completed questionnaires. For many of these respondents, additional data are available in the form of language exam results. This is believed to be by far the biggest collection of data ever undertaken to validate a descriptive language proficiency scale.

Empirical work has started by looking at the internal coherence of the 'Can Do' scales themselves, the aims being:

1.   To check the function of individual statements within each 'Can Do' scale;
2.   To equate the different 'Can Do' scales, i.e. to establish the relative difficulty of the scales;
3.   To investigate the neutrality of the 'Can Do' scales with respect to language.

Questionnaires have been administered in the subjects' own first language, except at very advanced levels, and mainly in European countries. Respondents have been matched to appropriate questionnaires – the Work scales given to people using a foreign language professionally, the Study scales to respondents engaged in a course of study through the medium of a foreign language, or preparing to do so. The Social and Tourist scales are given to other respondents, while selected scales from this area have also been included in the Work and Study questionnaires as an 'anchor'.

Anchor items are used in data collection for a Rasch analysis in order to link different tests or questionnaires together. As explained in Appendix A, a Rasch analysis creates one single measurement framework by using a matrix data collection design, or a series of overlapping test forms linked together by items which are common to adjacent forms, which are called anchor items. Such systematic use of anchor statements is necessary in order to enable the relative difficulty of the areas of use, and particular scales, to be established. The use of Social and Tourist scales as an anchor was based on the assumption that these areas call upon a common core of language proficiency and can be expected to provide the best point of reference for equating the Work and Study scales.

Textual revision

One outcome of the first phase has been a textual revision of the 'Can Do' scales. In particular, statements with negative orientation have been removed, as they proved problematic from a statistical point of view, and did not seem wholly appropriate to descriptions of levels of attainment. Here are two examples of the kind of changes made:

1. Negative statements were rephrased positively, preserving original meaning:

    *   Was: *CANNOT answer more than simple, predictable questions.*
    *   Changed to: *CAN answer simple, predictable questions.*

2. Statements used as negative qualifications to a lower level statement were changed to positive statements intended to describe a higher level.

    *   Was: *CANNOT describe non-visible symptoms such as different kinds of pain, for example 'dull', 'stabbing', 'throbbing' etc.*
    *   Changed to: *CAN describe non-visible symptoms such as different kinds of pain, for example 'dull', 'stabbing', 'throbbing' etc.*

Relating the 'Can Do' statements to ALTE examinations

Following the initial calibration of the 'Can Do' statements, and the textual revision described above, attention has turned to establishing the link between the 'Can Do' scales and other indicators of language level. In particular we have started looking at performance in ALTE examinations, and to the relation between the 'Can Do' scales and the Council of Europe Framework levels.

Beginning in December 1998, data were collected to link 'Can Do' self-ratings to grades achieved in UCLES (University of Cambridge Local Examinations Syndicate) EFL exams at different levels. A very clear relationship was found, making it possible to begin to describe the meaning of an exam grade in terms of typical profiles of 'Can Do' ability.

However, when 'Can Do' ratings are based on self-report, and come from a wide range of countries and respondent groups, we find some variability in respondents' overall perception of their own abilities. That is, people tend to understand 'can do' somewhat differently, for reasons which may relate in part to factors such as age or cultural background. For some groups of respondents this weakens the correlation with their exam grades. Analytical approaches have been chosen to establish as clearly as possible the relationship between 'Can Do' self-ratings and criterion levels of proficiency as measured by exam grades. Further research based on 'Can Do' ratings by experienced raters will probably be necessary to fully characterise the relationship between exam grades and typical 'Can Do' profiles of ability.

A conceptual problem to be addressed in this context concerns the notion of mastery – that is, what exactly do we mean by 'can do'? A definition is required in terms of *how likely* we expect it to be that a person at a certain level can succeed at certain tasks. Should it be certain that the person will always succeed perfectly on the task? This would be too stringent a requirement. On the other hand, a 50 per cent chance of succeeding would be too low to count as mastery.

The figure of 80 per cent has been chosen, as an 80 per cent score is frequently used in domain- or criterion-referenced testing as an indication of mastery in a given domain. Thus, candidates achieving an ordinary pass in an ALTE exam at a given level should have an 80 per cent chance of succeeding on tasks identified as describing that level. Data so far collected on Cambridge exam candidates indicate that this figure accords well with their average probability of endorsing 'Can Do' statements at the relevant level. This relationship has been found to be fairly constant across exam levels.

By defining 'can do' explicitly in this way we have a basis for interpreting particular ALTE levels in terms of 'Can Do' skills.

While the relation to exam performance has so far been based on Cambridge exams, data linking 'Can Do' statements to performance in other ALTE examinations will continue to be collected, allowing us to verify that these different examination systems relate in essentially the same way to the ALTE 5-level Framework.

Anchoring to the Council of Europe Framework

In 1999 responses were collected in which anchors were provided by statements taken from the 1996 Council of Europe Framework document. Anchors included:

1. the descriptors in the self-assessment grid of major categories of language use by level presented as Table 2 in Chapter 3;
2. 16 descriptors relating to communicative aspects of Fluency, from illustrative scales in Chapter 5.

Table 2 was chosen because in practice it is achieving wide use as a summary description of levels. ALTE's ability to collect response data in a large number of languages and countries provided an opportunity to contribute to the validation of the scales in Table 2.

The 'Fluency' statements had been recommended because they had been found to have the most stable difficulty estimates when measured in different contexts in the Swiss project (North 1996/2000). It was expected that they should thus enable a good equating of the ALTE 'Can do' statements to the Council of Europe Framework. The estimated difficulties of the 'Fluency' statements were found to agree very closely with those given (North 1996/2000), showing a correlation of r= 0.97. This constitutes an excellent anchor between the 'Can Do' statements and the scales used to illustrate the Council of Europe Framework.

However, using Rasch analysis to equate sets of statements (scales) to each other is not straightforward. Data never fit the model exactly: there are issues of *dimensionality*, *discrimination* and *differential item function* (systematic variation of interpretation by different groups), which must be identified and dealt with so as to allow the truest possible relation of the scales to emerge.

Dimensionality relates to the fact that the skills of Listening/Speaking, Reading and Writing, though highly correlated, are still distinct: analyses in which they are separated produce more coherent, discriminating distinctions of level.

Variable discrimination is evident when we compare Table 2 and the 'Can Do' statements. Table 2 is found to produce a longer scale (to distinguish finer levels) than the 'Can Do' statements. It seems likely that the reason for this is that Table 2 represents the end product of an extended process of selection, analysis and refinement. The result of this process is that each level description is a composite of carefully selected typical elements, making it easier for respondents at a given level to recognise the level which best describes them. This produces a more coherent pattern of responses, which in turn produces a longer scale. This is in contrast to the present form of the 'Can Dos', which are still short, atomic statements which have not yet been grouped into such rounded, holistic descriptions of levels.

Group effects (differential item function) are evident in the fact that certain respondent groups (i.e. respondents to the Social and Tourist, Work or Study forms of the questionnaire) are found to discriminate levels considerably more finely on certain of the scales used as anchors, for reasons which have been difficult to identify.

None of these effects are unexpected when using a Rasch modelling approach to scale equating. They indicate that a systematic, qualitative review of the texts of the individual statements themselves remains a necessary and important stage in arriving at a 'final' equating of the scales.

Levels of proficiency in the ALTE Framework

At the time of writing the ALTE Framework is a five-level system. The validation described above confirms that these correspond broadly to levels A2 to C2 of the CE Framework. Work on defining a further initial level (Breakthrough) is in progress, and the Can Do project is contributing to the characterisation of this level. Thus the relation of the two Frameworks can be seen as follows:

Council of Europe Levels	A1	A2	B1	B2	C1	C2
ALTE Levels	ALTE Breakthrough Level	ALTE Level 1	ALTE Level 2	ALTE Level 3	ALTE Level 4	ALTE Level 5

The salient features of each ALTE level are as follows:

ALTE Level 5 (Good User): the capacity to deal with material which is academic or cognitively demanding, and to use language to good effect, at a level of performance which may in certain respects be more advanced than that of an average native speaker.

Example: CAN scan texts for relevant information, and grasp main topic of text, reading almost as quickly as a native speaker.

ALTE Level 4 (Competent User): an ability to communicate with the emphasis on how well it is done, in terms of appropriacy, sensitivity and the capacity to deal with unfamiliar topics.

Example: CAN deal with hostile questioning confidently. CAN get and hold onto his/her turn to speak.

ALTE Level 3 (Independent User): the capacity to achieve most goals and express oneself on a range of topics.

Example: CAN show visitors round and give a detailed description of a place.

ALTE Level 2 (Threshold User): an ability to express oneself in a limited way in familiar situations and to deal in a general way with non-routine information.
Example: CAN ask to open an account at a bank, provided that the procedure is straightforward.

ALTE Level 1 (Waystage User): an ability to deal with simple, straightforward information and begin to express oneself in familiar contexts.

Example: CAN take part in a routine conversation on simple predictable topics.

ALTE Breakthrough Level: a basic ability to communicate and exchange information in a simple way.

Example: CAN ask simple questions about a menu and understand simple answers.

References

Alderson, J. C. 1991: Bands and scores. In: Alderson, J.C. and North, B. (eds.): *Language testing in the 1990s.* London: British Council / Macmillan, Developments in ELT, 71–86.
North, B. 1996/2000: *The development of a common framework scale of language proficiency.* PhD thesis, Thames Valley University. Reprinted 2000, New York, Peter Lang.
ALTE Handbook of language examinations and examination systems (available from ALTE Secretariat at UCLES).

For further information about the ALTE project, please contact Marianne Hirtzel at Hirtzel.m@ucles.org.uk

Neil Jones, Marianne Hirtzel, University of Cambridge Local Examinations Syndicate, March 2000

Document D1   ALTE skill level summaries

ALTE Level	Listening/Speaking	Reading	Writing
ALTE Level 5	CAN advise on or talk about complex or sensitive issues, understanding colloquial references and dealing confidently with hostile questions.	CAN understand documents, correspondence and reports, including the finer points of complex texts.	CAN write letters on any subject and full notes of meetings or seminars with good expression and accuracy.
ALTE Level 4	CAN contribute effectively to meetings and seminars within own area of work or keep up a casual conversation with a good degree of fluency, coping with abstract expressions.	CAN read quickly enough to cope with an academic course, to read the media for information or to understand non-standard correspondence.	CAN prepare/draft professional correspondence, take reasonably accurate notes in meetings or write an essay which shows an ability to communicate.
ALTE Level 3	CAN follow or give a talk on a familiar topic or keep up a conversation on a fairly wide range of topics.	CAN scan texts for relevant information, and understand detailed instructions or advice.	CAN make notes while someone is talking or write a letter including non-standard requests.
ALTE Level 2	CAN express opinions on abstract/cultural matters in a limited way or offer advice within a known area, and understand instructions or public announcements.	CAN understand routine information and articles, and the general meaning of non-routine information within a familiar area.	CAN write letters or make notes on familiar or predictable matters.
ALTE Level 1	CAN express simple opinions or requirements in a familiar context.	CAN understand straightforward information within a known area, such as on products and signs and simple textbooks or reports on familiar matters.	CAN complete forms and write short simple letters or postcards related to personal information.
ALTE Break-through Level	CAN understand basic instructions or take part in a basic factual conversation on a predictable topic.	CAN understand basic notices, instructions or information.	CAN complete basic forms, and write notes including times, dates and places.

Document D2   ALTE social and tourist statements summary

ALTE Level	Listening/Speaking	Reading	Writing
ALTE Level 5	CAN talk about complex or sensitive issues without awkwardness.	CAN (when looking for accommodation) understand a tenancy agreement in detail, for example technical details and the main legal implications.	CAN write letters on any subject with good expression and accuracy.
ALTE Level 4	CAN keep up conversations of a casual nature for an extended period of time and discuss abstract/cultural topics with a good degree of fluency and range of expression.	CAN understand complex opinions/arguments as expressed in serious newspapers.	CAN write letters on most subjects. Such difficulties as the reader may experience are likely to be at the level of vocabulary.
ALTE Level 3	CAN keep up a conversation on a fairly wide range of topics, such as personal and professional experiences, events currently in the news.	CAN understand detailed information, for example a wide range of culinary terms on a restaurant menu, and terms and abbreviations in accommodation advertisements.	CAN write to a hotel to ask about the availability of services, for example facilities for the disabled or the provision of a special diet.
ALTE Level 2	CAN express opinions on abstract/cultural matters in a limited way and pick up nuances of meaning/opinion.	CAN understand factual articles in newspapers, routine letters from hotels and letters expressing personal opinions.	CAN write letters on a limited range of predictable topics related to personal experience and express opinions in predictable language.
ALTE Level 1	CAN express likes and dislikes in familiar contexts using simple language such as 'I (don't) like . . .'	CAN understand straightforward information, for example labels on food, standard menus, road signs and messages on automatic cash machines.	CAN complete most forms related to personal information.
ALTE Break-through Level	CAN ask simple questions of a factual nature and understand answers expressed in simple language.	CAN understand simple notices and information, for example in airports, on store guides and on menus. CAN understand simple instructions on medicines and simple directions to places.	CAN leave a very simple message for a host family or write short simple 'thank you' notes.

Document D3 ALTE social and tourist statements

Overview of concerns and activities covered

CONCERN	ACTIVITY	ENVIRONMENT	LANGUAGE SKILL REQUIRED
Day-to-Day Survival	1. Shopping	Self-service shops Counter service shops Market place	Listening/Speaking Reading
	2. Eating Out	Restaurants Self-service (fast food)	Listening/Speaking Reading
	3. Hotel-type accommodation	Hotels, B & B, etc.	Listening/Speaking Reading, Writing (form filling)
	4. Renting temporary accommodation (flat, room, house)	Agency, private landlord	Listening/Speaking Reading, Writing (form filling)
	5. Settling into accommodation	Host families	Listening/Speaking Reading, Writing (letters)
	6. Using financial and postal services	Banks, bureaux de change, post offices	Listening/Speaking Reading, Writing
Health	Getting/staying well	Chemist's Doctor's Hospital Dentist's	Listening/Speaking Reading
Travel	Arriving in a country Touring Getting/giving directions Hiring	Airport/port Railway/bus station Street, garage, etc. Travel agency Rental firms (car, boat, etc.)	Listening/Speaking Reading, Writing (form filling)
Emergencies	Dealing with emergency situations (accident, illness, crime, car breakdown, etc.)	Public places Private places, e.g. hotel room Hospital Police station	Listening/Speaking Reading
Sightseeing	Getting information Going on tours Showing people around	Tourist office Travel agency Tourist sights (monuments, etc.) Towns/cities Schools/colleges/ universities	Listening/Speaking Reading
Socialising	Casual meeting/ getting on with people Entertaining	Discos, parties, schools, hotels, campsites, restaurants, etc. Home, away from home	Listening/Speaking
The Media/Cultural events	Watching TV, films, plays etc. Listening to the radio Reading newspapers/ magazines	Home, car, cinema, theatre, 'Son et Lumière', etc.	Listening/Reading
Personal contacts (at a distance)	Writing letters, postcards, etc.	Home, away from home	Listening/Speaking (telephone) Reading, Writing

Document D4   ALTE work statements summary

ALTE Level	Listening/Speaking	Reading	Writing
ALTE Level 5	CAN advise on/handle complex delicate or contentious issues, such as legal or financial matters, to the extent that he/she has the necessary specialist knowledge.	CAN understand reports and articles likely to be encountered during his/her work, including complex ideas expressed in complex language.	CAN make full and accurate notes and continue to participate in a meeting or seminar.
ALTE Level 4	CAN contribute effectively to meetings and seminars within own area of work and argue for or against a case.	CAN understand correspondence expressed in non-standard language.	CAN handle a wide range of routine and non-routine situations in which professional services are requested from colleagues or external contacts.
ALTE Level 3	CAN take and pass on most messages that are likely to require attention during a normal working day.	CAN understand most correspondence, reports and factual product literature he/she is likely to come across.	CAN deal with all routine requests for goods or services.
ALTE Level 2	CAN offer advice to clients within own job area on simple matters.	CAN understand the general meaning of non-routine letters and theoretical articles within own work area.	CAN make reasonably accurate notes at a meeting or seminar where the subject matter is familiar and predictable.
ALTE Level 1	CAN state simple requirements within own job area, such as 'I want to order 25 of . . .'.	CAN understand most short reports or manuals of a predictable nature within his/her own area of expertise, provided enough time is given.	CAN write a short, comprehensible note of request to a colleague or a known contact in another company.
ALTE Break-through Level	CAN take and pass on simple messages of a routine kind, such as 'Friday meeting 10 a.m.'	CAN understand short reports or product descriptions on familiar matters, if these are expressed in simple language and the contents are predictable.	CAN write a simple routine request to a colleague, such as 'Can I have 20X please?'

Document D5 ALTE WORK statements

Overview of concerns and activities covered

CONCERN	ACTIVITY	ENVIRONMENT	LANGUAGE SKILL REQUIRED
Work-related services	1. Requesting work-related services 2. Providing work-related services	Workplace (office, factory, etc.) Workplace (office, factory, etc.) customer's home	Listening/Speaking Writing Listening/Speaking Writing
Meetings and seminars	Participating in meetings and seminars	Workplace (office, factory, etc.), conference centre	Listening/Speaking Writing (notes)
Formal presentations and demonstrations	Following and giving a presentation or demonstration	Conference centre, exhibition centre, factory, laboratory etc.	Listening/Speaking Writing (notes)
Correspondence	Understanding and writing faxes, letters, memos, e-mail, etc.	Workplace (office, factory, etc.)	Reading Writing Reading
Reports	Understanding and writing reports (of substantial length and formality)	Workplace (office, factory, etc.)	Reading Writing
Publicly available information	Getting relevant information (from e.g. product literature, professional/trade journals, advertise-ments, web sites etc.)	Workplace (office, factory, etc.), home	Reading
Instructions and guidelines	Understanding notices (e.g. safety.) Understanding and writing instructions (in, for example, installation, operation and maintenance manuals)	Workplace (office, factory, etc.)	Reading Writing
Telephone	Making outgoing calls Receiving incoming calls (inc. taking messages/writing notes)	Office, home, hotel room, etc.	Listening/Speaking / Writing (notes)

Document D6   ALTE study statements summary

ALTE Level	Listening/Speaking	Reading	Writing
ALTE Level 5	CAN understand jokes, colloquial asides and cultural allusions.	CAN access all sources of information quickly and reliably.	CAN make accurate and complete notes during the course of a lecture, seminar or tutorial.
ALTE Level 4	CAN follow abstract argumentation, for example the balancing of alternatives and the drawing of a conclusion.	CAN read quickly enough to cope with the demands of an academic course.	CAN write an essay which shows ability to communicate, giving few difficulties for the reader.
ALTE Level 3	CAN give a clear presentation on a familiar topic, and answer predictable or factual questions.	CAN scan tests for relevant information and grasp main point of text.	CAN make simple notes that will be of reasonable use for essay or revision purposes.
ALTE Level 2	CAN understand instructions on classes and assignments given by a teacher or lecturer.	CAN understand basic instructions and messages, for example computer library catalogues, with some help.	CAN write down some information at a lecture, if this is more or less dictated.
ALTE Level 1	CAN express simple opinions using expressions such as 'I don't agree'.	CAN understand the general meaning of a simplified textbook or article, reading very slowly.	CAN write a very short simple narrative or description, such as 'My last holiday'.
ALTE Break-through Level	CAN understand basic instructions on class times, dates and room numbers, and on assignments to be carried out.	CAN read basic notices and instructions.	CAN copy times, dates and places from notices on classroom board or notice board.

Document D7   ALTE STUDY statements

Overview of concerns and activities

CONCERN	ACTIVITY	ENVIRONMENT	LANGUAGE SKILL REQUIRED
Lectures, talks, presentations and demonstrations	1. Following a lecture, talk, presentation or demonstration 2. Giving a lecture talk, presentation or demonstration	Lecture hall, classroom, laboratory, etc.	Listening/Speaking Writing (notes)
Seminars and tutorials	Participating in seminars and tutorials	Classroom, study	Listening/Speaking Writing (notes)
Textbooks, articles, etc.	Gathering information	Study, library, etc.	Reading Writing (notes)
Essays	Writing essays	Study, library, examination room, etc.	Writing
Accounts	Writing up accounts (e.g. of an experiment)	Study, laboratory	Writing
Reference skills	Accessing information (e.g. from a computer base, library, dictionary, etc.)	Library, resource centre, etc.	Reading Writing (notes)
Management of study	Making arrangements, e.g. with college staff on deadlines for work to be handed in	Lecture hall, classroom study, etc.	Listening/Speaking Reading Writing

Index

The index covers prefatory note, notes for user, chapters 1–9, bibliographies and appendices. Page references followed by *t* refer to tables

(handwritten annotation: production, reception, interaction)